The Management Consultant

Prentice Hall
FINANCIAL TIMES

In an increasingly competitive world, we believe it's quality of thinking that gives you the edge – an idea that opens new doors, a technique that solves a problem, or an insight that simply makes sense of it all. The more you know, the smarter and faster you can go.

That's why we work with the best minds in business and finance to bring cutting-edge thinking and best learning practice to a global market.

Under a range of leading imprints, including Financial Times Prentice Hall, we create world-class print publications and electronic products bringing our readers knowledge, skills and understanding, which can be applied whether studying or at work.

To find out more about Pearson Education publications, or tell us about the books you'd like to find, you can visit us at www.pearsoned.co.uk

The Management Consultant

Mastering the art of consultancy

Richard Newton

**Financial Times
Prentice Hall
is an imprint of**

Harlow, England • London • New York • Boston • San Francisco • Toronto • Sydney • Singapore • Hong Kong
Tokyo • Seoul • Taipei • New Delhi • Cape Town • Madrid • Mexico City • Amsterdam • Munich • Paris • Milan

PEARSON EDUCATION LIMITED
Edinburgh Gate
Harlow CM20 2JE
Tel: +44 (0)1279 623623
Fax: +44 (0)1279 431059
Website: www.pearsoned.co.uk

First published in Great Britain in 2010

ISBN: 978-0-273-73087-3

British Library Cataloguing-in-Publication Data
A catalogue record for this book is available from the British Library

Library of Congress Cataloging-in-Publication Data
Newton, Richard, 1964-
  The management consultant : mastering the art of consultancy / Richard
Newton.
      p. cm.
  Includes bibliographical references and index.
  ISBN 978-0-273-73087-3 (pbk.)
  1. Business consultants. I. Title.
  HD69.C6N495 2010
  001--dc22
                              2009050850

10 9 8 7 6 5 4 3 2
14 13 12 11

Typeset in 9/13pt Stone Serif by 30
Printed and bound in Great Britain by Ashford Colour Press Ltd, Gosport

The Publisher's policy is to use paper manufactured from sustainable forests.

Contents

Acknowledgements

I would like to thank five consulting colleagues who I started working with years ago in Coopers & Lybrand. Although our careers have moved on in different ways, we still work together from time to time. More often we meet up, share stories and enjoy laughing about the occasionally pretentious side of the profession. They are: Graham Jump, Peter Meredith, Perry Childs, Richard Ellis and Andy Macey.

Dedication

This book is dedicated to my son Konrad for inspiring me to write the book, when he admitted that he really did not have the faintest idea what I did.

Preface

This book is a personal guide to the art of management consulting. It sets out to help new and experienced consultants to do one thing: to become better consultants. In simple terms, *better* means providing help that is of the most long-term value to your clients. The approach is also simple: to identify what it is that the best consultants do that their less effective colleagues do not – and how you can do it, too. Underlying this is my belief in *client-centric consulting*.

The contents are derived from three sources. The first source is my experience as a consultant (working for Coopers & Lybrand, A.T Kearney, Ernst & Young and my own company Enixus). Secondly, my experiences in industry as a client – negotiating, buying and managing consultants. Finally and most importantly, I have a network of trusted consulting colleagues whose ideas have flavoured the book. Like a magpie I have picked up ideas and concepts throughout my career. I have shifted through them, throwing away most, keeping hold of the ones I like and think are precious. Many ideas in this book are my own, but of course I have learnt from others. I can't remember the sources of all of these, so I am sure more credit is deserved than I have given.

There were several reasons for writing this book, but two of them stand out. Firstly, there are comparatively few books on consulting, unlike many other management disciplines. Look at the business book selection in a good bookshop or online, and you will find many on strategy, leadership, marketing, delivering change and project management, to name a few areas. But consulting books are relatively scarce, scarcer than an industry of its size justifies. There are a few good books on consulting, but they do not approach the audience in the way I want to.

The second reason comes down to my frequent frustration when I work with or engage other consultants. The simple truth is that the profession often does not live up to its own hype. This is not to deny that there are many brilliant consultants out there, and I have been lucky enough to work with and learn from a few of them. But there are many consultants who know they should be better to justify their fees. Worse, there are some very mediocre consultants who mistake being paid a lot with being good. As supposed experts in business, it is amazing how often consultants provide inadequate value to their clients.

Management consulting is a large and very varied industry. The range of skills and services that fall under this title are huge. The difference in the type of work of the most expensive strategy houses compared to a project management consultant is so great that they may not even recognise each other as being in the same profession. There are some books that set out to address components of this industry. They tend to describe various tools and techniques of consulting. The best tools and techniques are only applicable in some situations and even if you know them it does not make you necessarily an effective consultant. I wanted to write a book for *all* management consultants.

The book contains tools and techniques, but it is also intended to make you think like a consultant: *how do effective consultants think about their work and their clients?* Consulting experiences are varied, and each is unique. By thinking like a consultant, irrespective of the situation you are in, you will be able to deal with any situation in the most effective way.

Introduction

Ask someone in business to define the title 'management consultant', and you will get a wide variety of responses, not all of them complimentary! The title covers an extensive range of roles providing a variety of services. There are no universally recognised standards for being a management consultant and as a result there are very varying levels of quality. In addition, many people want to be management consultants but do not know what it entails.

There are many consulting success stories, and numerous people have become comfortably well off as consultants. Given this success, it might be thought that the world was full of praise for management consultants. Yet, if you ask many customers in the private and public sector about their feelings and experiences of consultants, you will often be met with sceptical and even highly negative comments. There are numerous causes for these responses, but they can be summarised into three major categories. Firstly, too many consultants simply do not provide sufficient value to their customers and rely on churning out the same old work time and time again. Secondly, even good consultants with valuable knowledge often fail to understand true client needs. Thirdly, it is unfortunate to say, but there seems to be a number of very poor management consultants. This problem is compounded by the already mentioned lack of widely recognised standards for consultancy which can be used to judge or benchmark consultants against.

A key reason for the negative perception of consulting is the fact that too many consultants are focused on what they have to offer and how they make money, rather than what clients need. Too many consultants provide context-free and generic advice, whereas what clients need is advice that is tailored to their specific culture and context. Overall, too many consultants spend too much time trying to be clever, rather than asking themselves *what actually makes a good consultant?*

This book will describe those factors that make good consultants and how consultants can go about providing *client-centric consulting*. It describes consulting from the viewpoint of the client, and so will help consultants understand what will make them successful. The book will help in deciding on how to provide the most appropriate services and advice to clients. Rather than considering the tools and processes of consulting, as most other consulting books do, it focuses on the skills of successful consultants – what they do that makes them successful, success in this context being defined as client results, not only in terms of financial returns for the consultant. Finally, the book contains many tips from the author's and his colleagues' years of experience in consulting.

> ❝ the book focuses on the skills of successful consultants ❞

There is a huge number of management consultants and business advisors of one form or another. Management consultancies have been one of the great business success stories of the past 40 years, with some now employing tens of thousands of people in worldwide businesses, delivering significant profits to shareholders and partners. At the other end of the scale there are thousands of small consultancies and independent consultants. As employment patterns change, more and more people are choosing to work as consultants.

There are many attractions to a career in consulting. For some, consulting may seem the only choice following redundancy from a senior position. There are many examples of initially despondent redundant managers finding not only a better income, but more enjoyable work in consultancy. For others, it is a lifetime career choice that starts from university, even though few students have any real concept of what being a consultant entails. Many people enter the consulting profession for a more flexible lifestyle, although this is harder to achieve in practice than it might seem. Whatever the reasons for considering it, consultancy is a great opportunity. Companies appear to have an increasing and insatiable demand for advisors and interim managers. Providing services can be very profitable and give consultants a high standard of living. But consulting also has risks. It's an increasingly competitive environment as more people are drawn to the profession. Select the wrong services or sales approach, and consulting will be a stressful profession. There is also the constant uncertainty about what happens when the current engagement is complete.

Many people assume that simply because they have some specialist expertise, they can be a good consultant. Certainly, expertise is an essential foundation. This book assumes you have an area of specialist knowledge and can competently apply the techniques and tools of your specialisation. But specialist knowledge is not enough. It is not intended as a tautology when I say that the core competency of a successful consultant is the *skill of being a consultant*. It is not a profession for everyone – there is a specific art to being a consultant.

Although the consulting industry is successful, that success is in jeopardy. Fee rates for many organisations, including some of the largest firms, are lower in real terms than they were previously. Clients are becoming more adept at controlling consultants and extracting the best value from them. More and more people are entering the consulting industry, meaning that to excel the standards are rising all the time. Consultants need to raise their game.

This book sets out to provide you with guidance to what makes a great consultant, irrespective of where you fit amongst the incredible variety of management consultants. It avoids the constraints of focusing on specific elements of consulting or approaches to consultancy, and instead takes a client-centric view of what is needed to provide expert consulting. Although this book contains approaches, the fundamental questions it seeks to answer are *what makes a great consultant* and building on that, *how do you achieve this*?

Contents and structure

There are 14 chapters and two short additional reference lists in the book. The book is broken into three main parts. In the first part (Chapters 1–4), I explore what it means to be a management consultant and how to go about setting yourself up as one. In the second part (Chapters 5–8), I discuss how to go about winning work and delivering value to clients. In the third part (Chapters 9–14), I discuss a range of broader issues which set the context for consulting and will give you some additional tips and techniques to being a successful consultant.

The book has been designed to be read from cover to cover, but you can dip into it as you require. If you want to reference parts individually, the detailed contents of each chapter are described in the following table:

	Chapter title	Chapter summary
1	Consultants and consultancy	Introduces the key terminology and concepts used in the book and provides an overview of what being a consultant means.
2	Why does anyone buy consultancy?	Explores how successful consulting starts by understanding the reasons clients have for buying consultancy. This is essential knowledge for anyone wanting to provide client-centric consulting.
3	Your consulting service	Looks at the range of services you can offer as a consultant and how to position your skills and experience as a saleable client service.
4	The three core processes of client-centric consulting	Discusses the core engagement process and then puts it in context with the client's change process, and the client's operational process. Understanding this relationship is at the heart of client-centric consulting.
5	Finding and winning work	As a commercial business, consultants must find opportunities and sell their services to clients. This chapter discusses the processes and approach to winning work.
6	Delivering consulting engagements and satisfying clients	Investigates the central work of a consultant – delivering consulting engagements which add value to the clients.
7	The alternative approach – process consulting and facilitation	Describes an alternative approach to expert consulting – process consulting – which can be used to deliver entire consulting engagements or as a tool on an engagement.
8	Closing engagements and sustaining results	All consulting should result in some change in a client, otherwise it delivers no value. Often the change takes place and must continue after the consultant has finished their work. This chapter considers how to achieve change, and how to sustain it after a consulting engagement is complete.
9	Developing long-term client relationships	Describes the advantages of having long-term client relationships and how to develop them.
10	The ethical dimension	Considers the ethics of consulting, and the potential ethical dilemmas that regularly face consultants and ways to deal with them.

Chapter title	Chapter summary
11 The language of consulting	The central tool of the consultant is language. This chapter describes some approaches to communications and explores the topic of consulting jargon.
12 Knowing when to say no	Not all consulting opportunities are worth pursuing. This chapter describes the characteristics of engagements which consultants should avoid if possible.
13 Key consulting tips	A summary of useful key tips from experience.
14 The client's perspective – buying consultancy	A short review from a client's perspective of issues to consider when purchasing consultancy.
Conclusion	A brief summary of the role of the management consultant and topics covered in this book.
A The tools and processes of a consultancy business	A summary of the key processes and tools any consulting business requires.
B References	A short list of references that have influenced the author's thinking, and may be useful to readers.
C Sample proposal letter	A sample proposal letter for readers to adapt.

one

Understanding consultants and consultancy

Consultants and consultancy

T his chapter answers the questions: what is a management consultant and what is management consultancy?

You may be an experienced consultant who wants to pick up a few new tricks. On the other hand, maybe you are new to consulting and want to gain a better understanding of what it is all about. This chapter is aimed primarily at the novice consultant, whether you are considering joining a major consultancy, are starting out as an independent consultant, or have been recruited as an internal consultant. It provides an overview of some of the fundamental concepts in consulting. Most of the book is about *how* to be a consultant. As an opening to the subject this chapter answers *what* being a consultant means.

To gain the most from this book it is important to understand what a management consultant is, to be familiar with some common consulting terminology, and to appreciate the difference between being a consultant and other roles. If you want to be a management consultant, it is helpful to recognise why you want to be a consultant and to think through whether or not it is a profession that can meet your desires. To achieve this it is useful to have at least a basic grasp of the economics of a consulting business. This chapter sets out to do all of this. There is nothing complex here, but it is important as it provides the foundations for the rest of the book. This chapter covers a disparate range of topics that combined give a basic, but essential, picture of consulting.

One small, but noteworthy point: rather than write the phrases 'management consultant' and 'management consultancy' repeatedly, I shorten these to 'consultant' and 'consultancy'. There are other types of consultants and consultancy, and many of them could find something useful in this book, but the focus is on the management variety.

What is a management consultant?

There is a large and growing band of people who call themselves management consultants. Some people are management consultants but do not use this title, preferring labels such as *business advisor, strategy consultant, operational consultant* or even *leadership consultant*. These and related job titles encompass a divergent and eclectic group of individuals.

The work such people do varies enormously. The fee rates range from low to very high, and the length a consulting project may vary from hours to years. Clients who use consultants can be the owners of firms, managers of one level of seniority or another, or the main board directors of major corporations. Clients can also be staff in the public sector and not-for-profit organisations. Some consultants are employees of the firms the consulting takes place in, others are external but regular faces within an organisation, while many are individuals who appear in a client organisation for a short time and never reappear again. Their areas of specialist expertise go from obscure pieces of business to generalist management advice. Given this huge variety, what is it that is similar that enables them to be bundled together as *management consultants*? It is not easy to come up with a concise definition that covers this assortment of roles.

> " it is not easy to come up with a concise definition "

The problem with describing the role of a management consultant is compounded by the fact that some existing definitions have been written by people who are not consultants, and who do not understand fully what consultants do. But listening to professional consultants can equally be misleading. Those who are consultants have a vested interest in making the role sound majestic and magical, and to bias any description towards the type of work they specifically do. I have read definitions of management consultancy in sales brochures, books, dictionaries and various online encyclopaedias. A few definitions are the hopeless summarisations of people without any real understanding, some are correct but focus on irrelevant aspects of the role, many are good, but do not quite manage to encapsulate the role and its variations.

Given the wide variety of consultants, rather than starting with a definition, I will list characteristics to provide an appreciation of the role of a consultant. As little in this world is absolutely black and white there are caveats with each one of these characteristics.

Consultants do the following seven things:

1 They provide advice and recommendations to managers, and may provide assistance with the implementation of the recommendations. *Caveat:* Consulting companies may provide a whole range of services, from pure consulting to training and outsourcing. Not all of this is consulting. Consulting is about providing useful advice, and helping managers to implement the advice.

2 They base their advice and recommendation on a set of skills and expertise, or intellectual property they have available to them. *Caveat:* This is what should happen. However, ask any experienced manager and they can probably tell you of the time they spoke to or even engaged someone who purported to be a consultant but who had very limited skills, experience or intellectual property.

3 They consult. This may sound obvious given the name, but it is often forgotten. What I mean by this is that consultants engage in dialogue with an organisation and its staff, and apply their expertise to develop recommendations, taking account of the specific needs and context of that organisation.
Caveat: Some firms called consultancies do not consult. Such firms may be very successful in selling research, benchmarking data or other types of information. Consultants do not sell products or give the same advice to everyone. There is nothing wrong with selling a product, but irrespective of how it is branded, it is not management consulting.

4 They are involved with a given client on a temporary basis. *Caveat:* The length of a consulting project may be anything from hours to months. Occasionally, it may be years, although it is difficult to argue that someone who has worked continuously in one organisation for years is still working as a consultant. (Internal consultants work for one organisation, but they will be working on different projects across a range of departments or divisions.) It is not unusual for a consultant to work regularly for the same client, but each piece of work is of a limited duration.

5 They are independent. A consultant should be providing advice or recommendations irrespective of the internal politics and vested interests of an organisation or the managers who are their client.

Caveat: Consultants are human, have their own business interest to consider, and naturally have their own biases. But a consultant's biases should be independent of a client's biases.

6   They are not paid for from an organisation's normal staff budgets. *Caveat:* A manager who wants to employ a consultant needs a budget for it. This is often true even for internal consultants who charge back their time, and if they do not, they remain an overhead to the rest of the business.

7   They add value to a manager and the client organisation by helping them to change. Value can take many forms, such as improved decision making, faster change implementation, reduced business risk and so on.
    Caveat: At least they should do! Reality is not always so clear cut.

If we take these seven characteristics of a consultant and take the most pertinent points it is possible to develop a definition of a consultant that is true in most situations:

> ### Definition
>
> A consultant is an independent advisor who adds value by helping managers to identify and achieve beneficial change appropriate to their situation.

Essential consulting jargon

To get the most from this book it is important that we start with a common understanding of the basic terminology surrounding management consultancy. Some words, or pieces of consulting jargon, will be used repeatedly through the book, and if you are new to the industry then it's important you become familiar with these concepts. I am not generally a big advocate of jargon (see Chapter 11), but there are words and phrases that are continuously used by consultants. Most of these may be obvious and intuitively understandable, some are not specific to the consulting industry, but they are essential to know.

Consultants tend to talk about *clients*, rather than customers. The concept of a client is explored in the next chapter. In general terms, the word is used both to refer to a specific manager who gives the consultant direction on a consulting project, and the organisation in which that manager works. Hence a consultant may think of the client as Mr Peter Smith of the XYZ Company, or may consider it to be the XYZ Company. To differentiate, when I refer to a client I am talking about a person (or group of people), when I am talking about the organisation the client works for I use the term *client organisation.*

Once employed by a client, the specific consulting project being undertaken is usually referred to as an *engagement* or sometimes a *live engagement*. A client is one of a larger group of *stakeholders* a consultant must deal with. Stakeholders form a set of individuals who consultants must take into consideration when delivering an engagement.

To win some work consultants engage in *business development*. Business development relates to time that is not (usually) *chargeable* to a client, and includes activities that are associated with marketing a business and pursing specific sales. The aim of business development is to identify *opportunities*, and then convert these opportunities into live engagements and hence have some chargeable time. An opportunity is the situation in which a client has a need for some consulting support. To convert an opportunity into an engagement and hence be able to charge fees, consultants must normally write a description of the service they will provide to the client. This description is called a *proposal*. *Chargeable time* is the time when a consultant is billing fees to the client. Once an engagement is complete, consultants often seek to *sell on*, that is to sell a subsequent consulting engagement to the client so the consultant can remain chargeable.

> **❝ consultants must normally write a description of the service they will provide ❞**

In order to sell regularly, and for proposals to be successful, consultants may have *service lines*. A service line is a specific area of expertise that a consultant or a consultancy company invests in (see Chapter 3). For instance, one consultancy may have a service line in improving the management of IT departments, and another may have a service line to increase innovation in business. Service lines may be the informal labelling of expertise of individual consultants, but they can also be the formal documentation of processes and approaches to consulting by larger consulting companies. Service lines and any other knowledge or approaches are often called *intellectual property* or *intellectual capital* by consultants. Intellectual property has a specific legal meaning, but many consultants use this phrase in a looser fashion than the legal definition requires (see Chapter 3).

One of the most important measures of a consulting business is *utilisation* or *chargeable utilisation*. Utilisation is a measure of the proportion of time a consultant is working on fee-paying work on a client site. Hence, a consultant who is billing three days a week is 60 per cent utilised. It is normally not possible for a consultant to be 100 per cent utilised because some time must be spent on business development, the creation and maintenance of service lines, and holiday.

How does consulting differ from other roles?

Developing a full understanding of the role of the consultant is helped by understanding the difference between a consultant and an employee, a manager or a business leader. The boundaries between being a consultant and, for example a manager, are grey, but there are important and definite differences.

Let's start by considering the role of a consultant versus an employee in the organisation using consultants. The obvious point is that a consultant is not an employee of the organisation they are helping, but an employee of a consulting business. Why does this matter? Most consultants want to do a good job that satisfies a client, but their performance assessments, pay increases, promotions, ongoing praise and criticism are not done by the client organisation. All these are influenced by their performance with clients, but consultants have different motivations from client staff. Consultants are never fully part of a client organisation's team. For example, a client may regard a consultant as having done a brilliant job by providing fantastic advice. A consulting company may judge the same consultant to have only done an average job because he did not manage to make any additional consulting sales.

A consultant can be part of a client organisation's project team, and in doing this share some goals with other client staff, but consultants are always to some extent independent from the client organisation. Their incentives and performance drivers are different. This is true even for an internal consultant. Obviously, an internal consultant is employed by the same company as their clients, but is not employed by the same department or part of the same management hierarchy. This is not necessarily a bad thing – a consultant who is as much part of your team as any other employee will struggle to give truly independent advice.

What about the difference between being a consultant and a line manager? Like managers, consultants often are hard working and want to produce a quality result, but this is relative to the scope of a consulting engagement. They do not and arguably cannot deliver an end result in a client organisation, and do not live with the outcomes of their recommendations. If a consultant is providing advice, then, if the advice is accepted, a line manager has to implement this advice somehow. Even if consultants help with implementation planning or a change implementation project, they do not end up working with the results following the implementation. Consultants are temporary visitors to an organisation – it is line managers who must live with the results of any consulting engagement.

There is another point about consultants compared to managers. Many consultants are ex-senior managers with a good understanding of the challenge of managing a department. On the other hand, whilst all consultants advise, some have never managed anything of any significant complexity. Even relatively senior career consultants, who became consultants from university, may never have managed a team of more than 20 people. For someone in an operational role with several thousand staff and a budget of hundreds of millions, a consultant's understanding of the reality of dealing with this number of people and scale of budget will appear limited. The consultant's response to this should not even attempt to be an expert line manager, but to provide focused specialist expertise beyond that of a normal manager.

Finally, what about a consultant compared to a business leader? Many consultants fancy themselves to be great leaders, and some have the potential. There are well regarded business gurus who have come from a consulting background, but a guru is not a leader – a guru is an influencer and a shaper of opinions. Sometimes you

❝ you can be a very good consultant without having the ability to lead or inspire ❞

see a successful chief executive with a background in consulting, and they are probably a great leader. But on the whole I am sceptical about professional consultants as leaders. The consultancy profession encourages the development of a range of skills which sometimes can be mistaken for leadership, such as strong communication and influencing skills. Normally though, consulting does not require significant leadership skills. You can be a very good consultant without having the ability to lead or inspire.

The fact that consultants are different from employees, managers and business leaders should not be taken as a criticism of consultants. Consultants are not employees, managers or leaders – because that is not what the role entails or requires. Consulting is a very different role from being an employee, manager or leader. Consultants must appreciate these roles, be able to work with them and be able to influence them. Some consultants may have a background in organisations which required them to manage or to lead, but this is not universally true. Consultants should not forget that the role of the consultant is to consult, not to manage or to lead.

Now, having said all this, comparing consulting to other roles does to some extent depend on the type of consultant being talked about. There are two dimensions of consulting we should be aware of and differentiate:

1 *Internal or external consultants*: An internal consultant is a full-time employee of an organisation who has a role as a consultant to the business. Typical examples include human resources (HR) or internal change management specialists. An external consultant is someone who is engaged for a specific consulting project, but otherwise is independent of an organisation. Internal consultants tend to have a greater understanding of an organisation's culture and are familiar with many aspects of a business that an external consultant will take some time to learn or understand. External consultants will typically have a broader range of experience and have done work similar to their current engagement in other organisations.

2 *Strategic, operational, implementation or specialist*: Many consultants work in a wide range of roles and float between providing strategic advice, helping with implementing it and supporting operational managers. But generally we can differentiate between consultants (and consulting companies) who advise organisations at a strategic level – what direction a business should be taking; at an operational level – how the business should be run on a daily basis efficiently and effectively; or at an implementation level – how to deliver projects and changes (which may be derived from the advice of a strategic or operational consultant). There are also specialist consultants who focus on a particular area of advice. Arguably all consultants should be specialists, but what I mean here are, for example, consultants who focuses on very specific areas such as regulatory compliance advice or on minimising technology costs.

Another thing to consider is whether the work being done is consulting or another related profession. There are several job titles in common use which are often employed in relation to consultants, or in relation to people doing work that can seem similar to that of a consultant. The main examples are:

- ⬛ *Contractor*: A contractor is a temporary employee who is usually paid a day rate to complete some work which is of a transitory nature, where it is not appropriate or not possible to employ a permanent member of staff. This covers a wide range of areas – from office cleaners to very short-term senior staff. The overlap with management consultants is that many projects require temporary staff, and these are often contractors. Organisations are often left with a choice of whether to use contractors or consultants. A rough difference is that a consultant is employed to advise or provide skills the client does not have access to, and a contractor is employed as an extra pair of hands to increase the capacity of an organisation beyond that available with existing permanent staff.

- ⬛ *Interim manager*: An interim manager is a specialised form of senior contractor. An expert manager is engaged to perform a management role for a limited period of time – for example because a senior manager is ill or on maternity leave. Interim managers should be expert managers, who fit quickly into even the most senior management roles. It is really impossible to define hard and fast boundaries with consultants, as many consultancies offer interim management services and some consultants regularly work as interim managers – but when they do they are not working as a consultant.

- ⬛ *Coach/mentor*: It is common to pay for professional coaching and mentoring, to help individual managers. Such work is normally done on a one-to-one basis. Coaches and mentors are slightly different, but they are both concerned with helping individuals to reach their full potential. A consultant may work as a coach or mentor to individual managers, but there are also professional coaches and mentors, who rightly do not consider themselves consultants.

- ⬛ *Facilitator*: A facilitator is someone who uses facilitation skills to help a group or team resolve some issue or problem. Facilitation is one of the most misused words in business and is explored further in Chapter 7. Facilitation is often closely associated with workshops, but it is possible to use facilitation in other situations. Facilitators do not advise directly, but help clients to solve their own problems. I regard facilitation skills both as an expert profession in its own right, but to a certain degree also a core skill of all consultants.

It is worth understanding the differences in these roles, which can be real, but the boundaries are often exaggerated for commercial or personal reasons. Professional interim managers, facilitators and coaches have valid reasons related to the nature of the roles to differentiate themselves from management consultants, but it also makes commercial sense to do so as well. Many consultants have the necessary skills and often work in one or more of these roles, but you should not assume that all consultants can or even need to be able to perform such roles effectively. Put another way, you can be a successful consultant without, for example, having the capability to coach or be an interim manager.

Varieties of consulting organisations

There are many different organisational structures you can work in as a consultant, and the choice is important as it will affect the type of projects you do, the nature of the day-to-day work, and the level of risk and uncertainty you expose yourself to. There are essentially four ways you can work as a consultant:

1 as a solo or independent consultant working for yourself or your own company

2 as an employee of a major consulting company

3 as part of an organisation offering a portfolio of services of which consulting is only one – the most common is the consulting, IT development and outsourcing company, but there are other variants

4 as part of a small consultancy company.

To some extent the choice depends on personal preferences, and what opportunities are open to you. I have worked in organisations in all these models.

The independent consultant is usually either someone who has worked in a larger consultancy but wants a more self-sufficient lifestyle, or an ex-senior manager who now wants to advise rather than manage. There are many reasons for choosing to become independent. I now prefer to work for my own company as it enables me to maximise my personal flexibility. The cost is that I am completely dependent on my own ability to find projects and generate an income. However, once you have an established reputation this is not that hard. Organisations always need help. Additionally, as my business costs are comparatively low, and I have other revenues, should I choose not to work for a few months I do not need to generate significant revenues to cover my

> **❝ organisations always need help ❞**

business costs. I have access to a wide variety of work. I even undertake some very large engagements as I have a network of trusted colleagues, and we work together often to deliver larger engagements than a single consultant can manage.

At the other extreme are the major consulting companies. If you have little experience, are a recent graduate or like to combine consulting with a corporate culture these are the organisations for you. The big consultancies can be attractive places to work. For example, they tend to give great opportunities for professional development, international working and arguably reduce your personal risk as you have teams of people around you also helping to win and deliver engagements. Additionally, the larger firms often win massive projects which may require leading-edge thinking and techniques, although on the largest projects you can feel like a cog in the machine rather than a real consultant. If you become a senior manager (or partner) in such organisations the rewards can be high. But it does mean all the baggage that comes with corporate life such as annual appraisals, fitting in with company culture and worrying about things like brand risk. Big consultancies are also notoriously political environments. Some are focused on people who fit their specific organisational culture, which can give the consultancy a very defined feeling that will not suit everyone.

Companies offering a portfolio of services beyond consultancy provide a large variety of career options. However, if your firm is not purely a consultancy, there is always the tension over how independent the consulting advice is and whether it is really just a sales channel for other services. Some outsourcing firms have very successful consulting divisions, but there is always a doubt in some clients' minds as to whether the consulting is impartial advice or a funnel to win outsourcing contracts.

Whilst I am happy not to work for a large firm any more it is fair to say that I probably could not do what I do now had I not learnt what I did working for the major consultancies I was employed by. It is by no means a bad place to start.

There are many smaller consultancies, which offer a compromise between the complete self-sufficiency of the sole trader and the corporate hierarchies of the larger firms. Some of the smaller consultancies are industry leaders in specific consulting niches. For instance you can find consulting firms who specialise solely in financial regulation, telecommunications, customer services or cost control in manufacturing. If you have a particularly focused specialisation there may be a firm for whom you are a perfect fit.

Why do you want to be a consultant?

If you roughly understand what a consultant is, then it is time to reflect on whether and why you want to be one, and if your reasons have a realistic chance of being fulfilled.

The best reason for wanting to become a management consultant is simply because you enjoy the process of consulting with clients. Of course, if you have never worked as a consultant what 'consulting with a client' means will be unclear. If you do know, and this is the reason for becoming a consultant, then you are well set for a successful career. However, most people have more pragmatic grounds for becoming a consultant.

A common reason to join the profession is the potential variety of the work. Although as a consultant you may work in a specialist area, you will work in many organisations. The context and culture of the organisations and details of the problems will vary significantly. I find consulting work highly varied. I have worked all around the world, for companies in a wide variety of sectors, with clients of differing levels of seniority, to help resolve a divergent range of problems. However, if the service you will provide to organisations is very specialised – for example, helping them to be compliant with a specific piece of industrial regulation – what variety you gain from different clients you may also lose in essentially doing the same piece of work again and again.

Some people join consulting for skills development. This typically arises from one of two sources. Development may happen because of the wide variety of challenging work you are involved in. And there is no quicker way of improving your skills than doing a wide variety of challenging work. Alternatively, and this is most true for graduates coming into consulting, it is because you join a company who understands that its key asset is people and hence is willing to invest significantly in their development. Consulting does provide a great way to develop a powerful set of useful skills, such as problem analysis, communication skills and influencing skills. One important exception to this is that if you want to learn how to manage people then you will be better off seeking an operational line management role.

However, this brings me to another potential advantage of consulting. If you want to, you can avoid much of the burden of line management that goes with a corporate role. Some individuals love managing people, some hate it. If you work for a large consultancy you may still have staff whom you have to performance manage and motivate, but the teams tend to be small. As an independent consultant staff management is not something you have to worry about.

Graduates often want to join consultancies for the lifestyle and travel. There are a few professions which enable you to travel even more and to wilder places, such as mining and oil exploration, but generally there is a fantastic opportunity to travel as a consultant if you want to – especially if you are multi-lingual. Such travel can be exciting and rewarding. Working in foreign countries gives you a perspective that other travellers never gain, but it is a double-edged sword.

❝ working in foreign countries is a double-edged sword ❞

Travelling all the time can be dull. You have to be a little shallow to be really interested in having gold frequent flyer cards with several airlines. Often the locations sound exotic, but an office is an office wherever it is in the world. Continuous travel will also play havoc with your social life.

Some people want to enter consulting for the money. The money earned as a consultant can be good, but of course it depends what you are used to. Few consultants achieve the rewards of the chief executive of a major company, unless they happen to become a senior partner in a big firm. On the other hand, most reasonably successful consultants earn more than senior middle managers and junior executives in most other industries.

There are much more down-to-earth explanations for becoming a consultant. Some people just fall into it. I was recruited by Coopers & Lybrand out of industry, and frankly I had no idea what consulting was but it was better money, which for a young man with a family seemed an attractive proposition. I was lucky in that it is a career that has suited me immensely. Other people come into consulting because they feel they have no other choice. Perhaps they have been senior managers who find themselves late in their careers having been made redundant and, irrespective of age discrimination laws, cannot find a suitable alternative role. These are not necessarily bad reasons for entering the consulting profession. We are all, at times, hard-nosed about our careers, and just because you entered the profession as way of overcoming redundancy does not mean it will not be a huge success. On the other hand, simply because you have some business skills does not mean you will thrive as a consultant.

A phrase that has become common recently is the 'portfolio career'. This is a career in which you mix various different types of work together. This is definitely possible as a consultant, especially if you are self-employed. Some types of work can complement consulting very well. I know many people who manage to control this mix very successfully. I have several professions: as well as running my consulting business I write, deliver training courses and seminars and take regular time out to study.

Whatever your reasons for considering consulting, don't fool yourself that it is always an easy ride, or that it will give you a completely flexible lifestyle. For example, as a self-employed consultant you may well be able to take more holiday, you may well be able to work part time – but, and it is a big but, within the constraints of your clients' needs. You may decide to work only nine months a year, but that does not mean you can definitely choose the three months you don't work to be 1 November to 31 January every year whilst you are in the South Pacific, and expect at the same time to be 100 per cent fee earning until 31 October, and have an immediate start again on 1 February of the following year. Clients won't usually wait for a particular consultant: if they have a problem they want someone to fix it, and if you are not available they can usually find someone else to do the work just as well. Consulting opportunities cannot simply be turned on and off. They have to be searched out and won. Clients and engagements do not easily fit a predictable pattern. If you want flexibility you do need to have some flexibility yourself.

Whatever flexibility you want from consulting is effectively a constraint on your ability to service clients. If you are clever and pragmatic there is no reason why the constraints cannot be overcome and you can manage to balance your own and your client's desires very well. But you cannot both maximise your income and maximise your personal flexibility (unless, perhaps, you really are a world renowned industry guru).

I know many people who love working as a consultant. But consulting does not suit everyone's personalities. If you are constantly working in different organisations, it changes the relationship with the place you are working. To some extent you will always be an outsider, which does not suit everyone's personality. Consulting can leave many people with an ongoing feeling of uncertainty and risk. As one project ends, where is the next and when will it start? If you are an independent consultant there is no career path as such – you may want to vary your work, and may over time increase your rates, but there is no management hierarchy to be promoted through. If you work in one of the large consultancies, promotion is possible, but for most firms seniority beyond a certain level does not just depend on your consulting skills and expertise, but on your ability to sell.

Consulting offers great opportunity, but it is different from other types of employment. It offers potentially high rewards and significant flexibility. If unmanaged, it can intrude into your personal life, but arguably so does any senior role. If you are pragmatic and flexible, then you can get a good level of rewards and flexibility in return.

The economics of consulting

The past few decades have brought an increasing stress on the work–life balance and less on the financial factors of employment. However, a key aspect in deciding whether to be a consultant is whether you will make the income you desire. Whether a career in consulting can provide you with the money you want depends on your expectations (or income needs), your degree of success, but also the inherent economics of consulting. Before entering this profession you should understand your potential income. I am going to look at this only very, very simply. This is not a business plan for a consulting business, but it does explain the basics.

> ❝ this is not a business plan for a consulting business ❞

Let's start by considering the case of a single independent consultant as this is the simplest to understand. I will only look at revenues. Costs for independent consultants are generally low, and most of those that are incurred are attributable to clients and can be recharged as expenses. So, I am going to ignore them for now. This is of course a gross generalisation, but it is fine to begin with as it will not change the overall outcome. There are two factors that determine how much money you generate as a consultant:

1 the number of chargeable days a year you achieve
2 your daily charge-out rate.

(Not all consulting projects are charged on a daily basis, but this basis is accurate enough to understand the general economics of the business.)

It is really as simple as that. So how do you know how many days a year you will work for and what daily charge-out rate you will achieve? There are huge variations between different consultants. Taking account of fee rates and number of chargeable days it is quite easy to find two apparently similar consultants, one of whom has an income three or four times higher than the other. At the extremes, comparing the lowest to highest revenue-generating consultant then the multiples are much greater.

Some estimates

To estimate the daily rate you will achieve it is best to do a little research, but it is not straightforward finding accurate information. There is no easily available database of rates as there is no transparent market in consultancy, and it is generally not in consultants' interests to make it transparent. A good place to start is the internet. There are websites dedicated to sourcing consultants and other temporary staff that will give you a rough idea of potential daily rates, but they do tend to focus on the lower end of the market. There are studies of the industry, but they are not always freely available. Even if you get hold of one, their categorisations of consultants may give you some ideas, but generally are too broad to base your own fees on. A good source of information is your personal network. Ask a few friends who hire consultants regularly, and you may be able to get a feel for the sort of rates the big firms charge. These tend to be higher than independents achieve, although this is not always true. The best way to get a feel for rates is to find someone with some experience of the industry and ask them what they think you will be able to charge. Never forget, whatever fee rate you expect or want, it actually depends on a client being willing to pay it.

Next you need to estimate how many days a year you will work. If you are new to consulting, do not be overly optimistic. Can you really work 5 days a week for 52 weeks a year? That gives you 260 chargeable days a year, but you should never assume that what you make is 260 times your daily rate. You will rarely be 100 per cent utilised – and even if you can be, do you really want to be? As a rule of thumb, assume you will be busy 100 days a year. You may well be a lot busier, but if you cannot afford to be a consultant working only this many days you are taking a significant risk. Many consultants make a very comfortable living on this, and many more are busy for considerably more than 100 days a year. But it is best to be conservative at the start of your career.

Other factors

There are several other factors you must consider. There are possible tax efficiencies of being self-employed or running your own business. You need professional advice to understand these fully, and tax legislation can change at any time. Remember, if you are becoming a self-employed consultant after a career in industry there are none of the benefits that you may have received in your previous job. There are no extra pension contributions, no bonus, no paid holiday, no health care or sick pay, no car allowance, etc. Additionally, you should not confuse income with cash flow. Consulting tends to pay big bills in dribs and drabs, and some clients can be very slow in delivering cash into your bank account. I am usually paid reasonably promptly, but some invoices have languished for six months before finally being paid. You need to have a float of money to cover for these periods.

For a consulting firm with multiple employees the economics are much more complex. Costs cannot be ignored. Business costs for premium office space and facilities may be high. Staff you employ will naturally expect many benefits on top of salaries. There will be the costs of non-fee-earning staff and senior staff: although they may be able to charge some fees, these may not cover the full cost of their salary and expenses. Bad debt has to be considered – that is clients who will not or cannot pay. I have never (yet!) experienced this and it does seem to be rare. However, in the largest firms, simply because of the volume of work they undertake, occasionally a client may not pay. Whatever the size of firm, slow payment remains a far bigger issue.

Profitability of consultancy companies can be very high when chargeable utilisation is above a certain level, but drop below this level and all those large salaries and fancy offices can soon lead to big losses. Hence the tendency of some firms to recruit heavily in the boom times, but also to be quick to make staff redundant when the economy is struggling. In the end, although an accountant could find a million flaws in my simple views, the profit of a consulting company can be approximated by a very simple piece of arithmetic:

Profit = (days charged × average charge-out rate) – cost of business

The rate you charge and the number of days you work are dependent on clients, but your costs are largely under your own control. With modern technology and services you can run a consultancy on a shoestring, and still look completely professional. Therefore the most important considerations will always be making sure you charge enough days at a high enough fee rate to generate the income you require. If you are committing yourself to significant costs before you have started to generate revenue, think again. You can always make those commitments once you are sure of your income.

Finally, what about the situation in which you take a job within a consultancy, as an employed consultant, rather than someone who runs their own business? Here your salary is to some extent divorced from the economics of the consulting business, and is down to what you can negotiate. The big firms tend to have a standard package for graduates. For more senior staff the salary and package will depend on how valuable you are to the consultancy and what you can negotiate. At a more senior level your value to a consultancy is more related to your relationships and personal network than your pure consulting skills. Generally, the large consultancies pay well and provide a good set of other benefits. There are professions paying higher, but consulting has to be considered as towards the top end of the market in terms of salaries. As an internal consultant it is different, and your salary will depend on the market rates associated with your specialisation and the remuneration policies of the specific firm you are being employed by. Generally, salaries are lower than in the consultancy companies.

> **big firms tend to have a standard package for graduates**

What is a good consultant?

By this point you know what a consultant is, why you might want to consider it as a profession and whether you will make any money. In this final section I want to consider what makes a good consultant. Much of this book is taken up with giving advice on how to be a good consultant; this short section is concerned with what would be assessed as a good consultant.

When I told a friend of mine, who is a successful and experienced consultant, about this book he responded with the comment that there is little to write. He said the book would only be about 10 pages long, but then went on to advise that I should not write a book, but a haiku! The truth behind this jibe is that it is quite simple to define what a good consultant is – but most of this book is about how to achieve this rather than defining it. My poetry skills are limited, so I will stick to prose rather than the haiku. A good consultant: *continuously adds value to clients commensurate with his or her fees.*

We will explore what adding value means in later chapters.

There is a significant difference between being good at something and being a good consultant. There is an old joke, aimed rather unfairly at teachers, saying: *those who can, do; those who can't, teach.* This joke can be extended to become: *those who can, do; those who can't, teach; and those who can't teach, consult.* The joke for teachers is unfair, but it hides an important truth – there is a difference between being good at something and being a good teacher. As many students will attest, being a good university lecturer is quite a different skill from being a brilliant academic. I am sure we have all experienced the giant brain who cannot explain anything, and the person with a nominally lesser grasp who explains it very well. While most teachers are perfectly capable of doing, that is not what they are employed for – they are employed to impart and embed knowledge and skills in their students. Whether or not they can actually 'do' is to some extent irrelevant. It is similar for consultants. There are many advantages in having management experience, but consulting is not about managing. Equally, having been a great manager is an advantage for consulting, but it does not guarantee that you will be a successful consultant.

From your perspective you are a good consultant if you achieve your personal objectives through consulting. I cannot tell you what your personal goals should be, and the rest of this book is about how you can continuously add value for your clients. However, you may wonder whether you have the right type of personality to succeed as a consultant. There is no single personality type who makes the best consultant, but I will pick on a few factors which I think are important.

Firstly, as a consultant you should be a people person. It is not necessary to be a natural extrovert, but you must be happy engaging with others. You will constantly be working and interacting with people, and if this does not excite you then consulting is not for you. Next, you should be flexible and adaptable. Client needs and expectations vary enormously, and you need to flex to the situation. It may surprise some people, but it also helps if you are not status conscious. Although you may end up as a hugely successful consultant earning much more than most of your clients, when you are on a client's site you are just a consultant doing a job for them. Consultants must be orientated to resolving problems. A client has engaged you to help; there are many forms this help can take, but all of them must result in resolving a client's problems. Next, whilst a consultant is there to help, they must not be over hasty in determining solutions. You must have the personality that wants to solve problems properly, rather than resolve the most apparent symptoms. You want to be like the doctor who finds out why a patient has spots rather than the one who just gives a cream to make them less itchy. Finally, you must be someone who listens. To be objective and to provide a diagnosis that is most helpful to the client requires listening and assessing the situation. Solutions must be tailored to the specific context.

There are many other factors which influence your ability to be a great consultant, but the above are critical.

Summary

If you are new to consulting there are some essential concepts you must understand. You should now be familiar with the main concepts covered in this chapter. They are:

- The role of a consultant and the difference between it and other roles, especially that of a line manager.

- The skills of a consultant in relation to those of other professions such as contractor or interim manager.

- The core consulting jargon.

- The variety of consulting organisations.

- Why you want to be a consultant and whether it is a profession that can fulfil those needs.

- The economics of consulting.

- What a good consultant is.

The rest of this book explains how to be a good and successful consultant.

2

Why does anyone buy consultancy?

onsultants regularly present the consulting profession as highly intellectual and just a little bit special. Yet underneath the hype, management consulting is merely an industry providing a service in response to a customer's need. All the normal lessons from sales and marketing apply. The customer may be called the *client*, but it is only on this client's willingness to provide money in exchange for the consultant's service that the industry is built. Selling consulting is not especially difficult, but it is essential for anyone who wants to succeed as a consultant. If you never make a sale then even the best consulting skills in the world are only of theoretical value.

In this chapter I explore the basis for selling consultancy – a client who buys. Later in this book we will discuss interesting and powerful ideas about consulting, but I want to start relatively simply and prosaically, as success as a consultant must start with your feet firmly on the ground! Although the chapter is aimed at external consultants, the lessons are applicable to internal consultants. Whilst the challenge of 'selling' services internally within an organisation is different in some respects, for instance the lack of a formal contract, the essential need to identify opportunities and encourage a client to 'buy' is still there.

No matter how wonderful, unique or valuable your skills are, no one buys consultancy simply because of your abilities. Clients buy consultancy because they have a need or desire which consultancy is perceived to be capable of fulfilling. This chapter explores what these needs are. One of the fundamental mistakes new consultants make is to misunderstand that it is not skills that create the opportunity for consulting services, but client needs. Skills are required to market and deliver consulting, but if you do not understand your client needs, then you will struggle to sell an engagement. Before you spend time perfecting skills, gaining qualifications or acquiring accreditation you should heed the most basic marketing lesson: to understand what your customers desire.

Having a need is an essential part of a client buying consultancy, but there are additional prerequisites which determine whether a client can and will buy the service you offer, even if it fulfils their needs perfectly. Before considering what makes a client buy, it is useful to look at the prerequisites for purchase. I explain these in the first two sections of this chapter.

> **❝ it is useful to look at the prerequisites for purchase ❞**

Much of this chapter considers the client as if there is an obvious individual client. The final section of this chapter looks at one of the possible minefields of consultancy, in answering an often surprisingly complex question: who is your client?

The prerequisites for selling consultancy

What are the prerequisite conditions which must be met for it to be possible to sell consultancy? I have identified eight basic prerequisites which must be present in order to sell a consulting engagement:

1 There is a client.
2 The client has a currently unfulfilled need.
3 The client believes that they require help to resolve this need.
4 The client knows about you and your services.
5 The client perceives that you are capable of fulfilling this need.
6 You (or someone else acceptable to the client) are available to fulfil the engagement.
7 The client has a budget/finances to pay for your services.
8 The client has authority to spend the budget/finances.

Without over analysing these prerequisites let's quickly review them.

The first prerequisite is the most obvious, so obvious it can seem like it need not be stated. Hidden in the obviousness is an unchallenged assumption. The assumption is: *if I have business knowledge and skills I can be a successful consultant.* Documenting prerequisite 1 may appear unnecessary, but I know of consultants with all sorts of esoteric and interesting skills, for which there is no client. So, unsurprisingly, they do not find work. They moan and ponder about how to increase their skills further, thinking 'surely then I will gain work', without noticing that there are many more poorly qualified, but highly successful consultants. Before you spend time analysing and perfecting your service line, check that there is likely to be some form of client. Whatever skills or service line you have – no client, no income!

When there is a potential client, to sell a service, they must have a currently unfulfilled need, and a belief that this need can be fulfilled by consulting. Unfulfilled needs exist aplenty in business. Ask most managers if there is anything they would like help with or problems to be rid of, and you will soon get a very long list. This list radically shortens when you ask them which of these problems is a candidate for resolution by a consultant.

Let us suppose we have met the first three prerequisites. There is a client with an unfulfilled need that they accept they need help fulfilling. We are getting closer to the possibility of selling an engagement. Prerequisites 4 and 5 relate to you personally. The client must know about you. A client cannot buy goods and services they know nothing about. This is a common problem in consulting. If you happen to be working for a major international consultancy most potential clients will have heard of you – although even then, they may well not know your full range of services. On the other hand, if you are a small consultancy or an independent consultant most of your potential clients have no knowledge of your existence. Clients not only need to know about you, but to even get a sniff of real work you need to be perceived as potentially capable of fulfilling their needs. Simply put: are you a known and credible supplier? Unlike the first three prerequisites, prerequisites 4 and 5 are largely in your control and depend on your marketing and networking skills. If you are in a situation in which the answer to this question is no, the follow up is obvious: *what will you do to become a known and credible supplier?* (See chapters 3, 5 and 9.)

Of course, to perform an engagement you, or someone else you can put forward who meets prerequisites 1 to 5, need to be available to do the work. Consultants use the term **availability** to refer to time when they are available to work on a live engagement – i.e. time when the consultant is not working on another engagement, busy with business development, sick or on holiday, etc. Availability is difficult to predict. Engagements don't just end on a fixed date, and the time it takes to sell a consulting engagement does not usually neatly align with the time it takes to complete whatever else you are working on. Get your timing wrong and you may win some work when you are still busy with another client. You do not actually need to be available to perform the engagement to sell the engagement to a client. It is possible to sell work without being available to deliver it, but unless you can make yourself available quickly, the sales activity is a waste of your and your client's time.

Prerequisites 7 and 8 relate to money. You are a commercial business, and therefore are only going to work if there is access to finance to pay your fees. There are obvious situations in which this is not going to be true; for instance, companies going bankrupt or organisations with very restricted budgets. Commercially, these are to be avoided. As an exception, you may choose to take on some *pro bono* work for a good cause. I say as an exception not because I want to put you off undertaking *pro bono* work, but for the simple reason that unless you are privately wealthy it can only be a small proportion of your work or you will not stay in business long. A more common problem is not that an organisation has no money to pay your fees, but that the individual manager who is your potential client has no direct access to a budget or no ability to influence someone else to spend. It is always useful to ascertain early in your client negotiations if a client has sufficient money which they are authorised to spend.

In this section I have summarised the core prerequisites for a client to buy consultancy. Without these prerequisites being in place, no matter how hard you try, there will be no sale. But there is another side to the equation. Not the client perspective, but yours. Although it is not a prerequisite for buying, it should be a prerequisite for selling – that the client can provide you with whatever you need to do your work. Few consulting engagements can be undertaken without any client support. For instance, you may need access to human resources, almost always require some data and information, and will always need time to complete your work. Clients may not want or be able to fulfil all your prerequisites. As a consultant you must be flexible and often ingenious in finding ways to complete engagements without all the ideal things you think you need to do your work. However, whilst you may be able to compromise there are some

❝ as a consultant you must be flexible and often ingenious ❞

minimal prerequisites that must be met. If the client cannot fulfil these prerequisites for the work, the engagement should not progress (see Chapters 5 and 12).

Obstacles to selling consultancy

The existence of an opportunity, which meets the prerequisites outlined above, is the starting point for a sale. We are going to look at identifying opportunities and selling consultancy in detail later in the book (Chapter 5), but just because there are opportunities does not mean you will necessarily gain work. Clients have choices. There are many consulting companies, and there are thousands of individual consultants. For every opportunity there are also many possible obstacles to sales

What are the main impediments to selling consultancy? Here are some key obstacles to sales:

- You may not convince your client that you are the right choice. Clients will not just select you – you have to overcome the obstacles of their natural scepticism and doubt. Doubt may arise if you do not have a sufficiently established reputation, or if you write a poor proposal. Scepticism of your skills will be reinforced if there is bad chemistry between you and the client. The latter is one of the most difficult issues to deal with. Each of these problems can be overcome, but each reduces the likelihood of a sale.

- You are often in competition, and each credible competitor is an obstacle to your sale. You not only have to be able to meet the prerequisites of a sale, but you must be the best from a competitive position. What the client regards as the best will vary from situation to situation. A key activity in a competitive situation is to extract the client's decision-making criteria for selecting a consultant. Typical criteria are your fee rates, experience and skills, availability, and your demonstration of your understanding of the situation. But there will be less tangible factors as well, such as how much the client likes you.

- Your needs and the client's may not match. This is explored in more detail in Chapter 5, but is summarised here. A client does not just have a need to buy, but you must have a desire to sell. An opportunity not meeting your needs can be an insurmountable obstacle. A client may not be offering a high enough fee rate to interest you. There may be some physical or geographic prerequisites you are not willing to commit to – working at nights or thousands of miles from home.

- There is another more complicated reason why an opportunity may never become a sale. Imagine your client meets all the prerequisites to sell to. Further than this, you have had a series of productive conversations during which you have reached a mutual conclusion that you can help the client and they will meet your prerequisites of engagement. What can go wrong now? Client needs can change. During the process of engaging and selling to a client it is not unusual for needs to change. This is particularly frequent if the sales process is protracted. The reasons are many and varied. Common reasons include a change in the client's business circumstances, an evolution in understanding of needs as your discussions become more detailed, or the involvement of another stakeholder with different ideas from the original client.

In the first two sections of this chapter I have explored the various prerequisites that must be met and obstacles that must be overcome in order to make a consultancy sale possible. It may be that after reading this list you think it is never going to happen. Don't despair – these prerequisites are regularly met, which is proven by the vast volume of consulting sales that are made all the time. I have listed them not to put you off, but to enable you to align all your ducks in a row, painlessly.

On numerous occasions, I have seen consultants (including, on reflection, myself) making epic efforts to gain a sale, only to end up wasting time as one or more of these prerequisites was not met. This cannot always be prevented, but frequently the wasted effort is avoidable. It is often determinable early in the sales process that some crucial prerequisite cannot be met. Frequently, getting a client to answer a simple question like 'what budget is available for this work?' is enough to determine there is no real opportunity. Unless you have some power to change the situation, then you are much better off moving on to the next opportunity than working hard where no engagement will be available. I have never heard of a client deliberately wasting a consultant's time – as it is their time too – but sometimes it can feel as if they are! A client may simply have not thought through all the implications of engaging you, or sometimes they value just talking to a consultant without committing.

The client's explicit needs for buying consultancy

Let's explore prerequisite 2 from the list earlier in this chapter in more detail: *the client has a currently unfulfilled need*. This is the most complex and important item on that list, and the one that consultants spend a significant proportion of their time identifying and exploring. What sort of needs do clients have? Clients have a huge variety of needs and desires. I cannot write a list of all the possible client needs that exist, but I can place them into a short set of categories. These are not mutually exclusive, but the core needs clients typically fall into one of more of the following categories:

▦ The client thinks something along the lines of: 'I have a problem which I want solved – and I think a consultant would be able to solve it for me.' This is the traditional reason for buying consultancy. Variations on this theme include:

  – I want a bit of fresh creativity, innovation or new ideas which I cannot find in my existing employees.

  – I need some facilitation or workshops to solve a problem.

  – I want access to some specific IP (intellectual property), tools or techniques that a consultant has.

▦ A client has a new or ongoing initiative/project but does not have all the required resources. They think: 'I will ask a consultant to fill a role on the project.' Depending on the precise type of work this may be truly consulting, but more often it is really contracting. However, if the work is interesting and the fee rate is right there is no reason not to pursue it.

▦ A client has some operational work and the normal manager is away, unavailable or still needs to be recruited. Alternatively, there is a temporary operational role to fill. This is the realms of interim management, but the boundaries between interim management and consultancy are fluid and many consultants make excellent interim managers.

▦ A client has too much to do, juggling too many tasks at once and needs a little bit of relief or else risks dropping one of the balls. The client wants a consultant to come in and seamlessly take control of one or more of the juggling balls so they can give a bit more time and attention to the remaining ones. This is a factor in many consultancy sales.

- Occasionally, a client may be told to get some assistance from a consultant. This instruction may come from a supportive or frustrated senior manager telling a subordinate how to fix something that should have been resolved long ago. Alternatively, it may be a demand from an external source, such as an industry regulator telling a company to quickly become compliant with an area of regulation.

- Finally, a need can be created. Consultants with time to spare and a bit of creative insight can come up with all sorts of appealing and exciting service lines. Occasionally, a client will listen to a cold sales pitch and be interested enough to buy your service. The client may not have known they had a need, but after listening to the consultant's pitch finds that they do. It's like advertising: you did not know you wanted chocolate until you saw the advert! However, unless you have a strong relationship with your client, this is a hard act to pull off. It is possible, and successful consultancies do regularly achieve this. One of the reasons for fads in consulting services is to establish competitive differentiation and to create demand. Chapter 9 explores the situations in which this is possible.

Hidden grounds for buying consultancy

What a client tells you, when discussing their needs for consultancy, may provide a clear and complete picture of why they are considering your services. However, this is unusual. Most people have other grounds that they do not divulge. Sometimes they are embarrassed to tell you everything or maybe they feel it is better if some things remain confidential. They may think if they tell you the truth you will not do the work. Sometimes they do not tell you because they do not realise the information is relevant or important to you. Often they do not tell you because they have not analysed all the reasons they want to use a consultant and are not consciously aware of the grounds themselves.

Irrespective of the situation, you will usually start a consulting engagement with an incomplete and sometimes incorrect understanding of why the client is engaging you. In practice, this is neither always avoidable nor necessarily an intractable problem. But, generally, you are in a better position to fulfil the client's needs if you understand what the hidden grounds are.

You may not understand all aspects of the client's grounds for buying consulting because the problem is complex and cannot be easily fully

> **❝ involvement can only happen when the engagement starts ❞**

explained without some time involved in the organisation. This involvement can only happen when the engagement starts. It is not unusual for understanding of needs and selection of approaches to fulfilling these needs to change as the consultant fulfils the engagement. This is one reason why it is often effective to start a large engagement with a smaller scoping exercise, when both the specific problem and nature of the client's organisation are explored.

There are many other motivations for employing consultants which will not be immediately apparent when you are first engaged. Typical examples of hidden grounds for buying consulting include:

- Risk reduction: a client does not know how to overcome a problem, does not have confidence to so, or thinks there's too much risk in doing it themselves. These are perfectly valid grounds for engaging consultants. As a consultant, if you do not reduce a client's business risk as part of your work – for example the risk of taking the wrong decisions or performing a poor implementation of change – then you have not really added value. If you have a very strong relationship with your client they may admit this, but reducing business risk is rarely explicitly stated as a rationale for engaging you.

- The client has tried already, but has failed or is struggling to overcome a problem. Rarely will a client admit this directly to you, but it is important to try and ascertain if this is the case. If a client has previously failed to resolve a problem then their need for help increases, but their emotions towards the work and the consultant are easily prejudiced. Although this situation is common it does need to be treated with care. If mishandled, you can be perceived as positioning yourself as 'better' than your client. This is never popular with clients!

- The client wants to gain buy-in to an idea or project. A client can simply want something confirmed that they already know. They may ask for advice, when what they are really asking for is your agreement to their existing position. A client is unlikely to say directly to you: 'I am engaging you to confirm my opinions.' This can be tricky, as of course you may not agree with their standpoint, and can easily stray into an ethical dilemma (see Chapter 10).

- Clients sometimes engage a consultant because they need to be seen to be doing something, not because they actually want anything done. Clients have many stakeholders they need or want to keep happy. These include more senior managers and external stakeholders like regulators. By explicitly employing a consultant, to perform an engagement which the client has no interest in, they can sometimes artificially satisfy such stakeholders. The risk to the consultant is limited, other than that findings and advice may never be implemented by the client.

This is by no means an exhaustive list. The central point is to be alert for the true, covert motivations clients have for engaging you. The only way to understand the hidden grounds is by observation and entering into exploratory dialogue with the client. If you meet all their explicit needs, but never fulfil their hidden needs, you will not satisfy your clients – and often the hidden needs are more important than those explicitly stated. As all good marketers know, client satisfaction is a crucial element in a successful business. In Chapter 5 we will explore this further.

Having sold an engagement to a client, the subsequent challenge for a consultant is to continue to remain involved. There are many reasons why a client may retain a consultant, the most obvious being the need to follow on from a completed engagement. A less overt reason is that the client values the ongoing advice and support of the consultant. Much of the value of consultants can come in peripheral activities: extra value that the client gains simply by the consultant being around. This can be small tips, advice, problem solving, tools and so on.

Who is your client?

New consultants often talk about their client as if it is always absolutely clear who the client is, and also use the term *client* and the name of an organisation interchangeably. As in 'my client is XYZ Corporation'. Your fees will be paid by XYZ Corporation. XYZ is the client organisation, but you cannot interact, advise or have a relationship with an organisation. Your client is one or more human beings. There are many situations in which there is clearly one client, and you can be sure that the interests of the client and the client organisation are aligned, but often this is not clear cut. This can result in two related problems: firstly, the difficulty of identifying the true client, and secondly, conflict in the views of different stakeholders and clients.

You need to know who your client is because the client is the person (or group) who your consultancy is aimed at. The client is the person who will judge whether the consultancy has been successful or not. If you do not clarify who the client is you may never be judged to have completed your work successfully. A different problem is that without a clear-cut client different people in an organisation can legitimately ask you to do all sorts of work. Not having an unambiguous and single client can be compared to the situation in which as an employee you do not know who amongst a group of managers is your boss.

One reason for this lack of clarity is that there are often multiple stakeholders in a client organisation who have different views and interests in a particular engagement. Although it is theoretically meaningful to differentiate specifically between a client and other stakeholders, in reality the boundaries are not always clear cut. There can be a wide variety of interested parties in any consulting engagement. On some engagements this is a minor issue. On others, different clients/stakeholders can be in direct and explicit conflict over the needs and direction of a consulting engagement, with the consultant left like some UN arbitrator in the middle trying to resolve the dispute with limited resources. The conflict may be explicit, but sometimes it is hidden, which is worse, as the consultant can progress the engagement with one understanding and only in the latter stages when feeding back to one client comes against another stakeholder who denigrates the work.

> **there are often multiple stakeholders in a client organisation**

Another situation arises when the person who engages you, who you take to be the client, is actually hiring you under the direction of a more senior manager. The senior manager is really the client. The person who engages you may not accurately represent the true client's needs. This can lead to all sorts of misunderstandings and problems.

Different stakeholders are quite likely to have different views on what is required from an engagement, and even how the work should be approached. Some stakeholders may think you are the ideal candidate to perform an engagement, others may doubt your suitability to do the work. Various stakeholders will have all sorts of different decision-making criteria. Ideally, you need to clarify all of this.

Another source of confusion is the difference between a client and an organisation. A client is a tangible person. You can speak to them and through dialogue get an understanding of their wants and desires, needs and wishes, interests and foibles. An organisation is an abstract entity, and if such an entity can be said to have interests you can only determine them indirectly – by speaking to the staff and managers of the organisation. Problems arise because the interests of the individuals in the organisation probably never align with those of the organisation. Even if a member of an organisation's staff is trying to be objective and ignore their own interests, they will be constrained in achieving this by their biases, inherent assumptions and lack of full understanding of what the interests of an organisation are. One reason for clear and simple vision and mission statements in organisations is that all staff can then determine what the interests of the organisation are and are not.

We are therefore in a situation of imperfect information and limited consensus. One of the tasks a consultant initially has in any engagement is not only to understand the client's wants and needs, but to clarify who the client is. Ideally there is one clear client who has the remit and authority to describe exactly what you should do. In practice, this is not always achieved. Power in organisations does not always fit the organisational hierarchy, and you will not always be so lucky as to have one main stakeholder in your work.

Why is this a problem? Because a lack of clarity over who the client is, and no real understanding of the client's need and desires, leads to all sorts of other difficulties. Your engagement may be perceived as a failure if you please one person you perceived as a client, only to find someone else – who is really the client – is displeased. You cannot complete an engagement successfully without understanding client needs, which you won't do if you have not identified the client correctly. You may have difficulty finishing your work as you try to satisfy more and more client stakeholders. If you are working to a fixed fee, trying to satisfy everyone causes you to lose money. There are many variations of these sorts of difficulties.

How can you solve this issue? There is no foolproof way to resolve it in every situation. Your role as a consultant may be explicitly to help reach consensus between all stakeholders. But it will not always be, and even if you are there to drive consensus your role can never be to sort out all the differences of opinion in an organisation. However, you do have to achieve at least a sufficient consensus to be able to complete your engagement effectively. There are five main steps to achieving this:

1 Openly discuss the issue with whoever first engages you, and try to get them to support you in identifying and resolving any differences of opinion. If this is not possible, you should strive for the manager who engages you at least to accept the implications of an imprecise understanding of needs.

2   Understand who might be clients and stakeholders in the work, and then explore and analyse the specific situation, identifying true clients and exploring their needs.

3   Ideally, identify one primary (or 'real') client who will resolve any conflicts and arbitrate in any disputes with other stakeholders.

4   Take a commonsense check. When you do have an understanding of the different client and stakeholder needs, do they form a coherent and consistent set? Can you fulfil this set of needs in a sensible and achievable engagement that feels right for the organisation?

5   Write down your understanding of the situation in your proposal. Then if things are not as they appeared to be, you at least have a document you can point to with your understanding as agreed with the client. However, for some sensitive needs this is not possible.

We will look at the points in this list again in Chapters 5, 9 and 10. For now, I want to focus on step 2. Who might your client be? This will vary from situation to situation, but the choice of the person who is your client starts by considering the person who first engages you. Typically you will be approached by an individual about the work the client organisation wants performed. This person may or may not be the 'real' client. I call this person the *client interface*.

Another possible client is the manager who has instructed the client interface (usually a more junior manager) to engage you. In some situations, it was a personal decision of the client interface to engage you, but it is quite common for a more senior manager to direct the client interface to hire a consultant. This senior manager is the *real client*. Ideally, you want to develop a direct relationship with this person, as they are the one who really wants the work done and are likely to be the judge of its success.

There will often be senior managers or executives with no direct involvement or interest in the work you do, but who influence the work indirectly by being concerned or even assessing the performance of the manager who engages you. This is the *underlying client*. The underlying client is important, as in the end this is the person or group your real client mostly responds to.

There are budgetholders and approvers who need to be convinced before you invoices are paid. You are a commercial business and need to be paid for your work and therefore must be comfortable that such people will authorise your invoices. Usually the person you work with as a client is

❝ whoever authorises your bill is the *financial client* ❞   also the person who authorises your bills for payment, but not always. Whoever authorises your bill is the *financial client*. The financial client is important as of course you want to get paid!

Finally there is a whole host of other client staff who review, approve or may simply be asked an opinion about your work. They may also work for you on the engagement. Such staff are not really clients, but you cannot ignore them as they have the ability to influence the judgement of your client both positively and negatively.

Behind these various people lies another group, who will be more or less important depending on the nature of the engagement. These are the client organisation's stakeholders. These include external groups who may have an interest in the work, for example shareholders and owners, and for some industries, regulators. Many consultants never interact with these groups, but for some consultants they are a major influence on the success of the consulting engagement.

A typical set of clients is shown in Figure 2.1. The solid lines represent typical direct relationships relevant to the engagement. The dashed lines represent other possible relationships relevant to the engagement.

When considering this set of clients and stakeholders the following points should be taken into account:

■ The client is always a person. You may be paid from a large corporation's bank account, but you are engaged by, interact with and take instructions from an individual or group. An individual or group responds to your advice and accepts your invoices. For many reasons we may say 'my client is XYZ Corporation', but in reality it is always a person.

■ Ideally there is one client, which is sometime achievable, but there will always be more than one stakeholder.

■ The best situation is to understand and fulfil the needs of the client and all relevant stakeholders. It is often not possible to satisfy everyone and therefore you need to identify who is the real client and how you will resolve conflicts with other stakeholders.

■ Some of the problems that arise from having multiple clients/stakeholders will create issues for you, but not your real client. For example, you may be asked to do more and more work by different stakeholders, to the point at which you lose your profit margin on the engagement.

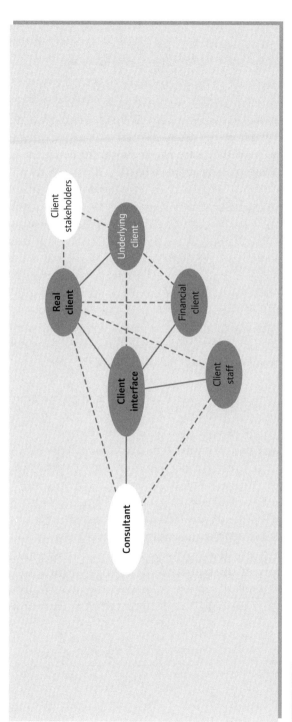

Figure 2.1 Clients

- There may be ethical issues associated with multiple clients with different interests (see Chapter 10). After all, if there are multiple interests, who actually represents the organisation?

- There is a potentially complex relationship with client staff. They may think of themselves as 'the client', when in reality they might be a resource for you to use on the engagement, or even the subject of your work.

- Finally, if you are working for a large consulting company your stakeholders may include people who are within your own organisation or other bodies. These people can make requests at the most difficult time during an engagement. More than one new consultant has been shocked when the work they thought they had agreed with their client, and considered as finished, was rejected by a partner or senior manager from their own company as not good enough. Hence a consultant may also have to work to keep a range of people concerned with different aspects of the consultancy firm's interests satisfied. For instance, there will be people responsible for the quality, risk and brand of a consulting company. Even if the client is happy with the work, such managers in the consulting firm may not be if it is not of sufficient quality or risks the firm's reputation.

There will be staff concerned with utilisation. Utilisation is how consulting firms make money. There is always pressure on consulting engagements to maximise billable utilisation for the maximum number of staff. Of course, the client wants the opposite!

Consulting firms are always trying to improve their knowledge and IP development. Consultancies view most engagements as a potential opportunity to increase their IP and knowledge. There will also be people with the fundamental business concern of whether an engagement is profitable and if it offers the opportunity for further sales. Finally, outside the consulting firm itself there are stakeholders such as professional bodies, who have some influence on how the work is performed and any standards associated with it.

These additional stakeholders can make the situation more complex. This increase in complexity is shown in Figure 2.2.

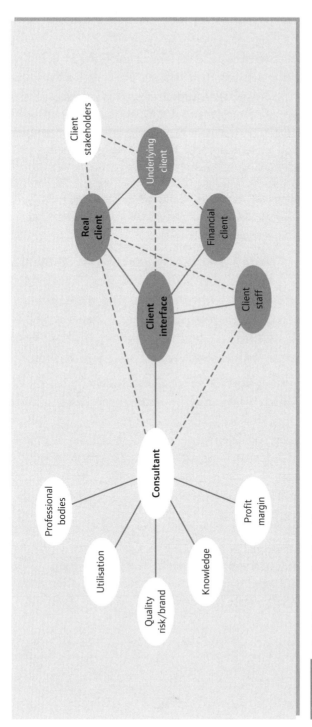

Figure 2.2 The full range of stakeholders

Summary

This chapter has covered some of the fundamental challenges in consulting. It is important to understand these because as a consultant you will face them all on a regular basis. Hence I want to give you a brief summary to ensure the key points are remembered. Each of these challenges is explored in more detail, together with ways to overcome them, in the rest of the book.

- Consultants sell to and are judged by a client. The concept of a client needs to be explored thoroughly as in any situation there may be different individuals who may be the client. The greater the clarity you have over who the client is, the greater the likelihood that your consulting engagement will be a success.

- The client has needs, and a consulting engagement is designed to fulfil these needs. If you can understand and fulfil your client's needs you will have the opportunity to sell and deliver consulting engagements. But you will not sell, no matter how good a consultant you are, if the prerequisites for buying consultancy are not met, and if you cannot overcome any obstacles to sales.

- To sell and deliver a consulting engagement you must have a proposition that will fulfil the client's needs. To position your consulting proposition correctly you must understand the client's explicitly expressed needs, but there are usually a hidden set of needs which can only be exposed through observation and exploratory dialogue with the client. If you do not expose the hidden needs, there is a significant risk you will not satisfy your client.

- When you begin a consulting career, identifying clients and exploring needs may seem contrived and difficult. As your experience in consulting grows, assessing clients and stakeholders becomes second nature and to some extent subconscious.

3

Your consulting service

In order to work as a consultant you must decide what service you are going to offer your clients, which is the main topic of this chapter. Confidence that the service is viable comes from understanding who your potential clients are and what they need (see Chapter 2). The central lesson from the last century of marketing is to start by focusing on what clients want, rather than what you would like to sell. This lesson is at the heart of client-centric consulting. However, whatever clients might want, your service has to be based on something you are capable of delivering.

Experienced consultants know that some clients, with whom you have a strong relationship, will hire you because you are a competent person who can turn your hand to many things. However, if you do anything and everything for one client you cease to be an independent consultant and effectively become part of the client's team. If you simply want to generate revenue this is not necessarily a problem, but it is a risky strategy. You will become reliant on one client, and if this is really what you want, go and get a job as an employee of that client. If you do not, sooner or later your client will cease re-engaging you. In order to avoid this risk you want to be hired by a variety of clients, each for a limited period of time. In turn, to achieve this you must have a skill set, competency or capability that will help them to overcome problems they have. Even internal consultants want to avoid the situation in which they work for only one manager, and want to help a wide variety of managers in the business.

Many consultants do not have a specific service line as such, and drift from engagement to engagement as opportunities arise. Some consultants manage to keep themselves highly utilised doing this, but it is not the best approach. Like walking past a shop that sells different goods each week, clients do not know why they should specifically come to you. The times when clients are willing to pay the highest rates are when they have a pressing issue which they perceive a limited number of people can resolve. If you want to charge the highest fees you need to be able to differentiate yourself from the mass of consultants and contractors. One important way to create differentiation between yourself and other consultants is to have an area of specialisation. This is your consulting service.

The challenge with services is to know what they are and how to deliver them, but it is equally important to be able to position them with clients. It is no good having a service that clients do not understand or do not think that they want. There is also the classic business trade-off between being a niche player or offering a more generic service. This trade-off is essentially between:

- highly specialised skills; and

- generic skill sets.

Highly specialised skills have limited competition, but potentially limited need. When they are required they may generate high fees, but there is a risk that the market can evaporate. A service line in year 2000 compliance was hugely profitable in 1999 and many consultants joined the frenzy. On 1 January 2000, when the year 2000 problem was shown to be insignificant, the service became unsellable.

> there is a risk that the market can evaporate

Generic skill sets may always be in demand, but there will be many consultants with similar skills. Whilst you may always be able to find work, the fee rate will tend to be lower. Project management skills are very valuable to clients and almost all clients run projects regularly. There are, however, many skilled project managers and unless you can differentiate your skills, the rates will tend to be relatively low.

What do you have to offer clients?

The obvious starting point for developing your service line is to think through what skills, experiences or capabilities you have. What can you currently do? If a client asked you to tell them, briefly, what you can do, what would you say? Not only should you think about what you currently know, but also what you want to do. Most of us can do many things that are not forms of work that we actually want to do.

My first piece of advice when thinking about service lines is to relax. New consultants often become overly stressed with the thought that they do not have any skills that are sellable. You almost certainly do. Clients always need help and always have problems. You do not have to know everything or to be a world expert in anything to be a very successful consultant. There are very few world experts. Most clients do not need world experts and cannot afford them. Clients need competent people who can help them to resolve the issues that they have. To be able to help someone you must know more about the problem they are trying to resolve than the client does. In some situations, one or two pieces of information may be the difference between being able to add value and not being able to help. In saying this, I am not implying that all you need to be able to do as a consultant is bluff your way with some buzz words. However, if you are a competent and capable person, you do not always need to know a huge amount about a specific problem to resolve it. You just need to know *enough*.

If you have already had a career or some work experience in one or more industries, you already have knowledge and skills that will be useful to some clients. Clients are looking for people who can do one or more of the following:

- Make the challenge of managing easier. Managers are hard pressed in modern industry: even if you can only help them with one of the many tasks they have to do, this has value.
- Provide knowledge and experience relevant to specific functions, sectors or services that their work relates to.
- Give them access to the relationships they need to do their job.

There are a series of questions you can ask yourself. How can you make a client's life easier? What sorts of common problems are you well positioned to solve for them? What functional knowledge do you have – are you an HR, IT or some other specialist? What sector knowledge do you have – do you know about banking or the defence industry? What services or specialisations in business do you know about – regulation, health and safety, software development or accounting policy? Who do you know who might be useful to clients? Try jotting down answers to these and similar questions and see if any pattern of knowledge arises, or if there are areas in which you have real skills. As a consultant you should not be seeking to be a master of all trades, nor do you need to be better at something than all clients. You merely need to find areas where you have a comparative advantage over some clients.

If you do not think you have sufficient skills to either present a service line credibly or to be able to do it in real life, you can always try to expand your skills. Everyone is capable of learning at every stage of their lives. There are millions of good business books and a huge amount of free online information. With some research you can pull together a body of knowledge that will be useful to some clients. However, I do caution you to understand the difference between being able to bluff about a subject and win some work, versus really being able to do it. Additionally, there are many good courses and training opportunities. Finally, you can always go away and study for a relevant degree or an MBA.

However, don't be fooled into thinking that with some qualifications the floodgates of work will open. Clients primarily want intelligent but practical people, not academics or people with 101 qualifications and accreditations. I am not belittling the value of qualifications or accreditations, or the intellectual rigour of a good academic. I am merely saying that clients who buy consulting are typically only moderately impressed by such things. There are situations in which the advice of an academic is valued above that of other consultants, and some academics do have lucrative consulting practices, but few generate an income as significant from consulting as a successful professional consultant.

Having a specific qualification can provide a level of differentiation, but clients are really looking for a proven ability to deliver recommendations, develop realistic plans or implement change, relevant to their specific context or environment. Clients may require qualifications in certain specialised areas, but do not be fooled into thinking that a string of great qualifications will win you any consulting work. Clients are mostly interested in track record. A few credible past clients who will willingly provide strong, pertinent references will sell you more work than any qualifications. By all means seek qualifications if you believe you will learn valuable ideas whilst doing them, and no doubt qualifications help in being selected for recruitment into permanent roles. But a consultant is not being looked on as a permanent recruit: no badge or title alone will give you any consulting work.

" clients are mostly interested in track record "

The exception to this is the situation where there is some barrier to entry or highly recognised differentiation. There are many people with MBAs, but there are comparatively few with well recognised MBAs. A Harvard or INSEAD MBA, rightly or wrongly, still – and probably always will – impress.

There will always be a limited number of people with the best qualifications. There are also other types of 'accreditations'. For example, if you want to work in sensitive areas of government you usually have to be security vetted. Vetting can be a tedious and long-winded process, but once you are vetted you have a competitive differentiation above anyone who is not. Those who have not been vetted are effectively barred from some types of government work.

The best way to develop the right saleable skills is to deliberately go after consulting engagements that make you credible in that field. If you want to be an expert in setting up data centres or in providing strategic advice to the directors of charities, then the best place to start is by setting up a data centre or working on a strategy for a charity. There is of course a potential vicious circle here: 'I can't do work X because I have never done any of work type X, and I have never done any of work type X because I can't do it.' The answer is to start with realistic expectations. You cannot expect to be taken as competent in a field you have never done any work in – so when you first work in an area you must start at a relatively junior level. On the other hand, many areas of specialisation underneath the hype and the jargon are similar to others. The secret is therefore to do two things when interacting with any client:

1   Present your skills and experience in the most compelling way as relevant to the client's need. Stress the similarities between what you have done in the past and what is being asked for now. If you have worked in telecommunications and the customer works in retail banking, don't point out how different the industries are, but stress similarities. They are both extremely regulated environments, are highly competitive, have growing customer service expectations, outsource extensively, are capital intensive, and are both dependent on and spend significant amounts on technology.

2   Make yourself rapidly familiar with the jargon of an industry. There are some real differences between industries, but fewer than initially appear. I have worked in the public sector, telecommunications, media, financial services, manufacturing, utilities, the health sector and mining. Yes, there are real differences, but one of the main differences is down to language. The barrier to entry into some specialisations is primarily learning the jargon.

Whatever age you are and however many years you have worked in one industry, there is nothing stopping you presenting your years of experience in the way that is most appropriate for a different sector or service line. There may be difficulties in learning new skills and capabilities at any time, but most are in the mind or about personal attitude and can be overcome. We all can, to a large extent, invent ourselves and continually reinvent ourselves in the way we want.

One way to develop a successful consulting business is to get into a new area of consulting first. If you are first into a specialisation there is no competition, and there are no recognised qualifications or experts. You are the guru by default. Spotting trends in management thinking early can be very lucrative. Relying on a trend is risky, as the market may never take off, but management as a whole is prone to fads and fashions. Some of these trends are vacuous and blow away within a few months or years. Others have a lasting impact on the way management is done. If you successfully spot a trend and enter a market early, the potential is huge.

Types of services

Winning work is not just about being competent – it is also about being credible. *Competency* is an objective statement of your capabilities. *Credibility* is the subjective perspective of clients and other consultants. Credibility depends on a whole host of factors, and one building block of a credible service is being able to position your skills relative to typical client needs. This enables clients to label you, and use the label to understand what you do, and ideally to think of other situations in which they can use your skills. If you have a skill or knowledge that is valuable, you have the basics to becoming a competent consultant. By positioning your skills as a consultancy service you can convert competency into credibility.

The most basic way to label yourself is as a useful pair of hands, or another head with which a client can enlarge a team for a short period of time. The typical situation is that a client is short of a resource for a project, and you can fill the gap. Whilst there is nothing wrong with project work, this type of positioning should be avoided. There are exceptions, and I am not saying don't do project work, just don't label yourself as a useful pair of hands. This is the route to low-fee contracting work. It should be avoided for two reasons. Firstly, you can probably do very similar work, but position it in a different way and fulfil a differently perceived client need and significantly increase your fees. Secondly, there is a lot of consulting work, often the most interesting and lucrative engagements, that is not available to people just

❝you must be perceived as a skilled consultant❞

because they are a useful pair of hands. To win it, you must be perceived as a skilled consultant.

A useful way to think about how you position your service is against three dimensions which consulting services can be categorised into:

▪ the sector
▪ the service line
▪ the phase in the change lifecycle.

The sector

The sector is straightforward to understand. What is the industry sector your skills are most relevant to? You can position yourself as an expert in financial services, the public sector, manufacturing or telecommunications to name a few. Often clients are not only looking for skills, they are looking for skills that are relevant to their industry. For example, billing in telecommunications is different from billing in other industries – if you want to work on billing systems in telecommunications you must have telecommunications experience. Similarly, financial regulation is specific to financial services, and even to sub-sectors within financial services. You must have relevant sector experience to successfully position yourself as a consultant in financial regulations.

The service line

The service line you work in is akin to a function in an industry, but is somewhat broader. You may be a specialist in IT, HR, regulations, operations management, project management, performance improvement or something similar. Many service lines are common to most industries. For instance, all businesses which employ people, irrespective of the sector, have HR needs and can be helped by HR consultancy.

To win some consulting opportunities requires both a service and a sector specialisation. In other situations you need either sector or service line experience, but not both. For example, staff performance management processes and systems are relatively non-sector specific. A specialist in staff performance management should be able to work across sectors. However, a business strategist is likely to require detailed sector-specific knowledge to understand the competitive situation and market trends.

In general, the more focused and rare your specialisation, the higher the fee rate you can charge but the higher the risk of finding no opportunity.

It is important to understand this is a very rough generalisation and there are many exceptions. Some consultants I know have very unusual skills, but there is enough work to keep them permanently busy at a high fee rate.

The phase in the change lifecycle

The last categorisation is what I call the phase in the change lifecycle a consultant works in. I will discuss change more in Chapters 4 and 8, but in essence all consulting is about change. Whether it is providing strategic advice through to helping in an implementation project, the outcome from consulting should be that something has changed in a client organisation. It may be that a better decision has been made, a manager has improved skills or a more fundamental change has occurred in the business.

Change is complex, but it can be thought of as a lifecycle. The lifecycle is an endless loop and therefore does not really have a start point, as change never ends. But we can think of the lifecycle for an individual change starting with an idea or concept. The idea can take the form of a definition of what an organisation should be trying to achieve. Consulting associated with defining why and what an organisation should seek to achieve is called *strategy consulting*. Having decided what direction the business should be going in, the actual operations of the business can be assessed to determine how well it is performing relative to the strategy and what should be improved. This is *operational consulting*. Having identified possible improvements, change initiatives can be planned to deliver the improvements, where a plan defines what and how the change will be made. This is *implementation planning*. Finally, a planned change can be delivered, with a sustainable change made to the organisation. This is *implementation* (or delivery) *consulting*. Once change is achieved the business is in a new state, and this cycle can start again. This lifecycle is shown in Figure 3.1.

Typically, the more closely a consulting engagement is related to strategy consulting the more important specific sector expertise becomes. The more a consulting engagement is related to implementation consulting the more important specific service knowledge becomes. However, this is a very broad generalisation.

Some organisations with consultancy businesses, including many of the largest companies, offer a range of additional services beyond those of

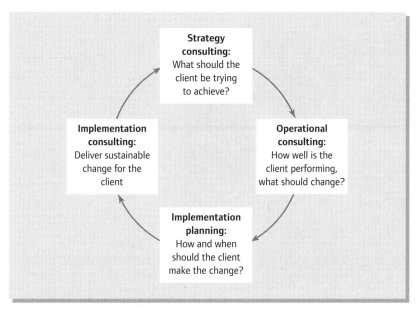

Figure 3.1 The change lifecycle

pure consulting. As well as supporting change implementation they offer software or other technology development services. Such organisations will offer to run some parts of the organisation's ongoing operations, which is usually called *outsourcing*. Consider a client organisation that wants to improve customer service. To make this improvement, the client organisation needs to set up a new customer call centre. The call centre needs new computer systems and staff. Some consultancies not only help with the identification of such problems and manage the implementation of the resultant changes – they may also offer to develop new IT systems for the call centre and to set up and run the call centre for the business. This is shown in Figure 3.2. This figure also positions how contractors and interim managers relate to this change lifecycle.

So far in this chapter we have looked at consulting services where the consultant provides recommendations or implementation skills – in other words the consultant helps the client directly. The relationship between the consultant and the client is one where the consultant tells or advises the client what to do. This is sometimes thought of as a teacher–student or doctor–patient relationship. There is another style of consulting, which we will explore in more detail in Chapter 7. This is where the consultant does not provide the client with direct recommendations, but instead

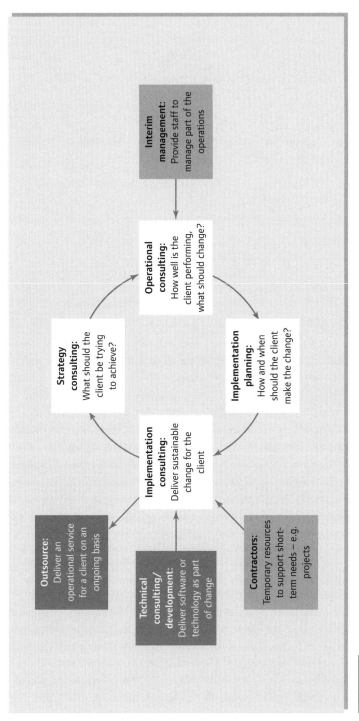

Figure 3.2   Relating consulting services to other service offerings

helps the client to help themselves. This is sometimes known as *process consulting* (and must not be confused with process design or business process engineering, which it has nothing to do with). Another name for this type of consulting is *facilitation*. A facilitator does not provide a client with a solution to a problem, but instead helps the client to identify and solve the problems themselves. A major advantage of facilitation is that clients are much more likely to accept the result from a consulting engagement when they have developed it themselves. Coaching and mentoring can also work on a similar basis.

All the points made in this chapter should influence how you should position yourself as a consultant. Do you want to be seen as an expert in a sector or service line, a strategy or operational consultant, as someone who can plan change, a specialist in implementation, a facilitator – or some combination of all of these? Making your choice is not about closing doors, as there is no reason why at different times, even within the same client, you cannot swap between the roles – but clients like to and probably need to be able to label you. What you want them to do is to label you in such a way that you have access to, and are seen as a credible support in delivering, the broadest range of high, value-adding opportunities.

" making your choice is not about closing doors "

Positioning your services with clients

Success as a consultant requires a market for your service and it must be a service for which someone is willing to pay a day rate that will give you a sensible return. We will deal with finding clients and selling to them in Chapter 5. At this stage I want you to consider sales only conceptually. What do you need to have in place for clients to understand and accept your services?

The first thing to remember is that you are not selling to yourself. You are selling to a client. It does not matter how wonderful you know your service to be, what matters for selling is only what clients think. Clients have to need or want the service you are offering, and to understand it. Contrary to the opinion of some novice consultants, few clients are impressed in the slightest by obscure jargon and incomprehensible services. Clients are looking for a number of things, which can be summarised with a list of words starting with 'c'. Are you: capable, competent, coherent, credible and *client-centric*?

How will you explain the value you can bring to a client and the specific service you can provide? There is a big difference between what you know you can do, and a saleable proposition.

I like to think in terms of pigeonholes. A pigeonhole is the name given to a compartment in which mail is put in an office when it is separated out according to department or even individual. The expression has come to be associated with a way of labelling people. In work we can be associated with pigeonholes relating to our skills, ways of interacting and relationships and groups we belong to. I could be pigeonholed as 'a management consultant' or 'an author' for example.

Pigeonholes are often seen as overly restrictive and generally a bad thing, but they are useful. We all need them, especially at the start of a relationship. Pigeonholes provide a short-hand for what we can do. No one remembers all of a CV or list of qualifications, but people do remember things like 'great strategic thinker', 'reliable project manager' or 'dreadful team player'. These labels are easy to remember and they stick. We are all much more complex than a few simple phrases and none of us likes being pigeonholed. The secret therefore is not to let it passively happen to us, but proactively to choose the pigeonholes we want to be put in. We can do this in the way we consistently and coherently communicate to clients.

This is one reason why I put coherence as something clients need to see in your service. If you are incoherent about how you label yourself, or you position yourself with labels that do not seem to fit together coherently, then irrespective of whether the labels are true or not clients will not accept the pigeonholes you want to give yourself. For instance, let's imagine the pigeonholes you want are 'great high-level business strategist' and 'fantastic C++ software programmer'. If you happen to be a great high-level business strategist and a fantastic software programmer, so what? Does any single client need to know this? No. Worse, the labels are not complementary and reduce the credibility of each other when put together. They do not seem to be a coherent pairing of labels, even if they do happen to be true. The client who buys you as a corporate strategist and the one who buys you as a software programmer will usually be different people. Keep them as separate pigeonholes for separate clients.

I cannot stress enough that you should not position yourself as a good person who can do anything. Being positioned in the 'jack of all trades' or 'useful pair of hands' pigeonholes will not lead to you getting the highest value consulting work. You may sometimes sell, but high rates are paid to people who have skills that fit a specific client issue, not to people who just happen to be useful. Good consultants avoid presenting themselves as a jack of all trades. The talent is to present your skills broadly enough to be attractive to clients for a variety of work, but narrowly enough to be a credible supplier of specialised services.

The truth is, of course, that many of us actually have at heart a pretty generic skill set. Do not despair. Even the most basic and generic of skills can be labelled in an attractive way that differentiates and enables you to charge your clients higher fees. For example, my core consulting skills are related to project and change management, which is probably as generic as you can get in consulting. There are thousands and thousands of consultants who have or claim to have a similar skill set. If you have such a skill set you should seek some differentiation by adding on sector-specific knowledge, or experience of specific types of projects. The day rate for a generic project manager is several times lower than an experienced consultant programme manager with knowledge of a specific industry or type of project.

Although you have a set of skills that you can use to link yourself consistently to every opportunity, you should try to position your skills as uniquely relevant to each and every opportunity. One common vehicle to explain your skills and services is the CV. The novice thinks of the CV as a list of experience and qualifications. The experienced consultant knows a CV is a sales tool. As such, it has to be tailored to the sales opportunity. A client is never looking for the cleverest consultant in the world. A client is looking for a consultant with sufficient *relevant* experience to be able to help with their problem.

"the experienced consultant knows a CV is a sales tool "

I have a master CV on which I have listed every single project I have ever done and every company I have ever worked for. No one sees this, except for some consulting associates I trust. Apart from the fact that it is far too long for most clients, it does not provide a simple, easily understandable and consistent picture of what I can do. I think it shows strong experience – but it shows that I can do too many things! Hence, when I have an opportunity that requires me to send my CV, I tailor it to the situation. I do not lie or make things up, but I stress the relevant areas of experience, and equally importantly I remove work that is not relevant. Even if you really are a master of many professions, clients will not believe you are. The impression from a CV with many different skills is not of a specialist who can do several things but a jack of all trades.

However broad your skills are, the route to success is to find a niche that suits you, or identify a market that is not adequately serviced by consultants and to develop those skills. Of course it is worth having more than one string to your bow, but only because it reduces the risks of not finding work and not because it will make you more attractive to a client in any one specific situation.

Once you have identified the services you will provide, do not think that you never need to reconsider them. Irrespective of how leading edge your services seem, you need to be flexible and constantly reinvent yourself. Service lines move on. For example, years ago no one asked if a project manager was qualified. Now there are various accreditations in project management and soon there will be chartered status for project managers in the UK. Software package like Baan or PeopleSoft were all the rage for a while, and a Baan or PeopleSoft consultant could have earned a good income. Who hears of them now? Business process re-engineering was something different and highly paid in the early 1990s; now it is a commodity skill that many consultants have. As a graduate from university I was initially trained as an MVS systems programmer. Many current readers will not have the vaguest idea of what that means.

Positioning services may seem to be something to consider only for the novice consultant. It is true that when you have worked with a client and have a great relationship with them your specific service lines are less important. But you can never rely on one client – you will always need new ones. Even if you trust an individual client manager to employ you on a constant stream of engagements, you do not know what will happen to their business in future. Even chief executives get fired or fall out with their boards sometimes!

Differentiating with intellectual property

One way to create a truly differentiated service from other consultants is to develop some intellectual property (IP). For consultants, IP consists of ideas or approaches to solving consulting problems that are unique to the consultant and which the consultant can control access to. Intellectual property can be methodologies or may be data such as benchmarking data. Some large consulting firms invest heavily in IP or intellectual capital to differentiate themselves from other firms.

A consulting organisation's methods, tools and processes can be valuable and undoubtedly provide a certain amount of differentiation. They are particularly valuable when new ideas in management arise. The first consultants with a defined approach to implementing these new management approaches can win significant business, often at premium rates. Six sigma has now become a common tool, but when it first arose those consultants with six sigma methodologies could charge a premium rate. However, generally I am a little sceptical about consulting IP for the reasons noted below.

First, IP ages very quickly. Knowledge is inherently transferable and in the long run impossible to protect. If you are a manufacturing company, you may have some secret or patented manufacturing process, and you can probably keep this secret from competitors for some time. The fundamental problem consultants have with IP is that there is an inherent conflict between having unique knowledge and being a consultant. As a consultant you are paid for your skills and knowledge because you share them with your clients. Once you have shared your ideas they are out in the open. You may have only shared knowledge with one company, but client staff will move on to other firms and take with them any good ideas you have taught. In large consulting companies you may only train your staff in your IP, but consultants very often move from one consulting firm to another, and cannot avoid taking concepts and ideas with them.

The second point I make about IP in consulting is that there is actually very little of it around, at least much less than consultants claim. Certainly, if I apply the true legal definition of IP I am doubtful that very many consulting approaches would meet this definition. Much IP is more about branding and consolidating knowledge than it is to do with the creation of really innovative thinking. For example, many consultancies have different approaches to ERP (enterprise resource planning) implementation. These approaches may be valuable, have been developed from many years of hands-on experience, and enable a firm to implement an ERP system more rapidly and at a lower risk than those without such a methodology. But if you look at several companies' approaches to ERP implementation there really is not a huge amount to differentiate between them. It is a mature market. No doubt some people do it better than others, but everyone involved in this type of service knows the steps to follow to implement an ERP system.

If you do have some IP, don't be paranoid about losing it. If your IP helps you win work or to deliver assignments, then great. But clients are not paying to have access to your IP. They are paying for your ability to deliver great consulting. No client thinks 'wonderful consulting, they shared their IP with me', clients judge success in much more tangible ways: 'I can

" if you do have some IP, don't be paranoid about losing it "

make better decisions now', 'my strategic direction is clearer', 'I have a realistic implementation plan', 'that was much faster than I could have done it', or 'the change was implemented well'.

Don't be afraid about your IP leaking to other consultants. A consultant with no experience and no relevant skills cannot pick up a piece of consulting IP and deliver a value-adding result. Intellectual property in consulting provides differentiation, enhances approaches, speeds up progress and reduces risk. It never removes the need to have skilled consultants. I have written many of my ideas in books which are widely available, but I am still certain that I have a set of skills that are valuable to clients and which cannot easily be found in other consultants. It is not that I have deliberately left things out of my books; it is simply that many factors in being a great consultant are more intangible and come from my ability to apply knowledge – not simply that I know lots of things. If consulting was just about knowing lots of information then the internet and services like Wikipedia would have already removed the need for consultants altogether.

The final point about IP is that you can develop it as your experience grows. You do not need it before you undertake paid work. You need to be careful from an ethical viewpoint that you are not claiming you have a methodology you have not yet fully developed. But within reason it is acceptable to create it as you go along. To some extent you have no choice. Consulting approaches and methods are based on experience, as this is really the only way to gain a method that is of any proven value.

Summary

Successful consultants build a profitable consulting business by thinking from the client's viewpoint and developing service lines that are meaningful to the client.

- Start by identifying what skills you have. Consider what you can do that will:
  - make the challenge of managing easier for clients
  - provide relevant knowledge and experience to clients
  - give access to additional useful relationships to clients.

■ Develop your services by thinking about the sector, service line or phase in the change lifecycle they are targeted towards.

■ Label, position and explain your services in ways that are meaningful and easily understood by clients. Proactively manage how you are pigeonholed.

As a conclusion to this chapter it is worth reflecting on the following question: how can you know that you are developing the right services? The proof that you have chosen the right services can only come from experience. If you have chosen the right service and are actively seeking clients, you should find that:

■ you are selling enough work

■ you are able to turn down work that does not fit with what you want to do.

If you are not busy enough then it is quite possible that you need to rethink, sometimes only in minor ways, what the service is you are offering or how you are positioning it with your clients.

Let me end this chapter with a final thought about the skills you require. In addition to the specialist skills you have, you need the skills of being a consultant. A good consultant is not simply a bundle of knowledge and capabilities about some area or another. This is essential, but it is not enough. A good consultant knows *how* to be a consultant, and this is what the rest of this book is about.

The three core processes of client-centric consulting

This chapter explains the consulting engagement process by looking at the stages and steps in all consulting engagements. The advantages of understanding the engagement process is that it gives a coherent structure to every piece of consulting work, and it provides a language in which consultants can discuss engagements clearly and unambiguously. The engagement process lies at the heart of all engagements and describes the everyday work of a consultant. But the engagement process is only one of the processes a client-centric consultant must be familiar with. As well as understanding this process, the consultant should also understand some of the client's processes.

The emphasis in this book is on client-centric consulting. Therefore I am going to position engagements into the wider setting of an organisation. An engagement does not exist in isolation, but has a context within the client business. This context can be understood by considering how a consulting engagement fits with the operations of the client enterprise. I will explain the three core processes a consultant should understand. The three processes are:

1 *The consulting engagement process*: The necessary steps and their logical order in the work the consultant is employed to deliver.

2 *The client's change process*: A consulting engagement is always only a part of a client's process of making a change. How does the work on an engagement relate to the wider change agenda in the business?

3 **The client's operational process**: Clients may thrive on change, but they don't exist to change. A business exists to deliver some product or service on an ongoing basis. How does the work of the consultant relate to this?

Although each of these processes is important, it is the relationship between them all that is most important to a consultant. Each process provides context to the others. By thinking beyond the engagement process you are able to give truly client-centric consulting. In addition, by understanding this context, the widest range of opportunities for additional consulting sales can be identified.

Given the wide variety of possible consulting engagements, let alone the varieties of businesses, it is not possible to define an engagement process which is accurate for every situation unless it is so high level as to be meaningless or it has so many options and 'if-then' type loops as to be impractical. I take a middle course and outline a process that will work in the majority of situations. I am not worried about the lack of applicability to each and every occasion. The engagement process I describe will be appropriate to most engagements, but you may need to tweak it here and there in specific situations. This should not be difficult once the basic structure is understood, as it is straightforward to tailor this engagement process to a specific situation. What remains important, irrespective of how process steps need to be adapted, is the relationship between the consulting engagement and the other two core processes. Simply being aware that the relationship is important is a good start.

> **❝ it is straightforward to tailor this engagement process to a specific situation ❞**

The most successful consulting provides assistance that is relevant to the client and in doing so must understand the interaction between these three processes. No matter how brilliant a consultant is, if the only context they have is the limits and boundaries of the engagement they are working on, they will never be able to achieve a full understanding and completely meet client needs. The value a client-centric consultant adds is by giving appropriate consulting advice relative to the client's processes and context.

The engagement process

In this section I describe the engagement process, firstly at a high level by dividing the process into three main stages (see Figure 4.1) and then in more detail by breaking the stages into nine steps.

Figure 4.1 The high-level engagement process

Successful consultants' objectives can be summarised as winning work, satisfying clients and cultivating long-term profitable relationships. A consulting engagement goes through three stages which achieve these objectives. The first stage is associated with all the sales activities and is called the *propose* stage. The aim of the propose stage is to win some work with a particular client. The propose stage is ideally brief, as no client is paying consulting fees whilst a proposal is created. In practice, selling consultancy can be a protracted business. The propose stage will either result in withdrawing from an opportunity or winning an engagement. When work is won, the consultant moves into the second stage, called the *deliver* stage.

The aim of the deliver stage is to satisfy your client by fulfilling their needs. The deliver stage is usually the longest stage of the engagement. The propose stage can be protracted, but the deliver phase is normally more resource-intensive in terms of person-hours worked. However, it is this work that results in the fees being earned by the consultant. A profitable consultancy needs consultants to work more chargeable than non-chargeable hours during the deliver phase – including also the time spent in the propose stage. It is in the deliver phase that the consultants add the most value to the client by applying the combination of skills, experiences and capabilities they possess. The deliver phase is then followed by the final stage, which I call the *close* stage.

Engagements end and you want them to end, or else you are not working as a consultant. It is the successful completion of an engagement that justifies your fees. Therefore a consultant has to work in such a way that the engagement can end and so the engagement must always be focused on reaching the end point. Do not confuse selling-on, which is concerned with selling a subsequent engagement to a client, with not finishing an individual engagement. The close stage can be very brief, but it is important. One reason for this stage is to ensure any loose ends are tied up, and often there are many on a consulting engagement. The most important part of closing an engagement is to provide an opportunity to cultivate a long-term relationship with the client. An engagement will end, but a relationship with a client should not.

Once the engagement process is broken into significantly more detail than the model shown in Figure 4.1, it needs to become less generic and more engagement specific. The process followed by a strategy consultant may be quite different from the process followed by an IT consultant. However, it is possible to show one more level of detail based on the steps in a standard engagement, which is broadly applicable to most engagements. This is shown in Figure 4.2 overleaf.

Let's briefly look at each of these steps.

To write a proposal and hence win an engagement a consultant has to *find* an opportunity. There are many sources of opportunities, but in the end they all derive from some unfulfilled client needs. Sometimes clients actively seek consultants to help them, and sometimes consultants come across a client who wants consultancy. On other occasions, client needs have to be teased out through ongoing dialogue and analysis. To begin with, an opportunity tends to be vague and clients may have a tangled web of issues. Consultants cannot simultaneously resolve every problem a client has, so a period of exploration and dialogue with the client, when the consultant works to *focus* to define the scope of engagement and a precise set of deliverables, is required. Having collected enough information the consultant must then develop a client proposition. The consultant must *frame* a specific offering in the form of a proposal. (The steps in propose-to-win will be described in more detail in Chapter 5.)

Assuming the client accepts the proposal, and during the frame step there is normally a period of negotiation and tweaking of proposals, so that eventually the consultant can start to deliver the engagement. A consultant will *commence* the engagement by performing a range of set-up activities, detailed planning and gathering resourcing for the engagement. Next usually comes *collecting* information about the client. The sort of questions the consultant is seeking to be able to answer are: what is the client's precise issue? What contextual factors need to be considered? What facts must be considered when determining the recommendations the consultant will make? And so on. Having collected sufficient information the consultant then analyses it and *considers* what recommendations to make, and the shape and content of any deliverables. The deliverables are then *created*. This includes activities such as

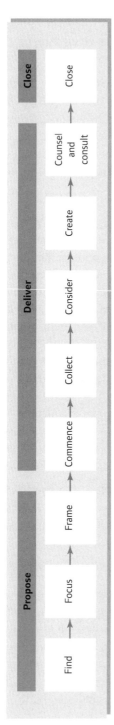

Figure 4.2 The detailed engagement process

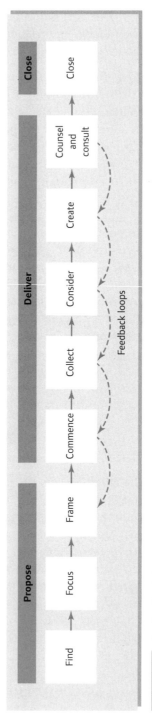

Figure 4.3 The feedback loops in the engagement process

writing reports or developing final presentations. Finally, the deliverables are handed over to the client. Clients are *counselled* on what to do next, and receive the *consultation* they have engaged the consultant to give. Occasionally clients are simply presented with final reports, but normally the counsel and consult step is a time of discussion, client education and a period in which the client has time to consider and then accept or reject the findings.

The steps shown in the deliver phase are very general. In reality they do not always happen in such a fixed linear structure. There are feedback loops and iterations between the steps. In the consider step, it is not unusual to find you do not have all the information you require and have to go back and collect some more. Even in the penultimate counsel and consult step, a client may disagree with a finding and it may be necessary to go back into the create step, or an even earlier step in the process and produce revised deliverables. It is sometimes necessary to return to the frame step and revise the proposal because of what is discovered in the deliver stage of an engagement. A consultant typically wants to avoid too many feedback loops as it extends the engagement and can reduce the consultant's profitability. These feedback or rework steps are indicated in Figure 4.3.

The time spent in each of these steps varies tremendously, as does the nature of the particular work. For example, if your key deliverable produced in the create step is a strategic analysis of a business, the work in the collect and consider steps will be very different than if your main deliverable is a change implementation plan. Chapter 6 will look at the deliver-to-satisfy stage in more detail.

The close stage does not need to be broken down into any more detail at this point. Closing an engagement and ensuring you cultivate your long-term relationships with the client is explored in Chapters 8 and 9.

The client's change process

In this section I want to relate the engagement to a client's change process. Let's start by discussing the change process within a client and then position it relative to the individual engagement.

Most organisations, especially commercial enterprises, exist in a state of constant change. Even when organisations do not wish to change they are forced to by commercial pressures, improvements in technology and modifications in customer behaviour and views. Even the most seemingly conservative organisations undergo some change. This change may be radical strategic modifications endorsed or even demanded by shareholders and other influential stakeholders. It may be the regular cycle of business improvements that are planned by managers, usually as part of annual target and budget setting. It is frequently the minor tweaks and enhancements made at a micro-level by individual departments on an ongoing basis. Whether it is strategic change, implementing new IT systems, business process re-engineering, six sigma initiatives, reorganisations, cultural change, cost reductions, quality improvement initiatives, expansions or retrenchments, building moves and relocations, mergers and acquisitions, modifying an individual procedure or any other form of change activity – it is all part of the relentless drive to improve the organisation.

Few, if any, managers in a business have a perspective on all of this change. In substantial organisations it is probably not possible to have such a perspective. The most senior managers are aware only of the largest initiatives, and all smaller modifications and adjustments are only perceived by them in terms of increases and reductions in the operational performance of a business.

Such a swirling mass of change is difficult, if not impossible, to encapsulate totally in a single process, especially as every organisation approaches change in its own unique way. But we can approximate to it accurately enough with a simple model of how change occurs in an organisation. This is shown in Figure 4.4.

The process shown has six stages. An individual organisation is normally working at all stages in this process simultaneously in different parts of the business, with many parallel changes going on at once. Hence one part of the business may be planning changes, another implementing changes and a third thinking about its strategy. However, if we consider an individual change we can walk through this process in a logical order. A business thinks about the future, and taking account of what is going on in the competitive environment in which it operates, the business defines some form of strategy. This strategy may exist as a tangible documented statement of the way ahead for a business, or it may be something more informal. It could just be an ever-evolving set of ideas within the heads of the senior managers in a business. We can think of strategy as the high-level change agenda for the business, but we can also think of strategy in a more modest way, as

> " a business thinks about the future, defines some form of strategy "

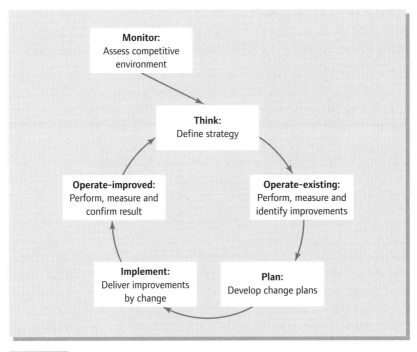

Figure 4.4 The change process in organisations

the thinking and analysis that goes on all the time in a good manager's brain and which results in ideas for improvements.

The business will have some existing operations. By 'operations' in this context I mean all the day-to-day work of the organisation – purchasing supplies, developing products and services, selling and serving customers, managing staff performance and so on. The operations are performed, measured or assessed and then, taking account of the desired strategy, improvements are identified. The improvements have to be planned, whether the plan is simply the allocation of a minor improvement to a specific member of staff, or the large-scale programme plans of radical change in an organisation. Once the plans are complete, the improvements can be implemented.

During strategy, planning and change implementation the business continues to operate. Following implementation the operations should undergo some improvement. The improvement might be that some higher level of performance is achieved, or operations are more efficient or more effective, or perhaps new products and services have been launched or existing products are better targeted at one set of customers or another. Over time, by measuring performance it is possible to determine if the changes have resulted in the level of improvement expected in a business.

The measured performance of the improved operations feeds back into strategic thinking, and the whole change process starts again. The change process is ongoing for several reasons. The implemented change may not lead to the level of performance desired. Even if it does, the strategy will evolve in response to new opportunities, new competitive threats, or other modifications in the environment in which the organisation operates. Organisations, their managers and customers always have new ideas and new desires constantly feeding the change process.

How does this relate to a consulting engagement? All consulting engagements should result in a change within a client. If nothing has changed at the end of an engagement then no value has been added to the client. This change may be subtle or it may be profound, it may be short or long term, it may affect a single individual or the whole organisation. Not only do all successful consulting engagements result in change, the engagements relate to one or more steps on the client change process shown in Figure 4.4. If you are being asked for strategic advice and the advice is accepted, it will result in a change somewhere in the strategic direction of the business. If you are performing a review of operational performance and your findings are accepted, it will result in a change somewhere in the operations of the business. Obviously, consulting related to planning and implementation are directly concerned with change.

The advantages of understanding the relationship between the engagement process and the client's change process is that it enables you to tailor your work most appropriately to the client's underlying change agenda, and hence increases the likelihood of success. If you know why a client originally asked for your engagement, and you have an idea of what will happen once your engagement is complete, you are much better positioned to provide consultancy that is targeted to the client's specific needs.

A second reason for understanding the relationship between the engagement process and the client's change process is that it increases your chance of selling on. The change resulting from a consulting engagement represents only one aspect of the change within a client. Whether the client tells you or not, or even whether the client is conscious of it or not, there is always a wider ongoing change agenda in every organisation. Whatever the engagement is, it will have been initiated due to some previous thinking in the organisation, and if successful will in turn result in changes in the business. If what you are doing is only one part of a client's change agenda, but you have an understanding of the whole agenda – or at least know a bit more than the scope of your engagement – you have much better information with which to position your services for additional sales.

Having completed a consulting engagement, there is almost always a logical sell-on to the next stage in the change process. In Figure 4.5 I show an example of how the client's change process could be broken up into a series of four consulting engagements based around consulting service lines. The advantage of thinking in this way is that it relates an engagement to both the consulting service lines and the process of change a client is going through. This set of four diagrams shows a logical sequence of engagements. The nature of each engagement is different, the skills required to do them vary significantly, and it is unlikely that a single manager in the client organisation would be the client for all of them. But, by understanding that there is always a next step to a successful engagement, you can get ready for any sell-on by identifying the right client for the work, and pulling the necessary resources and proposal together. What makes large consultancies successful is their ability to sell a variety of work to new clients and sell on to existing ones.

> the nature of each engagement is different

The example shown in Figure 4.5 is one possible sequence of engagements. A consultant starts by being invited to a client to develop a strategy for them. The strategy engagement corresponds to the *monitor* and *think* stages of the client's change process. This leads on to an opportunity, which the consultant wins, to perform an operational review in the second engagement. The second engagement corresponds to the *operate-existing* stage of the client's change process. This identifies situations in which the business does not meet the strategic requirements. Hence a change is required. Again the consultant sells on and this change is *planned* and *implemented* with the consultant's help in the third engagement. Finally, there is a post-implementation review to learn lessons for the next change, corresponding to the *operate-improved* stage of the client's change process. From an initially successful engagement a consultant has sold on three further engagements, each of which is valuable to the client. The selling on does not have to stop. For instance,

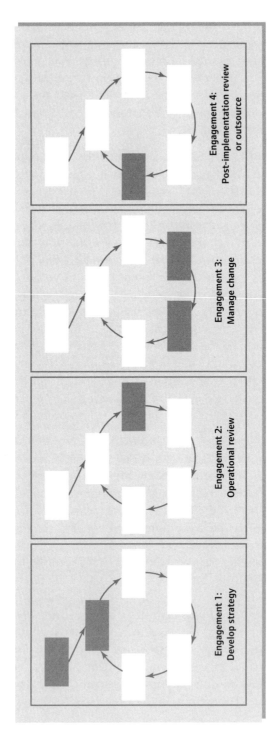

Figure 4.5 A possible sequence of engagements based on the client's change process

during the fourth engagement the consultancy might also offer to out-source some of the client organisation's operations.

Because the change process is an ongoing cycle, a consultant can enter this process at any point. Consider the situation in which you may be invited to help a client with some change planning. The completion of a change plan obviously leads on to an opportunity for an implementation engagement. But suppose that when you come to undertake the plan-ning you discover that there is insufficient information to develop the plan, or you think the basic change strategy will not work. If you can convince the client of this, there is an opportunity to step backwards through the process and look at operational performance or the strategic thinking that led to deciding on the change. It is not unusual for success-ful consultants to sell on by showing a client that what really needs to be done is not the engagement they have asked for, but to rework one of the preceding steps in the change process.

The client's operational process

So far in this chapter I have presented the engagement process and its rela-tionship to the client's change process. This is helpful, but is not sufficient to understand fully a client and position an engagement in the best way. A client may be involved in significant amounts of change, and senior man-agers may spend a high proportion of their time involved in change, but it is always worth remembering that clients do not exist to change. They exist to run an organisation, which is achieved by the daily operations of a business. This includes activities like selecting and buying resources, find-ing customers, developing and making products and services, selling products and services, providing support to customers, managing staff and finance, and so on. The enterprise may be sustained or improved by change, but will not survive on change alone. It is easy for consultants to lose sight of this, given their regular involvement in change.

The operational process is unique to an organisation, and there can be no single, useful, universal or generic representation of all clients' opera-tional processes. This reinforces the need for client-centric rather than generic approaches. What is important, in every situation, is to gain some understanding of the client's specific operational process.

A good place to start is to consider the perspective of the people responsi-ble for operating the business. To an operational manager a piece of consulting is not an important activity in its own right. Implementing change by applying a consultant's recommendations is not an important result by itself. The only result that matters to an operational manager is achieving necessary levels of operational performance and, ideally, improving on this. Consulting is only relevant to the extent to which it helps in achieving or improving operational performance – or, with a radical strategic change, in determining that the whole direction and nature of the operations must be modified.

Consulting typically identifies and implements change for clients. The change leads to performance improvements and hence the future operational results of the organisation are achieved.

consulting is done today, but is about tomorrow

Operations are done today and are about today. Consulting is done today, but is about tomorrow. In most organisations, the majority of staff and resources are allocated towards the current operations of the business, not towards thinking about tomorrow or how improvements can be made.

Even though the consultant's work is focused on tomorrow, the work of the consultant has an impact on today's operational process. Consulting engagements have various impacts on the operations of a business in a number of ways, including:

- *The way staff time and other resources are used:* As discussed in later chapters, few consulting engagements can be performed by consultants alone. Time is needed from the clients, who are usually busy managers. Client staff may need to be allocated full-time to work with consultants for the length of the engagement – staff who otherwise would make contributions to the daily operations of the business. Operational managers can appear to have incompatible emotions – both welcoming consultants for the value they bring whilst simultaneously cursing them for the time and resources they absorb.

- *The way consultants in the business affect it:* Consultants are usually strangers in a business, and all groups can be disrupted when new people join. For example, consultants are often associated with negative events in the minds of staff. The simple existence of consultants in a business can start detrimental rumours going and affect staff mood.

- *The risk of collateral damage and unintended outcomes:* Whenever anything new comes into a business, or anything is changed, there is a risk of some unintended outcomes – these may be positive or negative. The actions of consultants can unintentionally disrupt operations.

When it comes to change implementation, this cannot be done without an appreciation of the operations of the business. Organisations which have existed for many years are usually robust, but the work of the consultant has an effect not only within the scope of the engagement, and not only upon the wider change agenda, but potentially on the broader day-to-day operations of a business. Organisations, especially those which are large or have existed for some time, are complex entities. They are not made up from a set of stand-alone components. They exist as organisations because the different components interact and are interwoven. One process affects another; one system interfaces with other systems. The way one person works affects the way other people work and feel. Wherever a change is recommended or implemented by a consultant in one part of a business, it will usually have an effect elsewhere in a business.

A consultant should always consider the operations of a business, simply because without them the value of the consulting is limited. It is context free. It is like asking an architect for a design to improve your house without them understanding the design of your current house or how you use it.

Considering the operational process of a business may seem to make the consultant's life harder, but it is essential for client-centric consulting. However, there is another positive business reason to undertake this. Understanding the client's operational process provides the opportunity for additional consulting sales.

Maximising consulting opportunities

A consulting engagement only touches on one part of a client's business. This may mean it is possible to *up-sell*: that is, to increase fees by extending the scope of the existing engagement to parts of the business not currently within scope. For instance, if you are a consultant who specialises in launching new products and you are working in one division of a business there may be an opportunity to help another division with launching new products as well. There may also be many opportunities to *cross-sell*. Cross-selling is selling other services lines to the same client. For example, you may be helping an organisation improve the way it manages staff performance management, and as part of this you identify a general weakness in budget planning and budget management. There is, therefore, a potential opportunity to sell some additional financial services. The point is that both in cross-selling and up-selling, the additional sales do not directly result from your current engagement. Your current engagement gives you information about the way the business operates and relationships that enable you to identify the opportunity and increase the likelihood of a successful sale.

Figure 4.6 shows graphically the on-sell, up-sell and cross-sell concepts.

You may think at this stage that this differentiation between on-sell, cross-sell and up-sell is not that important as it is all just pedantic variations on the theme of making additional sales. They are all additional sales, but there is a good reason for stressing the difference between the three types. By seeing the difference it encourages you to think in the broadest way about possible opportunities with your client. If the on-sell is obvious, is there any possible cross-sell or up-sell? Alternatively, the cross-sell may be straightforward, but is there any potential on-sell or up-sell? Finally the up-sell may be there to take, but is there any opportunity for on-sell or cross-sell? Successful consulting businesses increase their potential revenue streams by thinking across these sales approaches. It is not simply revenue maximisation: if you are an independent consultant who can only actually complete a limited amount of work, the more opportunities you identify, the more you can choose the work you want to do and that which you can add most value to.

> ❝ think in the broadest way about possible opportunities with your client ❞

An easy way to think about on-sell, cross-sell and up-sell is to ask yourself on every engagement the following three questions:

1　What is the sequence of activities following on from the current engagement that will maximise value for the client? (On-sell)

2　Is the work of this engagement applicable to any other departments/functions/divisions of this organisation? (Up-sell)

3　Does the client I am currently working for have any other unfulfilled needs that different consulting services may satisfy? (Cross-sell)

Large consulting businesses may have a more significant involvement in the operational process in a client business through the related services of interim management and in outsourcing. These are valuable and specialist services which are critical to the operations of many businesses and there can be a symbiotic relationship between them and consulting, but they are outside the scope of this book.

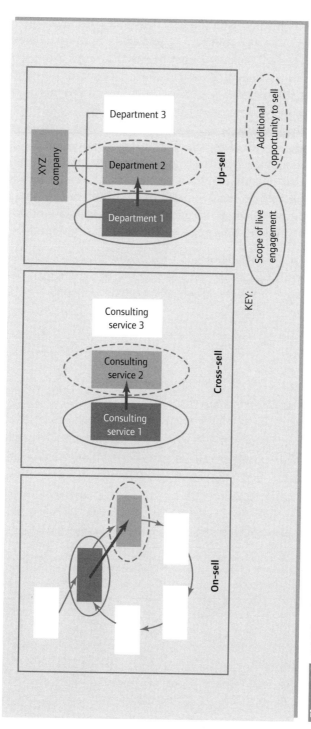

Figure 4.6 Additional sales from live engagement

Considering all the points in these sections, does this mean that the consultant has to be an expert in every aspect of the operational process? No. That is not required and would not be practical. However, a consultant should seek to understand enough about an organisation's operational process to be able to position an engagement relative to this process. This is both in the client's interest as the consulting will be more relevant, and in the consultant's interest as it can lead to more sales. This is one main reason why experience of an organisation can make the contribution of a consultant more valuable. There are various pros and cons of internal versus external consultants, but one significant advantage of internal consultants should be their understanding of the operational process, and their ability to shape an engagement appropriately so it has the maximum positive and minimal negative impact on the business.

The impact of the consultant upon the organisation and the sustainability of any resulting change are discussed in more detail in Chapter 8. Up-sell, cross-sell as well as on-sell are revisited in Chapter 5.

Summary

If you have read this book in chapter order, you have now completed the first part made up of the initial four chapters. You should have a clear understanding of the world of the consultant and be comfortable with the central topics and jargon of consultancy. The central message is both to appreciate and be willing to expand your skills in consultancy, but also to strive continuously to put this into the context of the client's organisation. This is at the heart of client-centric consulting. You have no business without clients and their unfulfilled needs. If you can position your services relative to real client needs and fulfil those needs, you have the makings of a sound consulting business.

Consulting engagements

5

Finding and winning work

This chapter is concerned with the ***propose-to-win*** stage of the engagement process, and explains the ***find***, ***focus*** and ***frame*** steps in detail (see Figure 5.1). It is one of the longest chapters in the book, as it relates to one of the most important things for a consultant to get right. If you are completely new to consulting, this is likely to be the part of a consultant's work you are most unfamiliar with. For experienced consultants, this is often the area of improvement that is most beneficial.

The propose stage covers everything from first contact with the client to the point at which a live engagement starts. Alternatively, it can end when either the client or consultant has decided not to progress with the opportunity. This is a critical phase, not just because it determines if you have any income or not, but because it sets the scene for the whole client–consultant relationship, and establishes expectations about how the engagement will be carried out. Depending on how you approach the proposal stage, you can end up with highly profitable, low-risk, enjoyable

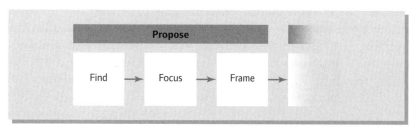

Figure 5.1 The steps in the propose stage of the engagement process

engagements; loss-making, unpleasant and highly risky engagements; or no engagements at all. To a great extent, this is under your control.

One of your aims as a consultant is to sell profitable engagements that add value to your clients. On top of this, you will have personal goals, such as having enjoyable work or being involved in engagements with some wider positive impact on society. The propose-to-win stage is structured to help you achieve your aims, and to filter out or eliminate engagements which will not meet your requirements.

The propose stage is a significant part of a consultant's business development. 'Business development' is a catch-all term used by consultants to encompass all their non-chargeable activities associated with generating work. This includes everything from writing articles, attending conferences, developing marketing materials, taking prospective clients to dinner, as well as direct sales activity. Some consultants avoid the word 'sales', almost as it if is somehow distasteful. Large consultancy firms have employees who are effectively professional sales people, as they are rewarded purely on sales targets, but they are often given some more ambiguous title, such as partner or director. However, the truth is that whilst selling consultancy may differ from many other forms of selling, beneath the words the purpose of the propose stage is to sell.

> **some consultants avoid the word 'sales', almost as it if is somehow distasteful**

The chapter is split into several sections. The first section, which is about *finding* opportunities, will be of interest mainly to external consultants, and is biased towards those from small companies as these are usually the organisations who find it hardest to market themselves. Consultants in large companies may sometimes suffer from a lack of sales, but generally they have no problem finding potential clients. The remaining sections should be of interest to all consultants: internal and external, solo consultants and those in the largest firms.

Selling work is important to every consultant. If you work as an independent consultant you must have an ability to generate sales otherwise you will have no income. To become senior in most large consultancy companies you need to have some business development capability. An ability to consult with clients is not enough: beyond a certain level no sales means no promotion. Internal consultants may have a captive client and hence feel that selling is irrelevant to them. But even for an internal consultant the ability to identify needs and frame appropriate solutions is essential to being valued in the organisation.

Finding opportunities

There are many great sales techniques. The expert sales person has an art which is not easy to encapsulate in a few paragraphs. However, behind all the skills is a simple truth: to make a sell there has to be a coincidence of needs. The client has to need (or want) help from a consultant, and the consultant has to need (or want) to work with a client. If both needs exist, there is an opportunity to sell; if not, there is none. If you accept this simple truth, then selling relies on two factors:

1　awareness of client needs – consultants finding prospective clients
2　awareness of consultant capabilities – clients finding prospective consultants.

Of course, there is more to selling than this. But this is where it all starts and is the most important part. I have sometimes sold work very quickly simply because I have stumbled across a client with a need or the client has come across me when I have been free.

Many consultants worry they are not capable of selling. Don't get stressed about selling. People and organisations really do have problems and really do want to buy solutions to overcome them. If you can convince the client you can help, you will sell. The challenge is finding people with problems suited to your capabilities rather than just optimistically pushing what you can do.

Consulting is inherently a networking business. It is a job in which you are as good as your network. The more people you know and the more who have a positive regard for you, the more likely you are to generate sales leads. Most sales leads come from your network, not from relentless cold calls or responding to requests for information (RFIs), requests for quotation (RFQs) or requests for proposal (RFPs). Hence the starting point for finding opportunities is to build and manage your network.

Build and manage your network

A strong network of positive relationships is an important asset to a consultant for all sorts of reasons. If you know lots of people with a variety of skills and backgrounds, there will always be someone you can call on for help, whatever your problem. A network provides information and it provides access to resources. A network is also the source of many opportunities and for some very successful consultants it is the original source of all their income. Major consultancies are more likely to recruit and promote you if you have a good network.

What makes up your network? From a sales perspective obviously the most important people are clients or prospective clients. But there is a wide range of other people who can help you identify and progress opportunities. You will know lots of people who are not prospective clients, but who themselves know other clients. There can be other partners interested in selling consultancy, for example consulting and interim management agencies. One of the most important components of your network is other consultants.

Do not overestimate how much competition you face from other consultants and play everything close to your chest. Similarly, do not underestimate how much work can come from developing relationships with other consultants. Many engagements cannot be done by a single consultant, and consultants will regularly come across engagements they cannot do. Experienced consultants actively seek others to be involved in such situations. This is not pure charity. Introducing other good people to a client can enhance a consultant's relationship with their clients. One should avoid being naive about sharing leads with every consultant, but if you appropriately share sales leads, intellectual capital and other resources you will receive them back in return.

If you are an independent consultant with a specialist niche skill it can even be helpful to form a relationship with a consultancy business. For commercial reasons such firms will naturally always try to allocate their own staff to client engagements first, but sometimes they are short of resources or do not have all the skills required. Most of the big firms have some form of associate network – where an associate is a contract consultant who joins an engagement team without becoming an employee. For some of the mid-size and small consultancies much of their work is staffed by associates. It may not provide a continuous stream of work, but it may well bring you some significant engagements.

You should deliberately build and manage your network and not leave it to chance or let it develop purely haphazardly. There is a big element of luck in any network of relationships. You may fortuitously bump into all sorts of useful people. But don't leave it just to luck. Much of building a network is informal. We develop relationships as a normal part of communicating and working together. But informal does

“much of building a network is informal”

not mean accidental. You should seek opportunities to introduce yourself or be introduced to people who can be useful to you. Then actively manage the network. Contact people in your network regularly. Don't wait years and years to speak to someone you once knew who is now in an important role. Don't leave people who have been valuable clients in the past out in the cold. If you have done a good job for them, then they are quite likely to request your services again – just don't let them forget about you.

Awareness of client needs

Your network should be your primary vehicle to become aware of clients with needs. The easiest and best way to find opportunities is simply to observe, listen and make sure everyone in your network is aware of your availability and capabilities. Beyond what arises directly in your network, there are three main sources of additional sales. You can try cold calls, that is directly approaching clients who you do not know and who do not know you, but who you might think are potential buyers of your service. Secondly, there are opportunities that come about because of requests for proposals (RFPs). Finally, of course, the client may contact you directly.

Selling consultancy relies predominantly on some level of relationship with the person you are selling to. You have no relationship with someone you cold call. Unless well thought through, cold calls rarely work, or at least the percentage of calls that will result in a sale is very low. If you are going to cold call clients, make it a targeted approach to a specific manager and aim a specific service line at them. It is incredibly unlikely to result in a sale, but if you make enough calls you may generate some further conversations and the basis to develop a relationship. Unless you are very lucky, generic 'I can help you' sort of calls will not work.

RFPs are distributed by some clients as a way to buy consulting services. (I will bundle variants such as RFIs and RFQs into the same category.) Of course, a client must have some awareness of your company and services to send you an RFP – but it may be very limited knowledge. On the other hand, to receive some RFPs you may need to be registered with a client's procurement department. Some clients have to use RFPs because of their tendering regulations. Other clients choose to use them as a way to optimise their procurement of consulting. RFPs are more typical for large engagements and public sector work. The question you must ask is: do you want to respond to such tenders or not?

There are pros and cons of tender situations, and not everyone is a fan of them. The opportunity from RFPs can be huge, but the cost of sales can be high. RFPs can be onerous to respond to, and if many consultancies are requested to respond, the probability of winning may be low. For some clients, the only way to work with them is by responding to RFPs. It is usually the smaller firms who avoid RFPs because they cannot afford the costs of responding to them, but there are exceptions. I know of one professional services division of a vast multinational services provider that shuns RFPs altogether. I also know of some independent consultants who get much of their work through them.

One specific RFP to watch out for is when a client organisation is looking to enter a framework agreement with a consulting company to provide consultancy on an ongoing basis. Some firms have a single favoured supplier for consulting, and winning the framework agreement can be lucrative. Alternatively, other organisations insist that you have a framework agreement with them before you can be considered for even a single consulting engagement. For such firms the framework agreement is not anything exclusive, it is a part of their standard procurement process.

The other way you can become aware of client needs is if the client contacts you directly. To do this they have to have some knowledge of your skills and services. This is discussed below.

Client awareness of consultants

Rather than consultants finding a client, clients with problems can find consultants. Many of my colleagues, with well-established reputations, get all their work from clients contacting them directly. For this to happen, the client has to be aware of your service as a consultant. Mostly, this is about clients ringing up consultants they have a relationship with, that is consultants who have successfully delivered engagements to the client's satisfaction in the past. But it is possible to more generally raise awareness of your capabilities and hence increase the likelihood that clients will consider you when they have a problem.

The common term for activities used to raise awareness of your capabilities is marketing. Marketing generally increases the likelihood of sales without being targeted on one sale in particular. You can easily spend a lot of time and effort on marketing. The point is to choose what marketing to get involved in and what is not useful. Unless you are a major consulting organisation, the amount of marketing you can afford to do will be limited. There are many forums which provide marketing opportunities, such as conferences and workshops. Professional societies often run networking events and breakfast meetings. There are hundreds of journals and business magazines you can write articles for. Writing and publishing a book can generate sales. You could consider maintaining a blog. Most of these things have to be done at your own cost. All of these may result in some leads, but focus your time on what you will get the most benefit from.

❝ ❝ you could consider maintaining a blog ❞ ❞

Consider a marketing activity such as presenting at a conference. Is it actually going to generate you any work? There are many reasons for presenting at conferences, but before you think that a conference will lead to sales, reflect on who makes up the typical audience. If you are a specialist in work of type X, going to a conference which is full of other similar specialists may well be important to your skills development but may also be worthless from an opportunity development perspective. Do specialists of type X buy the services of other specialists of type X? For instance, one of my skills is project management. I attend and talk at project management conferences as it helps keep my thinking fresh, but not to sell consulting. Project managers generally do not buy consultant project managers. Clients who have projects to run or project management teams to improve are the buyers of consultant project managers. Such clients do not typically attend project management conferences. For similar reasons, if you write articles, books or a blog you should think through who reads them and whether the readership includes prospective clients.

Any sophisticated marketing, and all but the most limited of advertising, is the domain of the large consultancies with a known brand. There are many advantages to working for a well-known consultancy. Some clients will contact you directly. A client is more likely to take a cold call from such an organisation seriously. The big consulting organisations may have full-time business development and sales staff. Generally, the smaller firms cannot afford staff dedicated to selling.

Full-time consultancy sales staff will approach new clients directly, but they spend much of their time listening for client pulls rather than pushing services. They are waiting to hear about client problems, which they know will be there.

More cost-effective marketing mechanisms for smaller consultancies are leaflets and websites. Personally, I do not favour leaflets as I think few clients read them and they are a dated format, even when distributed electronically. The exception can be when a client has shown interest in your services and you give them a leaflet which they can read and understand what it is that you offer. Overall, my advice is to spend the money you would have on a leaflet on a good business card. Websites are useful and I have had enquiries from mine, but they were all from people who were already looking for me or my company. They found my website and hence were able to contact me, but they did not come to know of me because of my website. Mostly, I use the website to direct potential clients who want to know what services I offer. Professional and social networking sites also provide the opportunity to expand your network.

If you choose to have leaflets, websites or business cards, avoid the temptation to save a few pounds by designing them yourself. Unless you have a real design flair, the chances are that they will look unprofessional. What information they contain may be great, but the perception that badly structured and poorly implemented communication gives is negative. The danger is that you convert a mechanism that can allow a small firm to look big, into something that makes you look like a complete amateur. Big corporations with large consulting budget generally do not want to be involved with amateurs.

Have you found an opportunity?

Let's assume you have found something that you think has potential because a client has contacted you directly or you have come across a client with a need. The end point of the find stage is to determine if the opportunity is real and to decide if you are going to invest time chasing it. You must follow some opportunities or else you will never get any work, but there is a direct and indirect cost to pursuing every opportunity. There is the direct cost of your time and associated expenses, and the indirect cost of not doing whatever else you may be doing with that time. This is not the step for detailed analysis, as you do not have the necessary information; this will be collected later. But roughly estimate the amount of time you will use chasing the opportunity, how much you want the work and what the probability is of winning it. Unless winning the work is critical, if the costs look too high or the probability of a win is too low, don't go further. Hopefully, you will find plenty of other leads you wish to pursue further.

Selling consulting can be straightforward, although it can be a time-consuming and frustratingly elongated process. The main thing to remember is that a client is very unlikely to buy a service that they do not think they need. If they don't think they need a service, then you are usually wasting your time trying to sell it to them. On the other hand, once a client has perceived a need then it can be plain sailing. Most clients have far too much to do and issues galore. If you can take one of the balls away that they are juggling and solve any associated issues, you will be adding value to them.

Focusing the opportunity

Having found an opportunity, you need to develop a deeper and more *focused* understanding of the situation. Consultancy takes many forms, while clients' needs are hugely varied and normally neither instantly clear nor totally transparent. To be able to focus on the essential and uncover hidden needs and desires requires information. This information is found through exploratory dialogue with the client and client representatives. You need to find out what the client really wants (as discussed in Chapter 2), collect the information necessary to decide if you are going to bid, and assemble the data required to pull a winning proposition together. This includes gaining an understanding of the wider situation. You cannot understand a client issue fully without some understanding of the context and culture of the organisation.

The exploratory dialogue is not just about gathering information. If it was, you could write a list of questions and email them to the client, review the responses and perhaps send a few follow-up questions. You could go around this loop until you had all the information you need. Sometimes with competitive RFPs this is exactly the approach that must be taken. But it is sub-optimal. The exploratory dialogue performed during the focus step does more than ask and answer a set of questions. Just as important is how you ask your questions and how you interact with the client to develop a strong relationship (see Chapters 9 and 11).

❝ the exploratory dialogue is not just about gathering information ❞

The way you focus the engagement helps to set expectations between yourself and the client. You should aim to develop a common understanding of the problem and the approach you will take to resolve it. Later on, you can concentrate on the formal language of the proposal and the correct legal terms in the contract, but in most cases the common understanding developed during this focus step is far more important than the documented terms. Dialogue is critical to building your relationship with the client and gaining the client's input into the work. This input is partially about information, but it is also about ensuring the client is involved in the work. The more involved a client feels, the more likely the work will progress successfully. A well-run focus step is of enormous value to you, as it enables the development of a great proposal, but also to the client, as it can clarify their own thinking. Some consultants call these activities *contracting with the client*.

Another way to think of contracting is as a risk management exercise. By going through discussions with the client you aim to reduce both your and the client's risk. The consultant's risk is reduced by exposing as much pertinent information about the future engagement as possible. This reduces the likelihood of unpleasant surprises once you get into the engagement. The client's risk is reduced by having an opportunity to interact with the consultant and judge whether they are competent and someone they can work with once the engagement starts. You will never know everything until you actually start the engagement, so focusing cannot remove risk, but it needs to reduce it to the level that you are comfortable estimating a price and suggesting an approach for a piece of work. A phrase commonly used by consultants to refer to this stage of contracting is *qualifying an opportunity*.

One colleague of mine colourfully likened qualifying opportunities to two dogs sniffing each other and finding out if they are going to bark at each other or wag their tails. There is simultaneously a desire to know more and a little wariness.

It is difficult to predict and plan this stage of the engagement process. Sometimes it can happen over an intense few hours or days. On other occasions it may drag out over weeks or even months of intermittent dialogue. Unless well managed, it tends to crawl along. The tendency for this focus stage to be elongated is one of the reasons why some consultants have multiple opportunities progressing at once, and start progressing new opportunities before existing engagements have finished.

From your perspective, there are four main questions you must answer during the focus steps:

1　Do you want this client?
2　What is the client's underlying issue?
3　Is it an engagement you want and have the capability to do?
4　Are you likely to win it within a reasonable level of effort?

These questions assume that you are dealing with a new client. Focusing is simpler with an established client, as you can ignore the first question.

I am going to look at each of these sequentially, but although there is a broad logic to the order they are presented in, in reality these four issues are explored and resolved in parallel. The second question is usually the most complex to answer and is the focal point of this section.

Do you want this client?

The first question to answer is whether you want to work with this client. In answering this question you start to collect the information you need to develop a proposal, and so it is both about qualification and information gathering. You should never be hasty to discount clients, and I reject very few opportunities just because it is a client I do not want. However, there are some people who do not make good consulting clients and with whom it is a struggle to have a constructive working relationship (regarding the latter, see also Chapter 12).

Perhaps the most obvious thing is to identify who the client is. As was discussed in Chapter 2, this is not always as straightforward as it initially seems. You may assume that the first person you interact with is the client, and often you will be right, but not always. However, follow the advice in Chapter 2 and you should be able to pinpoint the client.

There are good clients and there are difficult ones. You should not reject difficult clients out of hand, as many will have significant consulting needs and you will still be able to add value to them. You should try to understand how difficult they are likely to be, as, if nothing else, difficult clients tend to extend the length of consulting engagements and you need to size the work accordingly.

There are some minimal characteristics a client must fulfil. They must be willing to buy and they must have access to funds in order to pay. The client must be willing to provide support and resources for the engagement. There are many ways to design an engagement using variable levels of client support and resources, but there is a minimum level required. The client must understand that delivering a good result from a consulting engagement is a partnership between the consultant and the client. The client is neither buying a product nor are they outsourcing a problem to someone else. They will have to remain involved. Finally, the client needs to appreciate

❝ you must get something out of the engagement or else it is not worth doing ❞

that, as a consultant, you must get something out of the engagement or else it is not worth doing. At a minimum this is your fees, but the more attractive the client can make the engagement, the more likely you are to be motivated to execute an excellent piece of consulting.

There is a lot of information to collect and clarifications to be achieved to develop a good proposal. Information, such as available budget, styles of working, the level of access to client staff that will be possible, contextual constraints and so on, must be collected. Such information can come from the client directly, but can also be derived from other people in the client organisation. Some clients like to delegate the interaction with consultants. There is nothing in principle wrong with this, other than it is in your interest for your relationship to be with the client and not the client's staff, but it should not stop you progressing. However, the client must have some direct involvement in focusing the engagement. As a bare minimum the client should:

■ define the objectives of the engagement
■ define how the success of the engagement will be assessed.

If the client is not willing to do this, then it is quite likely that they will not be actively involved in the engagement if and when it starts. This indicates a difficult client.

You should also identify who is involved in deciding who will win the engagement. For instance, are the procurement department involved? If they are, what is the procurement process you must adhere to? It is also useful to clarify who will be the decision makers and other stakeholders in the live engagement once it starts. A very large group of decision makers and stakeholders will tend to make the engagement more complex and take more time or consultant resources, which needs to be factored into your proposal.

One critical set of information is the client's buying or selection criteria. You should identify what makes a consulting proposition attractive or unattractive to a client. You can easily develop a better proposal than a similarly skilled consultant by understanding what will make your proposition attractive to a client. Examples of possible criteria include whether the client is cost sensitive, or wants the best possible piece of consulting irrespective of the fees. Does the client like clever intellectual rigour and sound argument, or do they prefer pragmatic advice from an experienced hands-on consultant? Does the client favour detailed written proposals or short presentations? The easiest way to find this information is to ask the client directly what their preferences are and what style of working they like.

The information you collect in this step should give you a clear indication of whether you want to work with the client, and if it is a client you can profitably provide consulting to. In the end, there is rarely a black and white answer to this question, merely indicative facts and impressions you must make a judgement about.

What is the client's underlying issue?

The most important factor for the consultant to understand is the client's underlying issue. Many consultants fail to sell because of a lack of understanding of the client's real issues. Even if the consultant sells, the client ends up disappointed as the result does not meet their real needs. You must clearly identify what it is that makes the client want to use consultants.

Clients involve consultants for a whole host of reasons. Sometimes they want creativity – that is the ability to help them to gain a new insight. Perhaps they want expertise to help in making a decision. They may want people with specialist skills to identify and overcome problems in a specific area of their business. They may desire access to a consultancy's intellectual capital, such as processes describing a tried and tested methodology. Clients may want an independent viewpoint, and a different perspective on issues which are perplexing them. The client may want to use a consultant for political reasons, for example to validate a decision or push through unpopular strategy. All these relate to the context in which you are consulting, but on top of understanding this you must understand the specific issue the client wants addressed. Clients do not buy consulting for general reasons, but because of a specific issue or a set of issues. It is these that you need to tease out through your exploratory dialogue.

What do I mean by an 'issue' in this context? An issue is a problem the client has, or an opportunity the client wants to seize, that generates a need for assistance. An issue can be phrased as a question, and it is always helpful to consolidate the information and ideas about the client into a single question. When you write your proposal, you are offering to answer this question for the client. Of course, clients never actually have one issue. They have a complex mishmash of problems, opportunities, irritations, concerns, ideas and feelings. Some clients have a razor-sharp focus on a single issue they want help with, but much of the focus step is often trawling through the wide and murky sea of client thinking until you identify one or a few related issues they really need or want help to resolve.

New consultants often do not understand why it is important to identify an issue. Surely the consultant is there to help, and if the client is suffering from this muddle of challenges then shouldn't we help with all of them? The answer is no. Consultants are not employed to do a client's job for them. If a client wants that, then they require an interim manager; when you propose consulting, you do not offer to run the client's business. The general value proposition of a consultant is to resolve issues in a limited period of time. That may consist of providing clarity about what the issues are, identifying ways to resolve the issue, helping to plan the implementation of the resolution or supporting its implementation. If a client wants help to resolve several unrelated issues, you may bundle them into one engagement, but you are doing several separate pieces of consulting.

It is critical to being able to make a coherent and understandable proposal that you boil down the set of client problems to a single issue, or small set of issues. If you cannot, then try and sell a consulting engagement that aims to gain clarification. In other words, to specify the client issue as 'I cannot make sense of all the problems I have' and the consulting proposition would be something like 'to make sense of the problems and develop a prioritised plan of action for their resolution'.

To sell consulting, not only do you have to understand the client's issue, but you need to link it to your capabilities or service lines. The whole aim of the propose stage is to show a client you can resolve the issues they have. There is a natural tension to balance. You do not want your assessment of the situation to be constrained by your service lines, otherwise you will start to see the solution to all problems as a limited set of services. True client-centric consulting does not limit itself in this way. However, you will need to make a proposal, and it will require you to show a link between the client's issues and your capabilities. Hence it is helpful to think about how you align your service lines to the client's issue. I must stress that this is not about the application of standard services to a unique client problem. You are not selling off-the-shelf products. Your service will need to be tailored to the specific situation, but the issue still relates to your service lines. You are being engaged because you have experience, and your experience is encapsulated in your service lines.

> " the whole aim is to show a client you can resolve the issues they have "

Start by indentifying the client issue and then translate this into your service lines. To sell consulting, the translation from a client issue into a consulting service line should be transparent and intuitively obvious to the client. By thinking about the client's issue and its relationship to your service lines, you can:

▪ **Develop understanding**: If you think of a client's issues in terms of your experience you are in the best position to ask the right questions and clarify the situation.

▪ **Position and label the problem and the solution you are proposing**: Real issues in business are complex, but people understand best when they can be described in simple terms. You should aim for a proposal that is very clear.

▪ **Make a compelling proposition**: The most compelling proposition will result from a true understanding of the client's issue, and showing that it directly links to your skills.

Figure 5.2 shows how you can start to align your service lines to client needs. There are six columns, and each column represents a general category of client issue. At the top of each of the columns is an issue from a client's perspective. At the bottom of the column are potential consulting service lines that can be used to resolve this issue. Not all client issues will fit into the six categories shown in these columns, but most align more or less to these sorts of categorisation. Of course, your analysis needs to get to a much more specific client issue than defined here, but even at the level shown in Figure 5.2, you can start to determine if what is required is a strategic analysis, selecting solutions, implementation planning or implementation management.

Being able to categorise in such a way is helpful and important. The difference, for example, between a client issue being 'am I doing the right things?' and 'am I doing things in the right way?' may seem insignificant, but they are fundamentally different questions to answer. The former is a question about strategy, the latter is about operations. The first is concerned with what an organisation should be doing, the second is concerned with how it should be doing whatever it does. Misunderstand whether the client issue is the former or the latter and you will offer what is fundamentally the wrong service line to the client.

The larger consultancies tend to arrange service lines along the way shown at the bottom of each the columns in Figure 5.2. There will be strategy experts, specialists who can analyse an area of a business

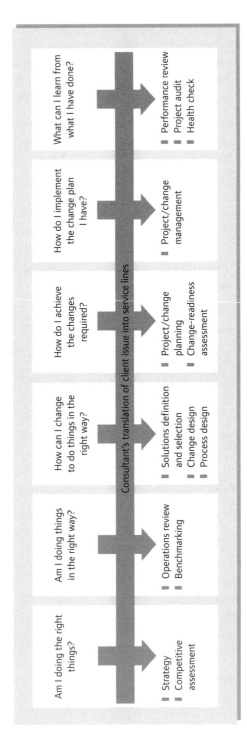

Figure 5.2 Aligning service lines to client needs

operations and recommend improvements, consultants who are expert in specifying solutions, consultants who do implementation planning and management, and usually consultants who can review aspects of operations to assess performance. By categorising an opportunity in the way shown in Figure 5.2, it is possible to start to identify which consultants should be used to develop the proposal.

What these consultancies are doing is aligning service lines with the client's perceived issues. In reality, there will be a more complex analysis going on, once additional characteristics are considered, such as the client sector and scale of the client organisation. For instance, the approach to strategy for a major multinational bank may be different from that used with a small, regional, manufacturing company – but the general principle of positioning a strategy service line relative to a client in either sector, who wants to know if they are doing the right things, remains the same. Figure 5.3 is a redrawing of Figure 5.2 emphasising the range of client's perceived issues that map on to the consultant's service lines.

The power of such a simple analysis of client needs should not be underestimated. It is very easy when analysing a client to get bogged down in all sorts of issues and information. As a consultant looking to make a sale, the basic question will remain: what is the client fundamentally looking for? Do they want some thinking and strategic insight, do they want some planning, or do they want help implementing change?

One area where a good consultant is differentiated from less able colleagues is in the willingness and ability to challenge the client in terms of their perceived issue. A good consultant does not simply work out the client's perceived issue and offer a service line that matches it. This can lead to sales, but you can add more value. A client may have a perception of what they want, but after some exploration the consultant may think that the client is wrong.

" the consulatnt may think that the client is wrong "

Now there is naturally a good and a bad way to tell a client that you think their understanding of the issue is wrong, but if you do it well, a consultant can add significant value – and it is value that is added *before* an engagement has even started. This is what I describe as identifying the client's **underlying need**, to differentiate it from the client's **perceived issue**. Figure 5.4 represents this situation (see page 96).

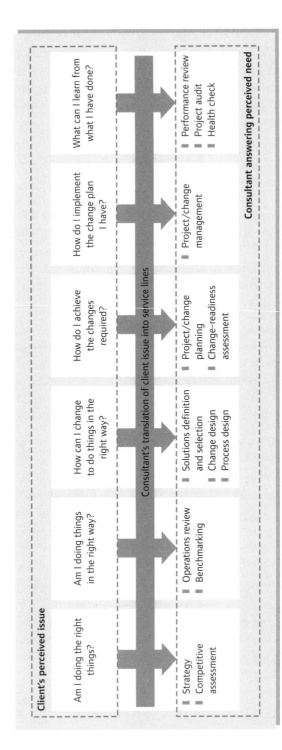

Figure 5.3 Direct relationship of service offering to client perceived issues

As an example consider the second column from the right in Figure 5.4. The client has a change implementation plan and is asking for the consultant to help implement it. The obvious response is to offer a project and change management service. However, the consultant may look at the client's plan and think that the plan is not good enough or will not work. In this case, the consultant wants to push the client back around their change lifecycle (see Chapter 4), and instead of selling project and change management the consultant wants to sell the client improved planning.

Figure 5.4 shows four situations in which the client's perceived issue is, in the consultant's view, misplaced. The consultant responds by challenging the client and offering a different service line to the client.

A client can easily take offence when a consultant rejects their own assessment of the situation. Even if the client does not get offended, there is always a risk associated with telling a client that you think the need they have is different from what they believe. It may lead them simply to reject you out of hand. But in many cases this is a risk worth taking. If the client accepts what you say, then you have shown your skills already and may strengthen your relationship. If the client rejects what you say and your analysis is correct, then it is possible the engagement would not have been successful anyway.

There is an ethical risk here, of the sort described in Chapter 10. Look again at Figure 5.4. If you look at the columns from left to right across the page there is a logical sequence of engagements. It starts with a piece of strategic analysis, through an operational review and then identifying and implementing solutions, and ends up with a performance review following implementation. As a consultant you may only be asked to be involved in one, or even only part of one, of these issues. However, if you are engaged to deal with one of the client issues to the right-hand side of the diagram, by challenging the client's perception of the issue you may move to the left-hand issues. By doing this you are extending the opportunity. The work you were originally approached about may still be required, but at a later date when you have improved the preceding work. Proceeding in this way because it is right for the client is an example of excellent value-adding consulting. If you do it simply to sell more work, then this is questionable ethical behaviour.

An alternative approach to challenging the client is to stick always to offering the client what they have asked for and only offer services which directly correspond to the client's perceived issue. Any changes in approach or focus of the engagement are left to when the engagement is

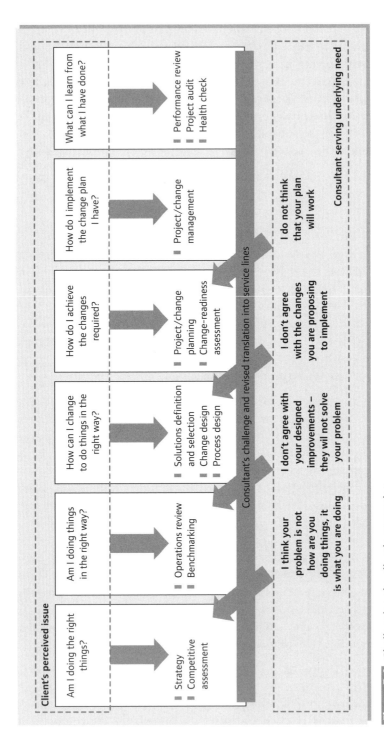

Figure 5.4 Challenging the client's perception

won. The advantage of such an approach is that you will know much more and have a better understanding of client issues once the engagement is underway. No matter how long you spend in the focus step, you will not have as good an understanding as you have once the engagement is underway. It may be that even with a really detailed focus step you need to change the service line or approach anyway once the engagement starts. You are normally also not being paid for your time in the focus step, so you will want to conclude it as rapidly as possible. The problem with this thinking is that it is far harder to change an engagement once it is underway, and it is riskier for you as a consultant. If you offer a client one service line, and that service line turns out not to fulfil the client's issue because the issue identified is not really the underlying one, the client will not thank you and may actually blame you for any resultant problems or costs. It is much better, if possible, to identify the client's real underlying issue now, rather than later in the delivery stage.

Assuming you can get to a clarification of the real client issue, it is also worth exploring why the client is seeking assistance from consultants at this point. Few issues are new, so why is the client seeking a consultant now? Is it something they have decided, or are they being coerced or encouraged by a more senior manager? If so, you want to understand that senior manager's drivers to ensure the engagement you will propose will fulfil their needs as well as the person you are interacting with as a client. The best solution is to ask a client directly why they have contacted you. This can short-circuit many potential sales problems, it can highlight obstacles that people want to overcome and it will quickly clarify if it is a coerced purchase or not.

❝ why is the client seeking a consultant now? ❞

Is it an engagement you want and have the capability to do?

As you are analysing the situation and developing an understanding of the client's issue, you will naturally tend to consider whether you want the engagement. Is it a dream engagement that will earn you high margin fees, or is it a nightmare waiting to happen that is likely to leave you with an endless piece of work for minimal income? Most assignments are neither of these two extremes but sit somewhere in a spectrum between them. You will not be absolutely certain how any one engagement fits in this spectrum until the engagement starts. But you can give yourself sufficient information to understand, to an acceptable level of risk, how close to the dream and far from the nightmare you are.

The first obvious question is: can you do it? Do you understand the client need sufficiently and have adequate skills and expertise to fulfil those needs? Some client engagements align perfectly with your skills. Many client engagements will not be suitable for you as they require a different skill set. Being a specialist is as much about being clear about what you don't do as it is being an expert in what you can do. However, it is likely that the very many and possibly the majority of engagements that come your way are neither a perfect fit nor a complete miss with your expertise. You must then make a balanced and honest judgement – can you do the work or not? If you are unsure, the best approach is to have an open discussion with the client about where you can add value and where you cannot. My experience is that such honesty leads to deeper relationships with clients.

You will have some of your own requirements before taking on an engagement. You need to clarify if the current opportunity will fulfil these or not. You should try to be as clear as you can about what your requirements are, both for your own satisfaction as a consultant and so that you can determine your ability to complete the work successfully. You will almost never get everything you would like, and therefore it is best to categorise your needs into three groups:

1 *Mandatory needs*: Without these being met you will not pursue the work. For instance, the minimum day rate you will accept, or the client's willingness to meet with you regularly for the life of the engagement, etc.

2 *Desirable needs*: You will do the work anyway, but tailor the proposal depending on whether these will be met or not. Examples include whether you can work at home on Fridays, or whether the client has full authority to mandate access to the resources you require, etc.

3 *Nice-to-haves*: These are things you will ask for, as nothing is lost by asking, but don't worry if they are rejected. For example, a private office to work in on the client's premises, etc.

Finally, what are the risks associated with the engagement? Is the client looking for any guarantee or to offset risk on to you? Ideally, you should bear as little risk as possible. On the one hand, it is not unreasonable for a client dealing with an expensive expert to expect the expert to have sufficient confidence in their advice to guarantee benefits. However, as a consultant you do not have enough power to ensure that your recommendations are undertaken in the way you recommend they are done.

Secondly, you rarely have sufficient resources to provide any meaningful guarantee to a client anyway. Be wary of accepting any engagement in which the client is expecting you to take any significant share of the client's business risk.

Are you likely to win it within a reasonable level of effort?

Selling consultancy takes effort, sometimes considerable effort. So at some point you must determine if you have a realistic chance of winning the engagement. To answer this question positively, you need to have some understanding of the client's wants and needs, be comfortable that you can work with the client, and have a belief that you can develop a compelling proposal.

You also must consider the competition. The more competition there is, the less chance you have of winning the work. It is much easier to work in a non-competitive situation. This is not uncommon, at least for smaller engagements. Lots of competition is not only a pain for you, it can mean more work for the client as they enter a dialogue with several different consultants and review and assess different proposals. But if a client is seeking a consultant for any sizeable piece of work, or for any critically important advice, it is sensible for the client to look at alternative offerings from different consultancies.

You should understand whether the situation is competitive or not, but do not worry too much about competition. If you have a good understanding of the client's issues and can make a compelling proposition to overcome them, you have a good chance of getting the work.

Most consulting theories and processes stress the importance of the focus phase. Many consultants don't spend enough time in or effort on the focus step. Yet, in something so inherently vague and subject to progressive elaboration like a consultancy engagement, there is a limit to how much certainty focusing can give. What is essential is that there is sufficient dialogue and groundwork to limit the engagement's scope, and to define an approach, timing and fees that you have sufficient confidence in.

You can spend too much time agreeing to the work. This may be because the client is risk averse, does not know what they want or is getting lots of your time for free. Whatever the reason, it has to stop – in the end it is not even in the client's interest as they won't fully understand the work or the solution until the engagement starts. At some point you must decline the opportunity or move into framing a proposition. If you decide not to progress an engagement, see the advice in Chapter 12, especially the section on how to say no to clients.

Any further information must be left to discover in the live engagement, accepting that you never have perfect information and any proposal will be subject to change. What is most crucial is to determine that you and the client can work together and that the client understands and accepts the work you do and the way you do it. The style of interaction during the focus phase sets the client's expectations of how the interaction will continue during the live engagement. Often, it is building this working relationship that is the most important part of focusing. One of the key parts is the signals you send as much as any hard facts that are agreed. Of course, certain definition of scope, approach, budget, etc. is ideal, but this is not always possible.

> ❝ determine that you and the client can work together ❞

Framing a proposal and winning an engagement

Having collected sufficient focused information, you now move on to the *frame* step and formalise your consulting offer to the client. This is the point at which you convert your thinking and various findings into a documented proposal. The proposal must reflect the client's needs and have a realistic chance of winning by appealing to the client with a compelling proposition.

There is no set format for a proposal. Usually it is a written document, and it can be text-based or a presentation. Either way, a proposal should provide enough information for the client to be able to decide to engage you. It must be sufficiently compelling, even if the client has queries and questions, to position you as the consultant the client should be working with. The proposal should also be appealing. Clients are not just buying a service, they are also buying you.

The proposal for a complex engagement may be an extensive document, but it does not need to be long. Some of my proposals are encapsulated in a one- or two-page letter, but there are times when it needs to be longer. The situation may be complicated, there may be a need for a complex contract, or it may concern a concept that cannot be explained in a few words. Irrespective of its size, the proposal must include:

- an understanding of the client's issues
- the approach you will use to resolving the issue
- the commercial terms
- a value proposition – a statement which explains to the client the value they will gain by investing in the proposal.

These four components must be included in every proposal. Each can range from a very brief description to many pages of text. Unless the client asks for huge amounts of detail, brevity is preferred. Being able to encapsulate accurately client needs and approaches in a short description shows real understanding. It also makes the proposal easier to produce and manage. However, depending on the situation, there is a wide range of additional materials you may need to add to a proposal. The additional material to consider can include:

- Other information which will encourage the client to choose you – this could be case studies, or client references, etc.
- Information the client has specifically requested to be included – a client may ask for any range of facts and figures, such as a consultant CVs or a general description of your company's service lines.
- Clarifications and conditions that you consider are essential to document to reduce your risk on the engagement or to define ground rules for how you work together – this might include explaining whether you are based on the client's site or will work from your offices, or the fact that you must have certain dedicated staff allocated to the engagement by the client.

Setting out to write a compelling proposition can be challenging. You may have collected a huge amount of information and initially may not be sure what precisely you are going to offer the client or how you will present this. It is worth spending the effort to get the proposal right, especially if you are in a competitive situation. There can be a massive difference in the appeal of a well-written and well-structured proposal, compared to a poorly structured and incoherently written proposal – even though both could be produced by consultants with equivalent skills to resolve a client issue. Techniques such as the pyramid principle and mind mapping (see the references at the end of the book on page 279) can help tremendously.

When preparing a client proposition, I find it helpful to think in terms of three critical dimensions to a consulting engagement:

1 What is the client issue?

2 What is the consulting approach?

3 What is the scope of consulting intervention?

This is summarised in Figure 5.5. Let's look at each of these briefly.

Client issue

The client issue was identified in the previous focus stage by exploratory dialogue. You must reflect the client issue and situation in the proposal. Be clear about why you are documenting the client issue. You do not write it down in the proposal so the client can understand it, although sometimes a good proposal can help to clarify a client's own thinking. You write it down to show to the client that you understand their needs. You are not writing an essay for someone who knows nothing about the client's business. You are illustrating your grasp of the client's situation to the person who best understands it – the client! You must show an interest in and understanding of the client's real problems, not just your service lines.

> be clear about why you are documenting the client issue

If as part of your focus step you have decided to challenge the client's perception of their issue, you should do some expectation setting. When a client asks for X, and you respond with, 'we don't think you need X, we are going to offer you Y', they will at least be surprised and possibly annoyed. It is best to talk to them informally first before offering a

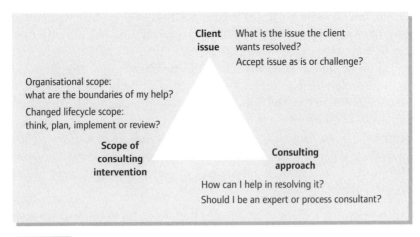

Client issue — What is the issue the client wants resolved? Accept issue as is or challenge?

Organisational scope: what are the boundaries of my help?

Changed lifecycle scope: think, plan, implement or review?

Scope of consulting intervention

Consulting approach

How can I help in resolving it? Should I be an expert or process consultant?

Figure 5.5 The dimensions of a consulting engagement

proposal that does not meet their expectations. In an informal discussion you can explain your rationale for an alternative approach and gain their support. Call the client and say you want to discuss the proposal before you submit it, to check it will meet their needs.

Consulting approach

The consulting approach is where your specialist skill is applied. You are competent because you have an approach to solving the issue. You are credible because you can explain this to a client in a way they grasp and have confidence in. Additionally, you must consider whether you are positioning yourself as an expert or as a process consultant (see Chapter 7). Are you going to tell the client what they should do, or are you going to help the client to work it out for themselves? These are fundamentally different approaches to consulting. Some clients need experts, other are better off with a process consultant.

Your approach should make it clear to the client what deliverables they will get, and how those deliverables will make things different for them. As you write the proposal, put yourself in your client's position. Clients not only want to know what the experience of working with you will be like, they want to know what they are getting for the money they are investing. What is going to be different for the client when the engagement ends? Will they understand some issue better, will they have been trained to perform better, will they have a next-steps plan, or will they have an implemented solution? Make it absolutely clear. A client is unlikely to buy if they do not know what the engagement produces and what the outcome from the engagement will be. What are the tangible deliverables (if any)? If your engagement is largely delivering intangible deliverables, such as skills transfer to client staff, the client needs some way of gaining confidence these will be delivered.

Scope of consulting intervention

The scope of the consulting intervention relates both to the client's organisation and to the client's change lifecycle. From the client's organisational perspective you should ask: what staff, departments, functions or business processes will be included in the scope of the engagement? From the change lifecycle perspective you should ask: are you essentially helping the client to think, to plan, to implement or to review – or some combination of all of these?

Other factors in a proposal

Try to avoid jargon or consultant-speak in the proposal (see Chapter 11). The only jargon that is permissible in a client proposal is the client's own jargon. Clients are rarely impressed by obscure terminology. Using such terminology only reinforces how remote and dissimilar you are from the client. Remoteness and dissimilarity in a consultant are not virtues from the client's perspective.

If you are concerned that the live engagement is likely to veer away from the proposal, you may want to include a short description of how you will deal with this should it occur. You may choose some form of formal change control process, or more simply note that you will review regularly and agree amendments to terms with the client. If you cannot finalise and agree to all the details, you must at least agree to how it will change (e.g. 'my rates are £xx per day and this is approximately 10 days work – if that is insufficient we will ...').

When you agree to work with a client you usually commit to a start date for the engagement. This means you must have an understanding of your forward availability. If the client says yes to the proposal, can you start next Monday or will it be next month? The ideal situation is that you finish one engagement and immediately start the next. In reality, this is difficult. Engagements do not always end when you expect them to, selling takes time, and clients can be unexpectedly slow in making decisions or committing to an engagement. If you always wait for one engagement to end before looking for the next you will become underutilised. Clients generally understand that you are not sitting waiting for their work, and as long as you are professional and do not make promises you cannot keep, clients will be flexible about your availability, within reason. One approach I use is to agree to start the engagement by a specific date as long as the client commits to it before another date. So, I might write in the proposal something like: 'As long as I receive confirmation that you are satisfied with this proposal by Monday 5 June, the engagement will start on Monday 19 June'.

> **" clients will be flexible about your availability, within reason "**

The final part of the proposal is ensuring it meets your organisation's legal, contractual and commercial terms. You should clarify what is and is not included in those commercial terms, such as expenses and VAT. Major consultancies will have a set of standards for all these points. If you are an independent consultant I would not overly worry about complex contracts. Write a clear and unambiguous letter of what you are offering, the price and conditions you think are important – that is usually sufficient.

Before you send the proposal to a client, check it. Go through it in detail and confirm it says exactly what you want it to say and that it cannot be misinterpreted. The best way to do this is to ask someone independent to read it and test that they get the understanding you expect from the proposal. Finally, ask yourself 'so what?' When a client has read a proposal, they should have a clear understanding of what you are proposing and why it is a good proposition for them to invest in. If, after reading the proposal you have written, you think the client might think 'so what?', then the proposal is not clear or compelling enough.

Keep on winning work

The aim of a proposal is to get a client to commit fees to you in return for a consulting engagement. Consultants need many engagements throughout their careers, so the steps of finding opportunities, focusing on client needs and framing a proposal should be ones you refine and improve all the time. If, during the proposal phase, you decide to decline the work or don't win it, follow up with your client to maintain a relationship. Just because you did not get this piece of work does not mean you will not get another. If you win the work, start thinking from day one about on-sell, up-sell, and cross-sell. The more successful your propose stage, the more certain your income is.

One way to measure the success of your propose stage is to think about the percentage of opportunities you win. A more sophisticated way to measure the success is to think about your whole sales pipeline. Your aim is not to win every opportunity that comes your way, but to win sufficient opportunities to keep yourself busy, with a minimal opportunity cost. The less effort and cost you expend in winning sales, the better it is for you. Let me show this in an example.

Example

Look at Figure 5.6. It shows the sales pipelines for two different consulting companies. They both start with the same number of opportunities and end with the same number of live engagements. On the surface these may seem to be equally well run businesses. In reality, consultancy 2 operates its propose-to-win process far better than consultancy 1. In consultancy 1 too many opportunities,

▶

relative to how many are actually won, are turned into proposals. This can eat up huge amounts of consultant time. In consultancy 2 poor opportunities are eliminated early in the process. Relatively few engagements are focused on, and all the engagements that reach the frame step are converted to live engagements.

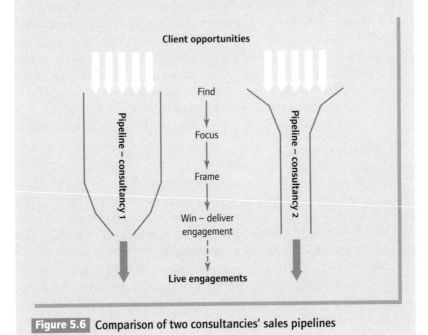

Figure 5.6 Comparison of two consultancies' sales pipelines

This is an extreme example to make a point. The fewer proposals you focus on, the more likely you are to win them as you can really focus your effort on them. If you are considering opting out or are unlikely to win, it is most efficient from a business perspective to eliminate the opportunity as early as possible.

Summary

The propose-to-win stage is a critical part of the consultant's work. You cannot succeed as a consultant without developing a real competence in finding opportunities and converting them into sales. This does not mean you need to be an expert sales person, as there are different ways to achieve these goals.

There are three main steps within the propose-to-win stage.

▪ **Find**: This step is concerned with finding opportunities and aligining your need for profitable engagements with the client's need for help.

▪ **Focus**: This is an exploratory step, requiring dialogue between yourself and the client. Its aim is to align understanding between yourself and the client, and to manage expectations and risk. In focusing an engagement you should seek to answer four questions:

  – Do you want the client?
  – What is the client's underlying issue?
  – Is it an engagement you want and have the capability to do?
  – Are you likely to win it with a reasonable level of effort?

▪ **Frame**: This step requires you to develop an appealing and compelling proposal. A good proposal shows your understanding of the client's issue, how you will overcome this issue, and the value proposition the client gains by engaging you.

The propose-to-win stage is summarised in Figure 5.7.

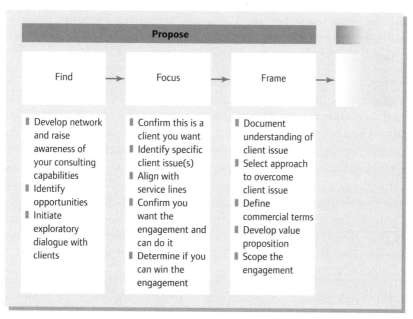

Figure 5.7 The propose-to-win phase of the engagement process

6

Delivering consulting engagements and satisfying clients

The core work of all management consultants is the delivery of client engagements. The engagement represents the time when a consultant's specialist skills, knowledge and service lines are applied. This chapter describes the process of delivering engagements, together with many tips and techniques essential for great consulting, and is relevant to all consultants. It should be read in conjunction with Chapter 7 on process consulting and facilitation.

Some senior managers in consultancies are no longer involved directly in engagements, but spend their time in managing the consultancy, business development and selling work. This is purely for the commercial benefit of a consultancy. Of course, a consultancy as a commercial enterprise needs to be successful and profitable. However, it should not be forgotten that the primary source of that success is not in the way the consultancy is managed or engagements are sold, but comes from adding value to clients by delivering consulting engagements that meet their needs. A client-centric consultant always has client needs at the forefront of their thoughts, and a consultancy business should be structured and managed to optimise the provision of client-centric consultancy.

This stage of the engagement process is called **deliver-to-satisfy**, as the main objective is not just to complete a piece of paid work, but to satisfy the client. The steps within this stage are shown in a linear fashion in Figure 6.1.

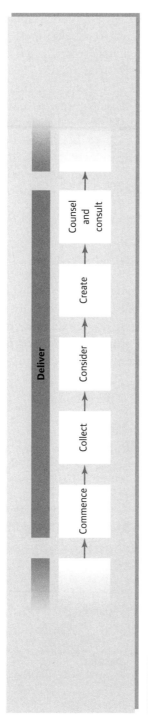

Figure 6.1 The deliver stage

The linear structure in Figure 6.1 aids understanding but, in reality, this stage is highly iterative. Whilst a consultant must generally progress in a logical order from an initial commence step to a counsel and consult step, there will be regular jumping between the steps. For example, when a consultant is presenting a report to a client, they may realise the report has missed some vital point. The consultant returns to the create step and then further back to the consider step to revise their recommendations. In doing this, they may realise they need more data and have to briefly return to the collect step. In a complex engagement, there will often be a periods of simultaneous working across the steps in the deliver stage. Hence, in reality the process will look more like that shown in Figure 6.2.

This chapter is ordered in the sequence shown in Figure 6.1

Commence

Having successfully won an engagement, the first step in delivering it is the *commence* step. Commence is concerned with planning and resourcing the engagement. In order to do this a number of decisions have to be made. The direction and nature of these decisions will be shaped by agreements made and information collected in the propose stage, but

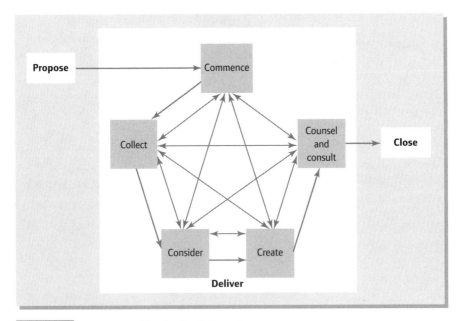

Figure 6.2 Iterative working in the deliver stage

normally it is only when an engagement is won that a fully detailed engagement plan is developed and named individuals are committed to working on the engagement.

The nature of a plan for a consulting engagement depends primarily on the scale and complexity of the engagement. A large consulting engagement with many consultants working on it for several months may require the involvement of a dedicated and experienced project manager. At the other end of the scale, a small engagement with a single consultant working on it for a few days requires little more than an ordered list of actions that need to be completed. Most engagements sit somewhere between these extremes.

Project management in a typical consulting engagement is not complex, but consultants are often not great project managers. This can be seen in the stress and semi-chaotic rushing around that typify the end of many consulting engagements. The end is always predictable and a little planning makes even the most complex consulting engagement run much more smoothly. A good plan reduces risk and increases profitability. An effective plan makes the consultant seem more competent in the client's eyes, and generally reduces the level of stress on everyone in the consulting team. I run courses on project managing consulting engagements, and I have observed that even very experienced consultants benefit from thinking more about planning their engagements.

> ❝ a good plan reduces risk and increases profitability ❞

You do not need a qualification in project management to manage a consulting engagement, but an engagement is a project, sometimes has complex logistics (such as aligning many people's diaries at different times), and a degree of logical and systematic ordering of tasks is required. At some time, each and every consultant may have to deliver a consulting engagement on their own. Hence, all consultants must have the basic capability to project manage the consulting engagement. The basis of managing a consulting engagement is a plan.

An engagement plan needs to be comprehensive but flexible. Ideally, it contains every aspect of the work required to complete the engagement. However, typically in consulting engagements it is difficult to determine all the tasks required until the engagement is underway. Therefore the plan has to have enough flexibility to add new tasks as the engagement is performed, without increasing resources or the project timescale.

One feature that can make planning a consulting project more complex is that, unlike many other projects, the timescale and amount of consulting resource to be used is often agreed as part of the proposal, before the detailed plan is developed. This may seem to be an illogical ordering of activity, and it regularly causes issues, but it is not an insurmountable obstacle. The costs and timescales estimated in a proposal should only be done by someone with experience and with a realistic view of how complex the engagement is. Additionally, there is some leeway in most engagements to scale the deliverables from the engagement relative to how much time is allocated in the proposal. For example, a report on an aspect of a business can be developed in more or less detail, and with more or less information gathered, depending on the constraints imposed by the proposal. Of course, client expectations must be aligned with this scaling.

What differentiates a really good engagement plan from a weaker one is that it is begun by considering the end point of the engagement first. A good plan is developed by thinking through what the result from the engagement should be, and how to bring the engagement to an end. The plan is then elaborated by working backwards through the tasks that must be done to enable this result.

The result of a consulting engagement may be the creation of a set of client deliverables or some predefined outcome. A deliverable is a defined output which is usually tangible, but sometimes intangible, and which the client can utilise. Examples of deliverables include reports, presentations, training courses, process designs, plans, lists of recommendations and so on. An outcome is a change in the client's business. Examples of an outcome include a 5 per cent reduction in the cost of operations, a decision made, or consensus achieved in the new strategy for a business. Traditionally consultants have been deliverable-focused, but increasingly are more outcome-orientated. By offering a client an outcome and not just a deliverable, it is possible to develop a better client value proposition and hence charge premium fees. It may seem a rather fine difference between deliverables and an outcome, but it is important to understand it whilst developing an engagement plan.

Let me illustrate with two hypothetical alternatives:

1   Deliverable: produce a revised strategy for a division of a business.
2   Outcome: achieve consensus on a new strategy and have all senior managers working towards achieving the revised strategy.

The former is concerned with developing and writing a report with a revised strategy in it. The latter entails the creation of the strategy report, but also requires ensuring all managers understand and agree with the strategy, and have the skills and resources to move ahead and implement it. The latter is a significantly more complex engagement, and as the consultant it is essential you understand the client's expectation with regard to deliverables and outcomes.

Once you understand the outcome or deliverables wanted, the next stage in developing a plan is to define the consulting approach or the process you will follow to achieve this result. Some clients are only interested in achieving the agreed deliverable or outcome and do not care how you achieve it. Many want to, and you often need them to, understand the process which you will use to get to this result. You usually need the client to understand the process you will follow, because the client will be a participant in this process, and will have to provide resources to support you in going through it.

One critical decision to make is whether you will adopt the style of an expert consultant or a process consultant. Chapter 7 describes process consulting, and this chapter is primarily orientated towards expert consulting, although the boundary is not clear cut. The fundamental difference is whether you expect to tell the client what to do (expert), or whether you will work with the client so that they can define themselves how to resolve their problems (process). These are radically different ways of working. However, within a single engagement a consultant may switch between these styles at different points.

It is also important to understand the organisational scope of a consulting intervention. Are you dealing with the whole business, or will you look only at a subset of the organisation, for example, specific departments, divisions or processes? An engagement to look at the recruitment process in the sales department has a significantly smaller scope than one to look at all HR processes in sales, marketing and customer service. Consulting engagements are for limited periods of time, and to achieve a high-quality result it is usually essential to place some boundaries on the scope of the work. An unbounded scope requires an unending plan.

> **❝ it is usually essential to place some boundaries on the scope of the work ❞**

All engagements need an engagement management process. The engagement management process is the mechanism by which the engagement is controlled. It typically requires a series of client meetings for the duration of the engagement. Whenever I run an engagement, I like to meet my client every week to update them on progress, discuss any findings and resolve any issues getting in the way of progress. Similarly, if you work for a large consultancy, your management may require meetings to ensure you are maintaining the necessary level of quality in your work and are not exposing the consultancy to any unnecessary risk. Your consulting company may have some mandatory processes to follow as part of the engagement. If the engagement has a team working on it, the team normally needs to get together regularly to update on progress, align work and to resolve problems. The frequency depends on the nature of the engagement. On some very intense engagements I bring the team together on a daily basis, on others it is less frequent. The engagement management process is normally very simple, and essentially involves setting up a series of regular meetings with an agreed agenda with client, team and consulting management. Experienced consultants know that the trick is to make sure the meetings are agreed and arranged at the start of the engagement. If they are arranged on an *ad hoc* basis whilst the engagement progresses, you will soon meet delays as people will not have time in their diary to meet you.

A final factor in developing the engagement plan is to decide whether you need to include any risk management activities within the plan. Consulting engagements are subject to a variety of risks, including access to resources and the possible negative influence of some stakeholders upon your work. Many risks have to be dealt with as they arise, but some are predictable and it is worth considering what activities you will undertake to overcome them. Risks are many and varied. Risks can be identified by asking questions such as: what will you do if the client does not provide the resources agreed at the times agreed? If you are basing your engagement on some hypothesis about underlying problems, what will you do if your hypothesis turns out to be wrong? What will you do if you find out some influential stakeholder is opposed to your work?

Having developed the engagement plan, it is possible to determine what resources are required to execute this plan. The resources are mostly people. They will be consultants, but they may also be client staff. One frequent problem on consulting engagements is getting real client staff released to work on the engagements in practice, as opposed to a theoretical promise by a client to give some staff to help. This is one reason why it is worth agreeing this up front. If a client offers staff to work on the engagement, make sure you get commitment to named individuals with the necessary skills and time available to work on the engagement. But resources may be more than people, and you must identify what else you need to deliver the engagement successfully. Examples of other resources include transport, building passes, office space, facilities, access to specific areas of a business and so on.

Table 6.1 presents a short planning and resourcing checklist. The aim is to be able to answer 'yes' to every question in this table. For every question you answer 'no' to, you must determine what actions you need to take to resolve it.

Table 6.1 Engagement planning and resourcing checklist

	Yes	No
Do you understand the constraints in terms of timescale and resources that your proposal places on your engagement plan?	☐	☐
Do you understand the deliverables or outcome required from the engagement?	☐	☐
Do you understand the process by which you will get to this result (including whether you will work as a process or expert consultant)?	☐	☐
Does the client understand this process and agree with it?	☐	☐
Is the organisational scope/boundaries of the engagement agreed? (Departments, divisions, processes included in scope and out of scope).	☐	☐
Have you included your engagement management process in the plan? Does this include all actions required by your consulting firm?	☐	☐
Are you clear about what data will be available and the level of effort to extract useful information (see the section on *Collect* below)?	☐	☐
Have you considered your consultancy's quality assurance process in your plan (see the section on *Create* below)?	☐	☐
Have you defined an engagement management process, taking account of the need to interact with the client, the engagement team and consulting management?	☐	☐
Are the engagement management meetings scheduled in attendees' diaries?	☐	☐
Are there any significant engagement risks you need to build into the engagement plan?	☐	☐
Do you understand the resources you require to complete the engagement?	☐	☐
Do you have access to all the resources you need (or a process to get access to them)?	☐	☐
Do the resources have the necessary skills and time available to work on the engagement?	☐	☐
Does everyone working on the engagement (client and consultant) understand their role and activities in line with the engagement plan?	☐	☐
Have you included all the activities required to close the engagement down, and to sustain any change resulting from the engagement (see Chapter 8)?	☐	☐

Collect

Whatever approach you take to helping a client, you need to *collect* information. The information is required to understand clients and their issues, scope engagements, understand impacts and the seriousness of problems, and to identify solutions. Information must be available on engagements as the basis for analysis and sometimes to measure results. Information has to be developed. Data is collected, which will at first be unsorted, in various formats, and is often of limited value in its initial state. The data must be analysed and converted into useful and meaningful information. There are many sources of data and many ways it can be analysed. The specific approach depends on the type of consulting you undertake, and much of the skill of a good consultant is about the ability to identify pertinent data and to convert it into the most relevant information in a specific situation. In this book I focus on data and information in a generic sense – the details are situational specific and will depend on your service lines and the individual engagement.

Accurate and sufficiently comprehensive data is critical to the success or failure of your consulting engagement. You cannot draw valuable conclusions without a relevant sample of data. The data collected is also related to the way success is judged. There may be different and conflicting views of success depending on viewpoint and data collected. Ideally, you must take account of these different measures and viewpoints. It is common for consultants to stumble when providing results to clients who ask questions like 'have you considered ...?', or 'did you speak to ...?'. To be judged a success you need to be able either to answer yes to such questions or to describe why the question is invalid for the engagement you are undertaking.

> **you cannot draw valuable conclusions without a relevant sample of data**

There are several challenges when it comes to collecting data, and the first is to know what data to collect. To decide that, you must have a clear understanding of the client's issue and the scope of the engagement. If you do not, most data collection is a waste of time. Assuming you do, the fundamental factor in determining which data to collect is to decide whether you will base your data collection on a predetermined hypothesis or set of hypotheses, or if you will be more unconstrained in your thinking. It is common in consulting to start by generating a hypothesis about a client's situation and then to seek data which either proves or disproves the hypothesis. Many strategy consultants use this approach.

The advantage of starting without any predefined hypotheses is that you may review a wider range of data sources and you will not be limited by preconceived ideas. The disadvantage is that you start an engagement with a completely blank sheet of paper and potentially an unlimited timescale. If you start with a hypothesis about the client's issue, then you can short-circuit data collection by focusing only on the data required to prove or disprove the hypothesis. An expert will have hypotheses about a client situation and arguably should always be able to define some starting set of hypotheses – if not, what is the expertise? But, at the same time, starting with hypotheses increases the risk that you may miss some unusual aspect of the client's situation or innovative solution to their problems. By having a preconceived idea of the client's situation you have limited the scope of your thinking and review.

Whether you choose to work with a set of hypotheses or have a completely open view depends on the nature of the engagement and what your client requires. Both approaches are valid and each has some advantages. If a client wants an expert to tell them what is wrong quickly and based on past experience, then working with hypotheses is best. If the client wants innovative and novel ideas and analysis of the situation, then it is better for the consultant to take a more objective and open-ended approach to data collection. What is important is to decide consciously which approach is best, and to define your engagement process accordingly.

It is helpful to be realistic about how objective you can be. There is always a degree of subjectivity in collecting data. You can never collect every possible piece of data, and the type of data selected and the method of analysis are subjective choices. This is often forgotten and what is presented as an objective review is really objective data selected from a subjective perspective.

The decision on what data to collect must reflect the nature of the client's issue and the context and culture of the situation. It is often helpful to explore issues and support further analysis by collecting quantitative data, such as financial information, statistics, figures and measurements. But client problems and issues cannot be truly understood without understanding the context. Few problems are totally independent and therefore you have to have some understanding of the interactions with other areas of the client's organisation. You must also develop an awareness of the client's culture. Culture may be part of the client's problem and part of any solution. Culture will determine the relative importance of issues and the acceptability of solutions. Context and culture cannot be understood purely by quantitative data. What this means is that it is usually necessary to collect both qualitative and quantitative data. Relying only on one or the other will bias the picture you develop of the client, and may also affect how your recommendations are accepted. For example, using purely qualitative data for people with a numerical bias may not result in client acceptance of the findings. Conversely, using purely quantitative data for people with a creative mindset may not be acceptable to them. Most clients have some biases towards qualitative and quantitative data, but also most engagements have a variety of stakeholders with different biases.

We are drawn to quantitative data because it can be manipulated and seems 'absolute'. In reality, even the most quantitative of consulting data contains subjective estimates and subjective choices are made as to what is relevant and what is not. We are drawn to qualitative data because it gives us a deeper feeling for the situation, and is more difficult to argue with. However, you will never be certain if you have collected a representative sample of qualitative data, and combining different pieces of qualitative data is always to some degree arbitrary. Whatever balance of qualitative and quantitative data you have, finding a sufficient amount of quality data – statistically relevant, found by a quality process, from appropriate reliable sources, etc. – is a key factor in determining the value of the engagement outcome.

Collecting data can throw up a host of unpredicted challenges. The expected data may not exist. It may be that what is ideally required is a historic set of data, but nothing is available. In such situations there needs to be a constructive dialogue with the client. Do you wait until the data is available, does the consultant estimate based on other similar situations, or does the client use gut feeling? Although it is never perfect, estimating and gut feeling are sometimes as good as it gets. Creating completely new data takes time. Problems with data collection is a key reason why you need some level of flexibility in your engagement plan. It is only once the engagement starts that you will really understand what data is and is not available from the client, and if you have committed a very tight timeline to a client with no understanding of the available data then you are taking a significant risk.

There are many sources and approaches to collecting data on a consulting engagement, and often it is necessary to combine data from multiple sources. Sources include:

- observation – structured, unstructured, measured, unmeasured
- interviews
- focus groups
- historic data analysis of client records and reports
- reviews of reports and publically available data
- analysis of a consultant's own records, for example benchmarking databases
- surveys (face to face, telephone, postal, etc.).

Some sources of data require specialist skills to undertake (e.g. focus groups), but generally all consultants must be able to construct and ask pertinent and appropriately phrased questions, and understand the responses given. (This is discussed in more detail in Chapter 11.) An understanding of basic data analysis techniques, elementary statistics and at least a basic use of tools like spreadsheets is usually essential.

Unless you have a well-established relationship, clients are rarely 100 per cent open with you, and some client staff will deliberately withhold information. This is human nature. Usually you do not want to know everything; nor does the client want you to. The problem with a lack of openness is that you may develop a false picture of issues and factors like resistance and drivers of change. The lack of openness is more common with qualitative data. However, occasionally you may be given wrong or more usually out-of-date or incomplete quantitative data. Hence, in deciding what data to collect and sources to use, it is sensible to do sufficient data collection to enable you to verify data from several sources and to spot inconsistencies and omissions. Additionally, when you draw conclusions you must always caveat them with the point that they are based on the data that was made available to you.

> *some client staff will deliberately withhold information*

When you find relevant data, make sure you understand what it really is, and how it has been developed. Names for data sources can be misleading, and well-presented data may appear artificially credible and powerful. If it has been derived from a suspect source or from a small sample size, whilst it may appear valid it will be presenting you with incomplete or inaccurate conclusions.

Data collected by consultants is not just used to draw conclusions, but may also be part of the measurement of the success or failure of an engagement. If you are expecting to deliver a specific and measured outcome to a client, then measurement must start at the beginning and provide a baseline. If you want to measure an improvement, the improvement activity cannot start until measurement is in place. In reality, managers who identify improvements will often not wait for measurement mechanisms to be put in place before starting implementation. This is understandable, but it will make your ability to prove an improvement difficult if not impossible.

Before you decide what data to collect, remember that there is a cost to data collection. Although it is a gross simplification, typically more and better data will take more time and resources to collect. Sometimes clients are willing to pay for the best possible data collection. Often they are not, and sometimes they do not have the time to wait for full data collection. This must be discussed up front and expectations set as to what is and is not possible, and clients should understand the implications.

There is a balance to be found, and more data is not always better. More data can be a hindrance as well as a help. Driving for more and more data will slow the engagement down. A stakeholder who objects to your work can easily undermine it by challenging data sources. It is very easy for a negative stakeholder to continually point out people you have not spoken to or data sources you have not utilised. If you think this is a risk to your engagement, you need to have a clear argument for what is a reasonable and sufficient sample of data, and why you do not need to search continually for more.

Occasionally, consultants themselves can cut corners with data collection and base their findings and ideas on generic principles and limited samples. This is always risky and usually suboptimal for the client. As an expert you should understand what is likely to be happening and what the probable solutions are to any client situation with limited information. But you must avoid the trap of thinking that every client is the same. What is a relevant and significant sample of data in a particular situation depends on the context. One data point is never a relevant sample, and generic information with no understanding of the client's context and culture is never a basis for value-added consulting.

Consider

Having collected sufficient data the consultant can analyse it and *consider* what the most relevant findings and recommendations are. This is where a consultant's specialist expertise is directly applied by converting a confusing mass of data into pertinent findings and recommendations. Before analysing the data and producing helpful findings, it is important to be clear about what a client requires, how a consultant adds value, and also to understand the sorts of consultant pronouncements a client is *not* looking for. This section starts by reflecting on what is of value to clients and then provides some essential tips on findings and recommendations.

How the consultant adds value depends on the client's needs, and for each of the statements I am about to make there is probably a client who wants something different. However, typically value comes from explaining issues and identifying solutions. A client wants a concise and easily understandable response to their request for help. They are not looking to you to show how complex the situation is, or how thoroughly you have analysed it with an immense and unintelligible list of points. The client already knows it is complex. The client is looking for clarity, innovation and a different answer than they would have come up with themselves. The client may want to reduce risk. You do not help them by identifying each and every possible risk, but by clearly specifying the largest and most probable risks. An engagement needs to be sufficiently wide ranging, but clarity, coherence and usefulness are of far greater value than absolute comprehensiveness.

Conversely, what is the client not looking for? Typically, the client is not looking for the consultant to 'borrow his watch to tell him the time'. Clients can read their own watches. They may want a consultant to confirm something they already suspect or believe, but that is not the same thing. Clients do not want consultants to rephrase their problems, by analysing what they know to be wrong and telling them this in different words. This is the doctor's trick of giving you a name for a disease which is essentially just different words for what you have said – or sometimes exactly what you said, but just in Latin. Clients may want you to analyse their problems and define them better or prioritise them, but that is not simply rephrasing them.

> **clients do not want consultants to rephrase their problems**

Clients are looking for meaningful analysis and recommendations. They are not looking for simplistic views resulting in inappropriate or incomplete advice. If an issue interacts with another issue in the business, you must reflect on the dynamic interplay, and not treat an issue as a standalone problem, as the resulting stand-alone solution will not work.

Clients are not usually looking for sticking plasters or symptomatic cures for their problems, but want final long-term resolution of problems. Clients are not looking for unbalanced criticism – though of course if they are doing the wrong things you must tell them, but in a constructive way. When you criticise a manager, reflect on the degree of management experience you have. Clients are looking for advice that is helpful and usable in their situation, not ideas that are only applicable in some theoretically perfect organisation.

Clients do not want to hear that the only problem is the organisational culture. A consultant cannot alter the culture, and clients can only do so over a long period of time. Although culture is often a contributory factor to issues, continuous talk of the need for a change in culture is usually lazy consulting. Also, you need to be aware of your own cultural biases. How are they influencing what you see and your solution? (One way to challenge yourself is to ask: 'If this is such a terrible organisational culture, how come this is a successful business. How many successful businesses have I set up and run?') You should identify and challenge undesirable elements of organisational culture, but be aware of your own preconditions and assumptions, and avoid simplistic analyses.

Similarly, if a client is going to solve a problem there is little point in only identifying a list of external environmental factors that contribute to the problem, which the client cannot alter. A client must understand the constraints imposed by the environment they operate in. However, a consultant must identify the things a client can change and rectify, not just give a list of reasons for why things are the way that they are and an excuse for the client to do nothing.

Most client value from a consulting engagement is developed in the consider step. It is when findings are made and recommendations are developed. Whilst a consultant must remain independent from the client, there is no point in attempting to point out findings and make recommendations, no matter how wonderful and insightful, that do not add value to your current client at the point in time at which they are being made. Before you undertake any analysis, bear in mind what is and is not useful to the client.

How you analyse data will depend on the data collected and your specialist skill or service lines. If you are a strategist you may have collected information on market drivers, competitive situation and customer trends. If you are an operational consultant you may have gathered information on operational performance, resourcing levels and budgets.

If you are an implementation consultant you may have sought out information on readiness to change, resistance to change and project priorities.

One tip in analysing the data you have collected is not to jump to findings and solutions too early. You must respect the client's need for urgency, but you must also avoid missing out on understanding the problem. Try to avoid, or at least limit, your preconceptions. This is challenging because being an expert means you will have a whole set of opinions which shape your views. The answer must be to balance speed, expertise and previous knowledge with openness to consider the unique characteristics of the situation.

To solve a problem in consulting we typically collect data and then look for patterns in it. An important question is whether the pattern we find is valid. In other words, is there enough data to support the conclusion? A bigger issue is that there is often more than one pattern in any set of data. Whenever you find a pattern, judge whether you have found the right pattern or if there are other ones.

Look at the simple diagram (derived from Chappell, see page 279) in Figure 6.3. Everyone may interpret such a diagram in a different way. For example, is it: a 4 × 5 grid of dots; a rectangle of six dots surrounded by a rectangle of 14 dots; two horizontal rectangles of 10 dots; three rows or four columns between dots; or some combination of these?

Figure 6.3 A simple diagram

This diagram does not represent a business problem, but the point made is still valid. The data collected on a consulting engagement will be far more complex than this and throw up a whole variety of possible patterns. If you start to see a trend in the data early on, by all means be excited by a possibly important finding, but also ask yourself: 'Is there any other way the data could be interpreted?'

Data, subsequent analysis and findings may initially provide a very complicated picture of a business. Don't be surprised if the problems in business are complex. The number of people involved and the variety of interacting processes and systems often make this often inevitable. One reason clients are willing to pay for good consultants is to gain clarity through this complexity. Often it is the symptoms of problems that are much more complicated than the causes. The visible manifestation of a problem is highly complex, and each symptom may seem unresolvable in a short space of time, but the root cause may be

❝ the visible manifestation of a problem is highly complex ❞

comparatively straightforward. For example, a poorly designed commission system in a client's sales department will result in a huge number of undesirable sales with massive knock-on effects across the business. All sorts of problems can be found in a business with a poor sales commission system, such as undesirable customers, high complaints, high customer churn, low profitability, staff turnover and poor staff morale. This can seem like too complex a set of problems to solve in one go, but these are not the root cause, they are only symptoms. The root cause is much simpler: the way a client determines bonuses for sales staff. Find a root cause like this, which is the source of many client problems, and you are on track to rapidly adding huge value to the client.

When analysing a client's situation, remember that few problems are purely technical. If you just try to understand and solve the technical aspects you will not come up with a complete solution. Human aspects play an important part in most businesses. The way staff are motivated, levels of morale, performance management approaches and so on usually play as significant a role as technical issues.

When reviewing an organisation's capabilities in any area, focus on strengths as well as the weaknesses. This is not a sop to the client, to help in balancing the good with the bad, but because it is as least as powerful and valuable to build on the strengths as to overcome weaknesses. It is often far more effective for an organisation to try and build on its strengths than to expend huge effort in trying to improve in areas in which it will never excel.

Most problems are understood by a process of analysis and decomposition. This can be powerful, but there must be a synthesis in the end as different parts of the problem interact. Unfortunately, not all problems can be understood by decomposition. Some problems are dynamic and have many interacting contributory causes. Unless you understand the interaction between causes you will never solve this type of problem. In these situations, the synthesis is more important than the decomposition. System dynamics offers a way to look at such interacting problems, and using system dynamics can add powerful insights to clients (see the reference to Senge on page 280).

A common reason to involve a consultant is to help a client make a decision. In making a decision you help a client to move forward, but all decisions have implications. In making one decision the client often closes off other options. Therefore you need to be sure you have reviewed the right range of options with nothing missed and without the scope being artificially constrained. The client should understand the costs and implications of each option being presented. Finally, a consultant should try to understand the value of optionality to a client. Every decision to some extent constrains future options. Clients cannot predict the future. Therefore, what is often of significant value to a client is not simply making the decision that is of the highest value at this point in time, but the choice that still leaves options open in future and hence has the greatest value over time.

> **❝ every decision to some extent constrains future options ❞**

Whatever findings and recommendations are made in the consider step, before thinking about presenting them to a client, perform a commonsense check on any conclusions. It is easy in the excitement, pressure and intensity of a consulting engagement to come up with harebrained ideas. The best consulting ideas meet three criteria: they are innovative, implementable and acceptable to the client. Ideas that fail on any of these three criteria are worthless to a client. Before thinking about handing materials over to a client, step back from your work and consider whether it meets these three criteria.

Create

The *create* step is concerned with converting findings, recommendations or other outputs into a deliverable format that can be utilised by the client. There are many possible formats, although consultants and businesses have a tendency to focus on three: text documents, presentations and workshops, or some combination of all of these. This section is focused on the creation of client deliverables. Chapter 11 builds on this, by reviewing the language of consulting. If your engagement result is a client outcome, Chapter 8 relates to delivering and sustaining client change.

The consider step was concerned with ensuring that the contents of consulting thinking resulting from an engagement are to the quality level required. In the create step the consultant ensures findings and recommendations are converted into a format which is credible to and usable by the client. The importance of this step should not be underestimated. Great content can be undermined in a client's eyes by poor presentational format. Conversely, weaker content's credibility can be enhanced by high-quality presentation.

It is only when it comes to creating deliverables that you find out if the findings and recommendations from the consider step are complete and coherent. A set of findings can seem powerful and important in your mind, but weaker or even incoherent when written down on a piece of paper. Yet in the end this is what you must be able to do. It is one reason why it is worthwhile starting to draft deliverables as early as possible in an engagement. This is relevant even if you will only present verbally. For verbal client feedback, think of the line of discussion you will use – if it is not coherent then you cannot create the required deliverable. Early drafts of deliverables focus the consulting team on the result they are trying to achieve, and also ensure you do not reach the end of the engagement with a set of incoherent or incomprehensible findings and recommendations.

What makes a deliverable usable by a client depends on the client's biases. Some clients love the dynamic interplay of verbal feedback in a workshop, others clients prefer to reflect quietly over a written report they can read several times and think through its implications. One client will favour text, another diagrams and yet others will like figures and numerical analysis. Although different types of consulting outputs are naturally more aligned to certain presentational formats, it is very helpful to

> **your engagement plan should be clear about when deliverables will be presented**

understand client biases and learning styles before finalising deliverable formats. The deliverable is primarily to help them, not to show off your skills or knowledge. To achieve this, your engagement plan should be clear about when deliverables will be presented, and you should be clear about who they will be handed over to.

In developing a deliverable the consultant needs to select the media format (written word, spoken word, presentation, etc.), the structure of the deliverable, the type of language used, the formatting within documents, and the balance of factors like diagrams versus text. The language used needs to be appropriate to the subject matter, but consulting jargon should be avoided. The only jargon acceptable is the client's jargon (see Chapter 11). In general terms the consultant is seeking to create deliverables that are powerfully persuasive, clear and engaging to read or use by the client.

A minor issue, but one which can cause some tension between client and consultant if badly handled, relates to branding on deliverables. Most major consultancies will brand all their reports and presentations with their own company brands. Many clients do not mind how a document is branded and therefore it is a useful way to ensure your consultancy brand is exposed within a client organisation. A few clients find this unacceptable, especially if the work is going to be presented to senior sponsors or even external stakeholders by the client. When clients are sensitive to branding on documents, it is rarely worth annoying or disappointing them by insisting on your branding against their desires.

Branding can be as simple as the use of house style for reports and presentations. Without seeing the actual brand or the content, I can identify the source of certain consulting reports just by their look, colour and format. Some consultancies have very specific formats for all their documents. If you work for one of these firms then you must conform to their corporate standards. My only advice in this situation is to try to avoid impairing the quality of client deliverables by the need to force adherence to a predefined format. The format should always be secondary to the client's usability of documents.

Deliverables should be marked in accordance with the terms of the proposal and contract with regard to ownership of any intellectual property or copyright, i.e. the documents should be appropriately marked ©*abc consulting* or ©*xyz corporation*. If you are going to copyright a report in your consultancy's favour, this fact should not come as a surprise to a client. Many clients do not care, but some occasionally respond very negatively to the idea that they do not own the copyright for a piece of work they co-developed with a consultancy and for which they paid. Have this debate early on rather than leaving it as a possible argument at the end of the engagement. (See Chapter 10 on ethics.)

Deliverables need to be checked and quality assured (QA) before handing over to clients. At the very least, read through all documents carefully. Mistakes and omissions in documents look unprofessional, reduce credibility and may expose you to risk. The large consultancies often have complex and well-defined QA processes which need to be built into your engagement plan as they can take extensive time. A QA process may require you to spend time with senior consulting managers with very busy diaries. If you are exposed to such a process, do not be surprised if you are asked to make significant changes to the deliverables. After all, the purpose of a QA process is to improve deliverables by asking for changes in them. If you do not want this to become a major problem then try to involve senior consulting managers responsible for QA as early as possible in the engagement. QA processes may look at completeness and relevance of deliverables, but they will also review the risk that recommendations may expose a consultancy to.

Often it is necessary to iterate between this and the next step several times until a client is fully satisfied with the engagement deliverables.

Counsel and consult

Clients are *counselled* and *consulted* not only at the end of the engagement, but throughout it. A client and client's staff should learn from a consultant across the engagement. This may be from small items of advice, by facilitating workshops, formal training and skills transfer activities, or simply by observing how the consultant works. However, all engagements reach a logical endpoint, when a client must be told the results of the work, counselled on their feelings and responses to this work and consulted on what to do next. Whereas the create step develops deliverables, the counsel and consult step is about presenting and discussing them with clients. This section should be read in conjunction with Chapter 8 on understanding and overcoming resistance.

How you discuss your findings and recommendations is as important to client acceptance as what your findings and recommendations are. Findings and recommendations must be presented with clarity, confidence and assertiveness. Consultants must appear non-judgemental, non-emotional and to the point.

In presenting results you are looking for client acceptance, but of course may have to deal with a level of rejection of your results. You must have sufficient time in your engagement to identify and overcome any client resistance. Such rejection may relate to a client's emotional or logical response to your results. It may relate to the content of your deliverables, but sometimes it can be triggered by format or how you present. Try to separate these different types of response, as they must be resolved in different ways.

Generally, at the end of an engagement you must present two different things: findings and recommendations. You must understand that these are quite different, and will each generate different levels of understanding, interest and resistance. Make clear which you are presenting when. Start by advising or presenting findings and gaining acceptance to them. Normally, the recommendations will follow on logically and there will be less reason to argue against them. If you mix up findings and recommendations you will tend to confuse the client and this can increase resistance.

> **❝ start by advising or presenting findings and gaining acceptance to them ❞**

Many consultants have never worked outside consulting and therefore understanding what works and what does not, and what is appropriate in any situation, is theoretical or comes from observation rather than direct experience. Hence you must not confuse resistance with the fact that you may actually have drawn the wrong conclusions, or even if you are right it may not work in a specific client organisation. (See Chapter 8 for a detailed discussion on resistance.) The challenge for a consultant is to balance consistency and assertiveness in holding on to results that you believe in and can justify, whilst also listening to the client and being responsive to valid criticism and suggestions.

As part of an engagement a consultant researches a wide range of data to prove hypotheses or suggest alternatives. Although you must be able to justify your findings, the point of feedback is to provide clarity to the client. Resist the temptation to report everything. Less is more powerful. Differentiate between telling the client everything and telling them about the most important or highest priority issues. A consultant provides focus and not unfiltered masses of information. You can always write the details in an appendix. Anyone can find 1000 problems in a large business. Few people have the capability to identify the single most important issue. Remember the lesson in the consultants' dialogue: 'Why did you write a 100-page report? 'Because I did not have time to write a one-page one.' A synthesis that enables a client to understand a problem truly, rather than get lost in the trees, is significantly more valuable to them.

Often the most useful feedback to clients is confrontational, but confrontational does not mean argumentative. There are ways to present difficult messages and ways to avoid them. Try to separate the confrontational content of your findings from your role as a consultant. Do not shy away from radical ideas, since these are often the most valuable part of consulting. In the end you must present what you think is right, which may not be what the client wants to hear. However, if the confrontational or radical aspects of your results are a relatively minor component of the overall deliverable, separate them from your main findings so any argument about these radical ideas does not spoil the main bulk of your findings.

The outcome from counselling and consulting is the client's understanding of findings and recommendations, but it should not end there. It must lead to actions. If the client takes no action as a result of your work, then you have failed to add any value. This primarily relates to what the client does next, but it relates also to what you do next with the client.

Summary

The deliver stage must start by looking ahead and planning what you will do, but also include expecting and being flexible to needs to modify the plan. As you progress through delivery always think from the client's perspective. Is what you are discovering innovative, implementable and acceptable to the client? An engagement needs to be sufficiently wide ranging, but clarity, coherence and usefulness are of far greater value than absolute comprehensiveness. The best consulting ideas meet three criteria: they are innovative, implementable and acceptable to the client.

At the end of the engagement you will produce deliverables or achieve a client outcome. You need to be absolutely clear about whether your client is expecting deliverables or an outcome. Any deliverables must be usable by and credible to the client. Any outcome must be in the form of a beneficial change to the client.

As a final tip, check your engagement plan and proposal regularly. It is easy to gradually veer away from it, which is not a problem if agreed with the client as the engagement progresses. But you don't want to diverge away from the original concept and at the end be surprised when the client checks off what you have done against the proposal.

Finally, the deliver phase is summarised in Figure 6.4.

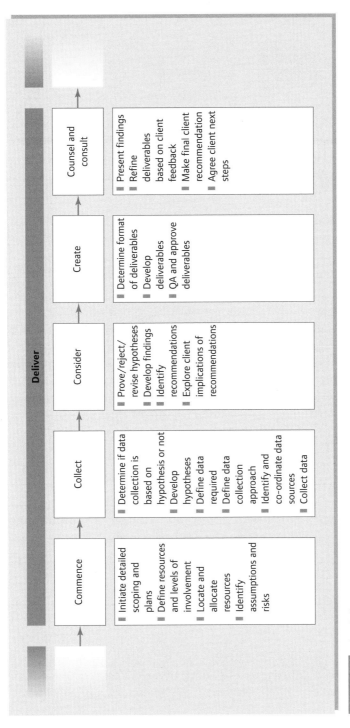

Deliver

Commence	Collect	Consider	Create	Counsel and consult
■ Initiate detailed scoping and plans ■ Define resources and levels of involvement ■ Locate and allocate resources ■ Identify assumptions and risks	■ Determine if data collection is based on hypothesis or not ■ Develop hypotheses ■ Define data required ■ Define data collection approach ■ Identify and co-ordinate data sources ■ Collect data	■ Prove/reject/ revise hypotheses ■ Develop findings ■ Identify recommendations ■ Explore client implications of recommendations	■ Determine format of deliverables ■ Develop deliverables ■ QA and approve deliverables	■ Present findings ■ Refine deliverables based on client feedback ■ Make final client recommendation ■ Agree client next steps

Figure 6.4 The deliver stage

7

The alternative approach – process consulting and facilitation

W
hen many professionals imagine a good consultant, they often picture someone who is an expert in a field and who can advise clients on all the important aspects of a particular subject. Thus they may conceive of an IT consultant who knows all about technology and the latest trends and advances, a strategy consultant who understands everything about a competitive market and how to help a client redirect their business, or a manufacturing consultant who is aware of all the ins and outs of designing a factory floor and running efficient production lines. Such consulting is called *expert consulting*. Expert consulting is hugely valuable to clients and is the basis of much of the success of the management consulting industry. The big consultancy firms advertise their expertise in all sorts of areas. The many small consulting companies and thousands of individual consultants can provide in-depth know-how in almost every niche of business and management.

Helping clients by providing them with access to deep subject matter expertise is not the only value-adding way of consulting. Many consultants use another method to assist clients that is radically different, and does not require them to position themselves as subject matter experts. This is *process consulting*.

The term process consulting may be unfamiliar to some readers. Throughout this chapter I use both the terms *facilitation* and *process consulting* largely interchangeably. Facilitation is a term usually preferred by clients as they are familiar with the word, whereas process consulting is a phrase or jargon more commonly used by consultants themselves. I tend to use the term process consulting, as I think it is a more precise definition, it derived from the pioneering and still valuable work of Edgar Schein (see page 280). Whilst I have been influenced by the writings of Schein and others, this chapter contains my own interpretation of process consulting. Clients may also think of process consulting as coaching, as the experience of process consulting is more akin to being coached than receiving expert advice.

Not all consultants understand, are comfortable with or proficient in process consulting. It is an approach that focuses more on a client's own willingness and ability to define solutions, to learn and to grow, whilst working with consultants, than on the direct subject matter expertise of the consultant. It is often seen as an easy way to consult, but in reality true process consulting is hard, and can be extremely demanding on clients and consultants alike.

The implicit bias so far in this book has been towards expert consulting, and this chapter seeks to redress the balance by discussing process consulting as a fundamentally different way of consulting. It is a complex topic that cannot be fully encapsulated in one chapter. Process consulting is a practical skill and is best learnt by doing it and receiving feedback rather than by thinking and reading about it. In this chapter I provide an overall description of my perspective on process consulting to give a general understanding of the approach. I describe the advantages, I compare and contrast it with expert consulting and explain which method is better in which situations.

"process consulting is a practical skill"

Managing process instead of content

Every activity can be split into two parts – the content of the activity and the process of the activity. The content is the *what*, and the process is the *how*. Usually with consulting the activity is to resolve some kind of problem or issue. An expert consultant is focused on the content and sometimes the process of solving problems. The expert helps describe how to resolve a problem and usually advises what the best solution is. A process consultant looks exclusively at the process. Scoping and solving problems is the responsibility of the client, with the guidance of the process consultant.

What is meant by 'process' in this context? This can be shown by examples, starting with a business meeting. It has some content – that is the subject that the meeting is about, the various information and arguments that are made at the meeting, and the conclusion or outcome that is reached. The meeting also has a process, for example, the process might be:

- Meet at 10:00 a.m.
- Chairperson will define the meeting objectives.
- Attendees will discuss what the objective means for 15 minutes to ensure there is a common understanding of it and an agreed scope.
- The attendees will then discuss how to achieve the objective for 30 minutes.
- The chairperson will select the best ideas to achieve the objective.
- The meeting will then work together to achieve the objective.
- After three hours the objective will be achieved, with consensus agreed, or if not achieved the chairperson will retire to decide the outcome and determine the next steps based on the contents of the meeting.

None of these points reflects the nature or content of the meeting, they are all about the process by which it is managed. This meeting could be concerned with any topic. In this example, the chairperson is managing the process, but is not acting purely in a process consulting style. As well as managing the process, the list above indicates that the chairperson will make decisions about the content of the meeting.

Let's consider a more complex task: creating a requirements specification for a new IT application in a business. An expert consultant would approach this by listing what they felt were the relevant requirements for this type of application, or even by telling the client what was the best software package for the situation. A process consultant would help the client to define the requirements themselves, by going through a process like the one below:

- Identify who may place requirements on the new system (requirement's owners).
- Interview identified requirement's owners and agree document requirements.
- Consolidate requirements into a single list.
- Remove duplicate requirements.
- Identify conflicting requirements.
- Bring requirement's owners together to resolve conflicts.

■ Agree prioritisation criteria with the team.

■ Prioritise requirements according to the team's criteria.

Again, none of these steps is about what the requirements are, they are all about helping a client by giving them structure to achieve the objective of defining the requirements. Whilst this can appear simple, there is a lot of complexity below these individual tasks. For example, a nominally simple task like 'agree prioritisation criteria with the team' may require great skills to clarify and combine different people's views and achieve consensus on them.

In a way, the title process consultant is unfortunate, as it can be confused with a process designer, business process re-engineering or an expert in one process or another. It has nothing to do with these. But I prefer it to the term facilitator, because the latter is often misused and misunderstood. Facilitation and facilitator are often synonymous with help and helper respectively. Facilitators are much more than people who help in solving a problem. A facilitator has a specialist skill and applies facilitation techniques. These techniques focus on helping a client by managing the process. I tend to use the term facilitation when I am discussing a technique I might use in an individual meeting, workshop or set of workshops. Process consulting is the phrase I am apt to use when approaching a complete consulting engagement or a significant part of an engagement.

One way to understand the role of the process consultant is to compare it to the role of an expert consultant. Typically, an expert consultant tells (or, more politely, advises) a client what to do, or shows them how to do it. A process consultant helps clients to work it out for themselves. This is summarised in Table 7.1.

Table 7.1 Process and expert consulting compared

	Process consultant	Expert consultant
Style of interaction	Encouraging	Enquiring
	Facilitating	Analysing
	Supporting	Instructing
	Coaching	Advising
	Exploring	Showing
	Involving	Recommending
The consultant's client proposition	I will help you to solve your own problems	I will recommend what is best and show you how to do it

Process consultants and facilitators provide structure and focus to the process of discussion and problem resolution. They are responsible for achieving an outcome, but the client, or more usually a team of client staff, maintain ownership of the outcome that is achieved. Hence effective facilitation requires an understanding of the objective or outcome desired, a process to manage the discussion and communication skills, as well as flexibility, responsiveness and insight into group dynamics.

Workshops are usually an important part of a process consulting engagement. A typical objective is to determine how to overcome a problem or issue that a client wants to resolve. Often the objective is defined in terms of scoping a problem. Most of the work will be done with the client or client team in workshops. But there is some preparation work for the consultant in terms of designing a process to manage a workshop, and there are usually some post-workshop tasks such as writing up the outcome and making notes.

> **" often the objective is defined in terms of scoping a problem "**

Workshops can produce a massive amount of unstructured material. One of the skills of the facilitator is to structure and summarise this material as the workshop progresses, but also to consolidate and write it up following the workshop. The structuring of workshop materials, which are often in the form of flipcharts and rough notes, is a crucial stage in process consulting. Process consultants must remain aware that they are facilitating and not leading. It is very easy when summarising information to put your own spin on it when you select what you think is most important and leave out what you feel is less critical.

The process consultant uses a range of approaches, tools and techniques. The first technique is to define a process to scope or resolve the client's problem that is appropriate to the situation. The approach could be to run a series of workshops, each of which moves the client progressively closer to the objective desired. The process consultant also needs to plan how each workshop will run and who should attend. Once the workshop is running the consultant should be skilled in identifying and resolving conflict, as well as developing consensus in a group. The process consultant must be observant of the group and group dynamics. Judgement is also important: for example, if consensus is not going to be achieved, deciding when it is a sensible time to let the team take a break from a workshop versus making them continue to reach a conclusion. The process consultant must be able to structure information from many members of the team, and help them to see patterns in it.

Most of all, the process consultant has to have excellent communication skills, especially those related to listening and questioning. A large part of the success of a process consultant is asking the right question at the right time to encourage thinking, debate and sharing of ideas. The sort of questions a process consultant asks can be exploratory, diagnostic or action orientated. Irrespective of the style of question, they should be aimed at helping the team to explore, to think and to understand. Questions of the form 'why do you ....', 'how will you ....', ' exactly what will you ...', 'what is the situation in which ...', 'what assumptions underlie ...', 'does everyone understand ...', 'do we have consensus ...', are common. The process consultant should avoid confrontational or leading questions (see Chapter 11). Using leading questions is not process consulting, but is really covert expert consulting. Leading questions can be hard to avoid, and often consultants ask them without realising that they are doing so. In asking questions, process consultants should observe as well as listen, looking for any indications that people are not being open or are not involving themselves in the discussions.

In managing workshops, the process consultant manages time and the environment the workshop takes place in. Workshops can easily fail because they run out of time to reach conclusions, and it takes skill to encourage a debate to progress, without controlling or steering the content of the group's discussions. Correctly deciding when it is appropriate to take a break, and when it is not, has a significant impact on workshop outcomes. Similarly, the way meeting rooms are laid out, and the existence or absence of distractions, make a huge difference to the success of a workshop.

Process consultants must try to be impartial, and keep the client team focused on the objectives. Process consultants must build trust with the team, so that team members will allow themselves to be guided by consultant. The process consultant treats all members of a team equally and should ensure that all members are involved in discussion and reaching conclusions. Conclusions are ideally reached by consensus with the team, although in practice consensus is not always possible to achieve for some contentious issues.

The consultant is primarily concerned with ensuring that the client achieves an effective solution that is acceptable to them, but what the solution is and what the criteria for acceptability are, are completely up to the client. A process consultant should avoid assumptions or preconceptions about the situation. In contrast, expert consultants are independent in the sense that the recommendations they give are meant to be what the consultant determines are best for the client, irrespective of the client's own viewpoint. An expert consultant must have preconceptions – that is the basis of their expertise. The word *recommendation* can be seen to encapsulate the difference, as recommendations lie at the heart of an expert consultant's work, while they are the antithesis of a process consultant's support for a client.

Table 7.2 summarises the main points in this section by comparing the role of a manager solving their own problems, to the roles of a process and an expert consultant in resolving a problem.

Table 7.2 Managing versus consulting

	Who defines the problem?	Who owns the problem resolution?	Who defines the solution?	What is the typical style of interaction?
Manager	Manager	Manager	Manager	Measuring, reviewing and directing
Expert consultant	Client	Consultant or client	Consultant	Information gathering, analysing and advising
Process consultant	Client	Client	Client	Questioning, structuring and consensus building

The advantages and disadvantages of process consulting

Some problems are obviously best resolved by process consulting. For instance, if there is a lack of consensus within a team, an expert giving their opinion on a solution may help with making a decision but is unlikely to help in achieving consensus. On the other hand, a process consultant is well skilled in helping to bring a team together and achieving consensus within the team. Many tasks can be supported by a consultant working in either a process consulting style or an expert consulting style. Hence the relevant question is: what are the relative advantages and disadvantages of the two styles?

There are some important reasons to select a process consulting as opposed to an expert consulting approach in some situations. Process consulting can be beneficial for the client on a personal level. It can result in greater acceptance of the outcome from an engagement, primarily because the outcome is the client's. Process consulting can help the

❝process consulting can be beneficial for the client on a personal level❞ client to learn and understand more about an issue. The nature of process consulting is that a client or client team goes through the process of scoping and solving a problem, and is the primary participant in the consulting engagement. In contrast, in an expert consulting situation the client can choose to be an observer and simply read the recommendations at the end of the engagement. The level of a client's personal involvement and development can be much higher during a well-run process consulting engagement than an expert consulting engagement.

Clients expect consultants to have expertise, and have often employed consultants to advise them. But it is not always appropriate to give advice. Sometimes a better solution is for clients to solve problems themselves. The problem with the external expert is that clients may reject advice or may not learn from the experience of working with an expert. A process consulting style is extremely powerful in getting clients to buy in to solutions – because the clients developed the solution themselves, and in doing so, the clients learn. Think back to your own childhood when you were learning. You can teach your children by telling them facts and giving them the answer to every question they ask. But teachers and parents know that a far better way to assist children to learn is to help them to understand and to think for themselves. Instead of simply telling children the answer to a problem, you can help them by responding to their request for help with questions like: 'can you remember anything this is similar to ...?', 'do you remember how you did this last time ...?', 'what can you tell me about the problem ...?', 'which parts do you understand ...?' By solving the problem themselves, children learn better. This advantage of self-discovery and understanding over being told answers does not stop in childhood.

Clients and client staff are often the best people to analyse problems and come up with solutions, as they are closest to them and understand them best. An external expert, unless they have spent extensive time working with a client, will always have an incomplete understanding of the context and culture of the client organisation, and of the details of how a client precisely does various tasks. Additionally, when clients have designed a solution themselves it is often easier and faster to implement.

There can be advantages to using process consulting from a consultant's point of view, irrespective of the client's needs. Process consulting skills can provide a way to help a client in situations in which you are not a subject matter expert, but still want to contribute value. It is common on many consulting engagements to find yourself in unfamiliar situations. For example, you may be invited to a meeting and find the topic is one you know nothing about. You can choose to stay uninvolved in the meeting and simply listen, but this is rarely acceptable behaviour for a consultant. You can bluff, but this should be avoided as it does not add value to the client and is risky to your reputation. A better solution is to accept you know nothing about the subject and to use a process consulting style. Sometimes asking questions as simple as: 'are we all clear what the objective of this meeting is ...?', 'how are we going to work together ...?', 'do we need consensus or is a majority decision good enough ...?', can be extremely helpful to clients. In this way, you can still help the client, whilst your own understanding of the situation and content develops. If you do this well, clients will value your input and often will not even realise that you did not add any content to the meeting.

However, process consulting is not a solution to all consulting challenges, or one that will enable consultants to manoeuvre through any situation. For instance, it can be tempting to involve a junior consultant, with limited subject matter knowledge, in an expert consulting team and let them muddle through by relying on process consulting skills. This should be done with care. New consultants often have less deep expert knowledge, but they may also have no process consulting skills.

None of this section should be used to imply that process consulting is always the preferred style. There are many advantages of being an expert consultant. An expert consultant can bring an independent and unbiased view. Although the process consultant is unbiased and wants to achieve consensus, the solution is the client's and may therefore suffer from any limitations in client thinking. An expert can help to break group-think. Critically, an expert can provide speed in identifying a solution. Process consulting, especially if it is used to achieve full consensus, can be very powerful, but it is not always quick. An expert can often immediately tell the client the solution to a problem. Clients also often want expert consulting. Whether it is right for them in the longer run or not, there can be an attitude with some clients of 'just tell me the answer'. It may be appropriate to try and persuade them otherwise, but, in the end, if that is what clients demand, then as consultants our task must be just to tell them the answer. Finally, there are many situations in which an expert consultant is the only appropriate approach. For instance, if a client needs to understand the ideal way to overcome a technical or specialist problem they have no experience of, then no amount of facilitation will produce the optimal answer, whereas a skilled consultant who has seen this problem many times before will be able to identify the optimal solution easily.

There was a joke going the rounds when I first did a process consulting course that it was 'content-free consulting'. In a way this is true, but not in a negative sense at all. It is content free, because it is meant to be, and whilst it sounds counter-intuitive to an expert consultant, the absence of content is the source of its value. A process consultant has a mature relationship with the client, in which the client is understood to be perfectly capable of understanding and resolving their own problems, but sometimes just needs a little help to be able to do this.

Expert and process consultants are sometimes presented as either/or ways to support a client, but in reality they are both valid and valuable ways to consult. The challenge for the skilled consultant is not to choose one or the other, but to be able to do both and to determine which approach is best in which situation.

When to be a process consultant, when to be the expert

A consultant who can switch between a process and expert consulting style needs to consider which approach to use in which situations. The choice should be determined by what is most in the client's interest. For either approach, you need to start with an understanding of what the client's issue is, and what are the client's capabilities and needs to get to a solution. If the fundamental issue is that the client does not know what is wrong or how to define the issue, both process and expert consultants can define the issue. An expert consultant, based on previous experience, will tell the client what the likely issue is. A process consultant will work with the client to develop clarity in the client's own thinking.

There are several factors to consider before deciding which style of consulting is best. Does the environment or culture of the client suit process or expert consulting? Some clients respond very badly to attempts to facilitate them, and do not employ consultants for these reasons. Other clients are passionate about facilitation and see it as an important aspect of a consultant's role. Trying to use process consulting with a client who is not open to the approach is rarely successful. Conversely, always acting the expert when the

" does the culture suit process or expert consulting? "

client wants a deeper participation in the engagement and shaping the outcome is inappropriate.

Other factors to consider include the speed of resolution required by the client, the level of input and involvement a client can give to an engagement, and the level of consensus around the issue. When a client wants greater involvement, when the issue is contentious and consensus building is required, and when there is time, then process consulting is often preferable. However, if an issue is well accepted and a client wants a consultant to just get on and resolve it, expert consulting is usually better. There may be several opportunities to include facilitation and expertise within an engagement. It could be that the whole engagement is about process consulting or it may be that a part of the engagement is done as an expert consultant – either can be used at different times, and each style of consulting can be used by different members of a consulting engagement team.

Theorists, especially those with a bias towards coaching and facilitating, can stress the criticality of not mixing an expert with a process consulting mode. It is true that if you want an individual to learn and develop it can be crucial to maintain a consistent process consulting approach and to avoid 'giving them your answer' by switching into an expert mode. But within a consulting engagement life is rarely so clear cut. As described above there are many advantages of a process consulting style, and rarely is the client worried (and sometimes not explicitly conscious) about whether you are using a process or expert mode. You must make a judgement as to which approach to use on a regular basis. Even when facilitating workshops I sometimes switch into expert mode, although if I do this I make it explicit to my clients. Hence I may say something like: 'I am going to be a little more directive now, is that OK?' or 'I would like to give some direct advice on the issue.' This has to be handled with care as you can easily undermine your position as a facilitator. A solution is to use two consultants: one works as part of the client team as an expert member, and another retains the role of a facilitator.

Sometimes process consulting is used for whole engagements, but more often it is more powerful to use it in parts of an engagement. For example, I may facilitate a client to explain their requirements, to scope an issue and gain consensus in a client team about a way forward. But I may then act as an expert when it comes to advising the client on how to meet those requirements. Typical situations in which process consulting is frequently successful include:

- ▨ scoping unclear issues and engagements
- ▨ identifying client requirements or decision-making criteria
- ▨ prioritising between tasks
- ▨ developing shared understanding and consensus
- ▨ working on an activity as part of a team-building stage of an engagement.

Process consulting is more appropriate in some stages of the client's change process than others (see Chapter 4). You can develop ideas and even help a client to develop plans via facilitation, but you cannot easily implement change or review operations as a process consultant. Similarly, different stages of the engagement process are more easily delivered as a process consultant than others. Process consulting skills can be especially useful as part of the exploratory dialogue in the propose stage of the engagement process, when an understanding of the client issue is required. If you choose to perform the deliver stage as a process consultant, it may require modification from that described in Chapter 6. For example, for a process consultant the consider and create steps of the deliver stage are not concerned with developing their own thinking and final reports, but with structuring and making sense of the client's ideas and helping them to draw their own conclusions.

Another factor to consider in selecting the preferred consulting approach is your capabilities. Not all consultants are great process consultants, and not all need to be. But some level of facilitation skills are a strength for all consultants. An ability to differentiate between helping a client with the content of a problem and assisting them by managing the process is important. However, it is very irritating when you are advised that you will be attending a workshop run by a facilitator but the facilitator tries to stay in an expert mode and is really telling the attendees what to do and think. If you really cannot facilitate or process consult, then do not try.

> if you really cannot facilitate or process consult, then do not try

Some situations require exceptional facilitation skills, especially when developing consensus around highly contentious issues. Expert facilitation is a specialisation in its own right. If a consultant is not a natural or talented facilitator, they should understand the situations in which a client needs an exceptional facilitator and, rather than doing the work personally, assist the client in locating such a highly skilled facilitator.

One thing a client is often looking for from a consultant is creativity and innovation in ideas. The approaches to creativity from a process and expert consultant are quite different, and in determining which approach to use it is important to understand what the client wants and needs. Consider the following examples of how an expert and process consultant will approach such a situation:

- **Expert consultant**: 'Have you tried this ... I have seen this work well in other situations?'
- **Process consultant**: 'Here is a creative process, I will help you to understand and to use it. With my help you will go through it to generate your own new ideas.'

These are fundamentally different approaches to coming up with new ideas. A client may be open to both, or may be explicit in what style of help they require. If a consultant is going to use a combination of expert and process consulting, the decision of which approach to use and when can usually be determined as the engagement progresses. If the consultant will only use one approach, this is best agreed with the client before the engagement starts.

The issue of collusion

Both process and expert consultants should be independent of the client, and avoid colluding with the client. Collusion happens when a consultant gives a client precisely what the client wants, irrespective of what is right for the client organisation. Sometimes collusion is deliberate by the consultant, on other occasions it is unintentional and results from too close a working relationship between the consultant and the client. The way collusion occurs is different in process and expert consulting. Colluding with the client as an expert is telling them what you think they want to hear. Collusion as a process consultant is reflecting what the client has said without worrying about consensus or involvement of the rest of the client team. You can also collude with the client by posing as a process consultant, but then telling them the answer because they do not want the bother of being involved in workshops.

A related situation to collusion is when clients wash their hands of responsibility for an issue by handing it over to a consultant. This is more of a problem for expert than process consultants. Generally, consultants should not take full ownership of a problem; the client manager in the end must always retain ownership. When a client hires an expert consultant, the client can sometimes effectively delegate ownership to the consultant. This is when clients think, 'it's not my problem anymore because I have hired a consultant'. Clients cannot abrogate responsibility to the consultant in a similar way when using process consulting. Hence process consulting is not an easy option for clients. If it is done well, it can be enjoyable and exciting, but it does require the client to participate 100 per cent in the process.

Many consultants struggle with process consulting. They are often seduced by the content. The content may be interesting and also holding on to the content can seem comfortable. Positioning yourself as an expert clearly establishes your relationship and role with the client. Moving to a process consulting mode can feel risky, and you may get the impression of exposure at times, since the value you are adding is less clear cut. However, many clients deeply value good process consulting. It is not uncommon for a client to appreciate more highly the member of the consulting team who facilitates the client's own thinking, rather than an expert consultant in the same team.

Summary

This chapter provides an overview of process consulting in contrast to expert consulting. Key points to remember are:

- Process consulting provides an alternative approach to consulting compared with expert consulting. Instead of advising clients of what the solution to a problem is, the process consultant helps clients to develop the solution themselves.

- Process consulting is powerful in situations when it is important to help clients to understand, learn, develop their own solutions and achieve consensus. It is very useful when it is necessary to explore ideas, opinions or scope issues, but is less helpful in direct implementation or operational performance review engagements.

- Process consulting can be used in combination with an expert consulting style, and for experienced consultants the question is less 'should I be a process or expert consultant?' and more 'in this specific situation, which approach is better?' Even in a single conversation, a skilful consultant can switch between expert and process consulting.

Process and expert consulting are summarised and contrasted in Table 7.3.

Table 7.3   Comparing expert and process consulting

Process consultant	Expert consultant
Approach	
Facilitate and structure	Analyse, advise and recommend
Provide a path (or process) for the client to get to an answer	Define the answers
Work with clients to help them understand their own needs, ideas and vision	Provide client insights based on expertise and knowledge
Core skills/competencies	
Developing client rapport	Developing client credibility
Listening and questioning	Deep, relevant and current knowledge of subject matter
Facilitation and workshops	
Ability to restructure complex information from multiple sources into a coherent whole	Analysis, explanation and clarification
	Ability to make advice relevant to the client's specific business context
Conflict resolution and consensus building	
The consultant's contract with the client	
■ I am going to help you to help yourself.	■ I will review your situation.
■ You will determine the most important problem, the symptoms and the solution yourself.	■ I will determine what the relevant problem and symptoms are.
■ Your role is to scope and solve the problem.	■ I will then tell you what the problem and solution is.
■ I will provide a process to help you in doing this.	■ Your role is to give me relevant information and to answer my questions.
■ The outcome will be whatever you come up with, but I will help to structure coherently the outcome and help you decide what to do next.	■ The outcome will be my recommendations, which you will have to deal with. However, if you want I can then further develop implementation plans for you.

8

Closing engagements and sustaining results

I n the last chapter we looked at the activities involved in running a live consulting engagement. Those delivery activities are the bread and butter work of the consultant, but every individual consulting engagement is of limited duration. All engagements end. How this ending is handled is important both to the client and the consultant. The client wants a smooth and seamless transition when the consultant exits the client organisation. A consultant is judged as much on *closing* an engagement and bringing it to a satisfactory conclusion, as on the delivery of the engagement. A good ending is a planned and deliberately managed event. It should never just be the uncontrolled and inexorable reaching of a certain time or date.

One feature of consulting engagements, which may surprise novice consultants, is that the activities in delivery tend to be the domain of the junior and middle-ranking consultants. The more senior consultants, directors and partners tend to spend more of their time involved in the activities at either end of the delivery stage – that is, in the propose and close stages of the engagement process. In some ways this reflects the difficulty, the opportunity, and – especially – the potential risks of those stages of an engagement.

Ending an engagement well is a science and an art. The science comes in the standard repeatable items to check off when an engagement closes. Some of these activities are for the client's benefit, but many are for the ongoing advantage of the consultancy (e.g. updating the consultant's CVs following an engagement). The art of closing an engagement derives from the less definite and less precise aspects of finishing a piece of work. For example, if you have done a really good job then clients are often disappointed when you leave. This feeling of disappointment can turn a great result into an unhappy client if it is not handled with sensitivity. Therefore much of the close stage is concerned with doing whatever is required to leave the client with a good feeling about you. The section in this chapter on closing engagements looks at both this science and art.

Even though the engagement ends, the consultant should not think purely of reaching that point and ignore anything that may happen to the client afterwards. The consultant not only can try, but must, peer into the future after the end of the engagement. The obvious considerations are that there may be sell-on, and there will be a client relationship to be managed in the longer run. More importantly, the real value from a consulting engagement is received by a client *after* the consultant has gone. It is how the consultant influences and improves the operations or direction of a business in the long run that is the true measure of excellent consulting. Providing advice and assistance that is forgotten as soon as the consultant exits the client's organisation is of limited or even zero value. Of course, consultants cannot control what happens after they have left, but they can influence it. Hence as well as describing how to end an engagement, this chapter also explains how the consultant can increase the likelihood of long-term success by ensuring the consulting results are sustained.

> the real value is received by a client after the consultant has gone

There are two criticisms repeatedly made of consultants. The first is the lack of added value by telling the client what they already know. This is the 'borrow your watch to tell you the time' account of consulting. The other criticism is that consultants run away just when the going gets tough. Consultants write reports, give presentations and make recommendations, but leave it up to the client to do the hard bit – implementing the change. This is the 'consultants don't implement' version of consulting. Both these criticisms tend to arise at the end of engagements and have an element of truth and a degree of unfair stereotyping. Both criticisms are sometimes right because it was precisely what the client asked for. Clients may use consultants to survey the thinking of the organisation, to make recommendations, and may not want any ongoing involvement from the consultant. However, in many situations, the criticisms point to poor consulting. The former criticism is the one that is heard more often, but it is the 'consultants don't implement' comment that is more problematical both for consultants and clients. If we take a client-centric view of consulting, then consultants who do not care about how the client handles any recommendations are shirking their responsibility to their client.

Even if a consultant has no implementation skills and is never involved in implementation they must consider what the client does with their recommendations. Hence this chapter is relevant to all consultants of whatever specialisation. The precise responsibilities you have in an engagement depend on the type of engagement and your client needs. But it is wrong to conclude that change is the exclusive preserve of consultants involved in implementation engagements. For instance, even the purest of strategy consultants or specialist advisors must consider what the client does with the advice given, once a report is handed over. If not, there is a risk that the client ignores or cannot implement the advice. Unimplementable or ignored advice is as worthless as no advice at all, but considerably more expensive.

In many ways the role of the consultant is less than that of a manager. A consultant analyses, identifies and advises, but the decision to implement and to live with the consequences of the changes is a manager's. This should not be seen as a weakness: it is inherent in the definition of consultant as opposed to manager. The role of the advisor, even the most brilliant and gifted advisor, is always subordinate to that of the person being advised. Consultants must never forget this. But there is one important respect in which the role of the consultant is more difficult than that of the manager. The manager is responsible whilst they are in post. The challenge for consultants is to influence an organisation to be different and remain different when the consultant is gone. This is the primary, exciting and most valuable aim of consulting, which is explained at the end of this chapter.

The flow of this chapter is shown in Figure 8.1.

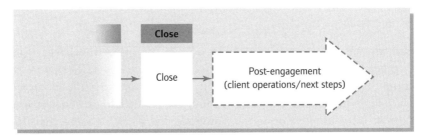

Figure 8.1 The close stage and afterwards

The end of a consulting engagement

When an engagement finishes should be a time for reflection on what you have achieved and what you have learnt for future engagements. In the stress of a busy consultancy there is often pressure to get on to the next engagement and to forget important activities that seem like niceties, such as engagement reviews. This is a mistake. Like all businesses, the consultancies that are most successful are the ones that learn from their mistakes and build on their successes.

The true judge of the success of an engagement must be the client, and each client's views and considerations are unique. If you want to learn and improve, it is always worth seeking feedback from the client on what they liked and disliked about the engagement. Typical client considerations will include:

- Did you do everything that was agreed?
- Was the work performed to an appropriate level of quality?
- Did the work add value in the client's view?

Many of the factors that clients consider will be less precise:

- Did you meet or exceed the client's expectations?
- Did you behave in a way that fitted with the client's culture?
- Were you flexible and responsive to the client's changing needs as the engagement progressed?

In the longer run, value to a client is not about what happens whilst the engagement is running, or even on the day it finishes, but is accrued over time. You should ask yourself:

- Over time, is the client making better decisions?
- Does the client have a better strategy?
- Has the risk of the client's business been reduced?
- Are the client's operations faster, cheaper, better?

The precise questions will depend on the nature of the consulting engagement, but it should be possible to pose questions of this form about the outcome of the engagement. Some of outcomes can be measured, some not. Where they can, it should be possible to link back to the original value proposition in your proposal and see if the measurements testify to the right outcome.

A consultancy does not exist just for the clients but is a business in its own right, and therefore you have your own commercial factors that can judge the success of the engagement. Most obviously: was it profitable and did you sell any additional work? From a longer-term perspective, the success of an engagement comes down to factors like whether you improved relationships and extended your network, and whether you learnt anything on the engagement that can be used in future engagements.

However, before you can make such a review of the success of an engagement, the first question is the rather obvious, but often difficult one to answer: when is the engagement over? The initial consideration is whether you have done what you agreed to do in the proposal, and created the deliverables or the outcome that were contracted. These may be reports, findings, analysis, benchmarks, presentations, processes, tools, training courses, skills transfers, etc. There is also a more subtle measure by which a client may measure you. Any deliverables are based on findings, assumptions and hypotheses you made.

> " any deliverables are based on findings, assumptions and hypotheses you made "

Does the client accept these, and the process by which they were discovered or developed? Many clients will not be interested in the consulting process as long as they are happy with the outcome, but some clients will want proof of thoroughness and intellectual rigour within the work you performed in the commence, collect, consider and create steps. It is worth thinking about how you will convince clients that your consulting approach is sound and comprehensive.

There are several reasons why it can be difficult to be precise about when an engagement is complete. Engagement deliverables can always be improved a little more – both in terms of content and presentational format. You can probably go on forever making minor enhancements. Deliverables are usually not unambiguously defined in the original proposal, and only when they are presented may you find that the client has different expectations. Even minor differences in expectations can lead to rework and extending an engagement. There may be little peripheral promises made to client staff throughout the engagement. Such promises can be as simple as printing off an article you think might be relevant to them, or offering to introduce them to someone in your network. These all need to be fulfilled. The engagement ends when there are no such loose ends left.

Whilst there may be some clear-cut criteria, usually determining that a consulting engagement is finished is a judgement. It is a judgement made by both the client and the consultant, and ideally one which you have consensus on. A successful end is one in which both the client and the consultant are happy and agree that the engagement is complete. Even a pre-agreed date can only be accepted as the real end of an engagement if you have produced what is required, and the client has not asked for any changes to scope or deliverables. It is easy to irritate and disappoint a client by ending prematurely from their perspective. Conversely, it is easy to convert a profitable engagement into a loss-making one by constantly tweaking and improving deliverables to a client's requests. Both of these risks can be avoided by a well-managed close stage.

The art and science of the close stage

The basis for a good engagement close is defined in the original proposal. The clearer the scope, deliverables and outcome from an engagement, the easier it is to be precise about when the engagement is finished. In reality, for many engagements the precise shape and scope of deliverables can only be defined as the engagement progresses and may be evolving until the last day. In such a situation, it is essential to have ongoing dialogue with the client about what the final outcome will be, and to modify the client's expectations every time the final outcome changes. If you are unclear, or think the client is unclear, pursue a dialogue until clarification and consensus is achieved.

Flexibility in consulting engagements is usually good. Clients do not want to work with consultants who constantly turn around and say: 'I am not doing X, because in our original proposal you agreed to pay for Y.' But flexibility needs to be managed and aligned to the fees you are charging and the time the engagement takes. Do not ask for more money every time the client asks for something that will take you an extra 30 minutes to do. However, in general terms, if the client wants more than was originally specified, then that is additional chargeable work. Similarly, if a client decides part way through development of a deliverable that they do not want it anymore, the work to date needs to be paid for. The final invoice should reflect such factors, but should also be what the client expects.

The next factor in a good engagement close is that you are prepared for closedown. You should never reach the end of an engagement by surprise, as from day one you knew you would get there. Yet it is common for consultants to end engagements in a state of barely controlled chaos, as all sorts of activities need to be finalised. In most cases, these activities were predictable. What needs to be done at the end of the engagement should be part of the engagement plan. Activities such as reviews of deliverables by senior consultants in your firm, or client review work-shops, should be set up in advance. You know they will always be required, so running out of time to do them is a sign of poor planning and sloppy engagement management.

Identify what will be handed over to whom from your engagement, and make sure they are prepared for this. You may hand everything to a single client, but it is not unusual to be producing several deliverables; for example, a report to a real client, a training pack to HR and some revised job descriptions to a line manager. Consulting deliverables are rarely just handed over, they usually need to be explained and may require a degree of client education. This all takes time. Try to predict potential blockages to accepting your findings, and resolve them whilst you still have time and resources to do so. The blockages can be simple logistical issues, for example you cannot hand over to a client who is away on two weeks holiday. Therefore, check in advance that the staff you will be handing over to are available on the dates required.

If it is a large engagement with several consultants, as you hand over aspects of the engagement you can decrease the size of the consulting team. Not all the consultants need to be with the client until the very last day. Unless there is a specific advantage to doing so, let individual consultants leave the engagement team once their part of the work is complete and handed over to the client.

Before you end a consulting engagement you should make sure the client knows what happens next. Partially this is good business sense, as it is a point of opportunity for on-sell. But even if there is no possible on-sell, and all the next steps are to be performed by the client with no consultant input, you never want to leave with the client thinking, 'What do I do now?' An assertive client will not let you finish, and probably will not pay your invoice if they do not know what to do next. A less assertive client may let you get away with leaving them in the dark, but it is hardly good consulting. Some form of next-steps plan should be included in every set of engagement deliverables.

> **some form of next-steps plan should be included**

There is a balance to be found, as a complete detailed client action plan may be a major piece of work that deserves to be charged for as for any other part of your work to a client. Such a plan may not be what the client has asked for, or is willing to pay for. However, the next-steps plan does not need to be detailed. Often it will be a short list of actions. It is always possible to provide a simple and concise indication of the direction the client should go in, even if one of the next steps is 'develop a detailed plan'. The test of your next-steps plan should be that it is enough for the client to read it in conjunction with your recommendations and does not think 'so what?' nor 'what do I do now?'.

Similarly, you should make sure your consulting managers and consulting partners know what happens next. Should you, or anyone else in the consultancy, be doing any specific action with the client? Are there any unfulfilled commitments or any opportunities for further work that must be seized? Be clear as possible about who needs to do what, whether it is simply a follow-up phone call or if it is a specific client meeting that needs to be planned and arranged. Plan the next steps in your relationship with the client with care.

There is always a set of activities required for the good management of the consulting business at the end of an engagement. Timesheets and expenses for the engagement need to be finalised, so you know precisely what should be billed. Final billing and invoicing should be done. Try to ensure the final bill really is the final bill. Consultants have a habit of finding old expenses receipts weeks after an engagement is complete and the last invoice was raised – or identifying a few days of another consultant's time that should have been billed to the engagement. Clients hate it when you raise a 'final' bill and then several weeks later send them another one saying you missed out some time or expenses. Think from the client's perspective – an extra bill makes their own budget management difficult. This is especially problematic if you raise an additional bill in another financial year – they may have no budget for your bill.

A well-organised consultant or consultancy business will automatically complete housekeeping tasks like updating CVs, and client case studies when an engagement is complete. Copies of client deliverables should be filed for easy future reference. All other papers and files should be archived or, if appropriate, destroyed. Staff performance reviews should be carried out and client feedback sought. You may have picked up some client assets whilst on the engagement, for example building passes and laptops. These should be returned. Records should be updated, especially information that is critical for the efficient future operations of the consulting business, such as contacts logs or relationship records.

Every engagement provides an opportunity to learn. Learning will happen informally for all members of an engagement team. Every consultant's experience grows on each engagement. But at the end of an engagement consultants should consider the formal capture and logging of good ideas, improved processes and tools, or anything else that will make future engagements better, or which can be used with future clients. However, there is a big difference between individual consultants learning on engagements, and the formal documentation of knowledge for reuse on future engagements. Well run consultancies willingly invest time in the latter. (There is an ethical issue in selling something to one client that another client has paid for – see Chapter 10. However, as long as it is done sensitively, does not breach any client confidentiality or contractual terms; consultants thrive on building specialist understanding by performing similar work in multiple clients.)

Ending a consulting engagement is a great skill and needs preparation. A poor ending will leave a client with a bad taste in their mouth and will limit the chance of further sales. A well-managed ending is good for your business and your clients. Ensure you are ready to finish, and the client is ready for your departure. An engagement close checklist is shown in Table 8.1 below.

Table 8.1 Engagement close checklist

	Yes	No
Internal consulting business management		
All timesheets and expenses collated?	☐	☐
Final invoice sent to client accounting for all time and expenses?	☐	☐
Consultant CVs updated?	☐	☐
Case study developed?	☐	☐
Engagement reviewed and lessons learnt for future engagements?	☐	☐
Intellectual capital/reusable deliverables converted into appropriate format?	☐	☐
All paperwork/files stored appropriately?	☐	☐
Contact logs and relationship records updated?	☐	☐
External client relationship management		
All deliverables provided to client in agreed format?	☐	☐
Final handover meeting with client held?	☐	☐
Client feedback collected?	☐	☐
Next steps agreed with client and aligned with next-steps plan?	☐	☐
If selling on, next engagement prepared and ready to start?	☐	☐
All client assets returned?	☐	☐
Date of next contact or talk to the client agreed?	☐	☐

The engagement end and the client's next steps

If an engagement is ended well, the client may be as enthusiastic and excited about the next steps as they were at the beginning of your involvement. If not, the next steps may never happen or at least be slow in starting. Ending well is important in giving the client an ongoing impetus, but it is not enough. From a consultant's perspective an engagement will often end with recommendations, but someone has to implement them. A document listing good ideas is not enough, as it is only through the resulting change that a client achieves lasting value. If you are not involved in implementation, you may conclude this is not your problem. You have handed over your recommendations and been paid, it's now up to the client. This is a bad conclusion to reach, as it is by client's achieving lasting value that your reputation and business as a consultant will grow.

The next steps for a client after an engagement ends depend on the type of engagement and what the client has asked. For example:

- *Strategy, advice, or recommendation engagements*: Next step is planning change.
- *Planning engagements*: Next step is implementation of change.
- *Implementation engagements*: Next step is a review of implementation.
- *Review engagements*: Next step is to recommend improvements.

As described in Chapter 4, there is the possibility of continuous sell-on as the consultant helps with the logical follow-on to every engagement. However, this is not the point of this chapter. You may continue to be involved with a client, but that does not remove the need to prepare the client for change. There are two key reasons for this.

Firstly, at some point your role will end. It is perfectly valid for a client to decide at any stage that they can continue by themselves, and irrespective of when your role ends, you should consider the client's subsequent change. Secondly, consultants must understand their limitations – you cannot make client change happen. This is not simply an issue of power; it is because you are not changing, but the client and the client organisation are. Only the client can be responsible for making change happen in a client organisation. If you do sell on and remain helping the client, then that is good for your business, and hopefully the

> " consultants must understand their limitations – you cannot make client change happen "

client, but even so you can only go so far. You will not be spending your future working life dealing with the change, only the client will. The consultant is there to help understand why to change, to show what to change, to facilitate the how to change – but not to change.

In reality, the degree of change required will vary enormously, from the alteration in thinking in an individual client when providing one-to-one advice to a single manager, through to the major restructuring and alteration in a business that can result from a novel and radical strategy. The rest of this chapter is written as if the change is significant, but the underlying principles are applicable even if the change is relatively minor.

Great consulting requires a strong sense of partnership between a consultant and a client. Yet, however strong the partnership between consultant and client, the fundamental truth is that the consultant and client are taking different journeys. For the life of an engagement their journeys run alongside each other. Afterwards, when they are driving in different directions, the most a consultant can do is to try to have a lasting influence on how the client steers. There is only so much the consultant can do to help a client. But a consultant should never finish an engagement with an attitude of 'oh well, it's all the client's problem now'. The role of the consultant is to build, with the client, the environment such that any recommendations made by, or change implemented with, the consultant will be sustained.

One implication of the limits to a consultant's powers is that whilst consultants may be able to guarantee making valuable recommendations and providing great advice, consultants cannot guarantee benefits because consultants cannot guarantee change. If there is no change, there can be no benefits. Achieving change is up to the client. When a consultancy does confirm benefits, it is only ever based on a long list of conditions that the client must fulfil, which effectively means ceding some management control to the consultant. Without this, the most a consultant can do is to describe how in a certain situation, when specific conditions are met, the client will get one positive outcome or another.

Yet although the consultant cannot guarantee successful change, change is the test for all consultancy advice. If an engagement does not lead to change then it has not added value. It is in considering the sustainability of consulting results where the partnership between client and consultant must be at its strongest. If, as a consultant, you do not influence the client to make sustained change, you either have defined the wrong solution to the client's problems, or you have not convinced the client to accept your ideas.

Making the change sustainable

The ability to implement a change in any situation depends on a number of factors including: capacity for change, capability to change, openness to change, urgency for change (real and perceived), and the level of power and support for the change. Many of these factors are outside a consultant's ability to influence. However, there are critical factors for change that consultants can and should help with. The most important factors are:

- giving the client confidence in the consultant's recommendations
- ensuring the client understands the case for change
- ensuring there is a coherent and complete set of prerequisites for the change, or a plan to develop them
- providing a clear understanding of the next steps
- understanding and preparing for resistance to the change.

I am not saying do any of this as a matter of kind-heartedness, but of professional comprehensiveness. These critical parts of your work should be accounted for in your fees. With the exception of the first bullet point, they are each potentially individually chargeable engagements. How you fulfil them depends on the situation, and in the end depends on what the client wants and is willing to pay for. If a client decides to limit or exclude any of these items then of course they can, but you need to ensure they understand the implications.

Let's look at each one of these in turn briefly.

Confidence in the consultant's recommendations

For a client to adopt recommendations made by a consultant, the client must have confidence in them. Confidence has to be at its highest when it comes to making change, as this is the point at which the client is risking most. Until that point the only thing that could go wrong was wasting the investment in a consultant's fees. It is one thing for a client to risk some budget on a consultant that they do not have 100 per cent confidence in, it is quite another to adopt the recommendations of that consultant, especially if the recommendations will result either in highly visible or fundamental changes.

How does a consultant provide confidence to the client? This is the domain of human psychology and each client will have a unique set of criteria which will determine if and how much a client trusts a consultant and has confidence in their recommendations. Factors to consider include:

■ strength of personal relationship between consultant and client

■ clear and understood process by which the recommendations were derived: sometimes an established expert reputation and close relationship can replace the need for an explicitly demonstrated reliable consulting process

■ recommendations based on reasonable and agreed assumptions

■ recommendations based on a sufficient data sample, a variety of sources of data and sufficiently detailed data

■ consistency in communications from the consultant: as an engagement progresses and a consultant discovers more, the hypothesis made may be disproved and positions changed, but a client is more likely to trust someone who presents a reasonably consistent line of argument throughout an engagement

■ logical coherence in how recommendations are presented.

In addition to these factors, how the engagement progressed and the nature and style of interaction between the consultant or consulting team and the client or client staff will have a significant impact on the confidence in the consultant's findings. For example, a consultant who is perceived as arrogant and who does not listen is less likely to deliver accepted recommendations than one who works well with the client staff and listens attentively.

A final factor will also be how radical the consultant's findings are. Radical findings may be of more value to the client, but clients will naturally find it more difficult to accept recommendations which challenge well-established ways of working and basic business principles and assumptions. If your recommendations will be radical, it is worth starting to set the client's expectations early in the engagement. Surprising a client with radical recommendations at the end of an engagement rarely leads to a happy outcome, even if the findings are completely valid.

> " a final factor will also be how radical the consultant's findings are "

Case for change

The aim of consultancy is not to give 'take it or leave it' advice but to convince a client to accept findings and using them to make change.

This is not achieved just at the point of handover, but comes about by building commitment to the change throughout the life of the engagement. Clients will not accept findings only on their intellectual integrity or intuitive appeal alone, there needs to be a case for change. The client needs to be able to answer the question: 'If I accept these findings and make the subsequent change, what will be the benefit to the organisation?'

A critical role for any consultant is to sell the recommendations to the client. The way selling is done will depend on the client. Some clients will respond to logical argument, some to an emotional appeal, others to a documented business case with scaled metrics. In selling the story, the consultant not only has to convince the client, but has to help to educate them. Once recommendations are adopted by the client, they may need to build a further case to convince other people in the organisation to accept the recommendations.

One informal test of whether a client has accepted the consultant's recommendations is to listen to what the client is talking about. If the client's business conversations modify and start to incorporate the language and ideas of the consultant then the client has probably adopted the consultant's recommendations and their thinking is becoming aligned with the consultant's. A further test is how the client prioritises their time – if the client will not allocate any time to a consultant it means that the engagement is not sufficiently important to the client. If the client starts to allocate more and more time to the consultant, then you have caught their attention and are influencing their priorities.

On ending an engagement it is important for the client, and any critical stakeholders who are party to accepting consulting deliverables, to understand the case for change. This is something you should try and persuade a client to be personally involved in. Ideally, the client will not delegate responsibility for understanding the case for change to a more junior manager. If it is delegated, it will be the junior manager who has to sell your recommendations to the real client. This is not an insurmountable problem, but, depending on the skills of the junior manager, it may increase the risk that your recommendations are not accepted.

Coherent and complete change prerequisites

For a client to embark on change, they require all the prerequisites needed to successfully implement the change, or at least a plan to develop them. By prerequisites for change, I mean all the materials, ideas, plans, power, skills and resources required for change. There may be a significant range of prerequisites.

Consultants often forget many of the softer requirements for change. Change prerequisites usually consists of a combination of tangible physical deliverables (recommendations, process designs, plans, business cases, etc.), and supporting intangible deliverables (knowledge, culture, enthusiasm, drive, etc.). Consultants tend to focus on the tangible, but usually the intangible are more important to the long-term sustainability of the change. A good consultant will at least advise the client manager on the intangible deliverables they need to think about. Few consulting problems are purely technical; most have a human dimension. Implementing change always has a human dimension, and it is the intangible deliverables that most strongly influence this human dimension.

One of the crucial intangible factors in change is the style of management adopted by the client. This may need to be adapted according to the context and nature of the change. For example, there is a significant difference between managing a change based on the implementation of a new IT system or a process change, and managing a change trying to alter the culture of an organisation.

The client must have the capability to perform the change. There is little point producing recommendations a client does not or cannot understand, or does not accept. The deliverables produced for a client must be appropriate and usable by the client. Engagement deliverables need to be matched to the level of skills and maturity of the client, or the client's skills must be improved as part of the engagement. If you are training or transferring skills as part of the engagement, you can't just transfer the ability to do, you must also transfer the skills for ongoing management, measurement and development of these skills.

The ability for the consultant to produce a complete set of prerequisites starts with the proposal and the engagement plan. Critically, the engagement needs to be scoped broadly enough. To produce a complete set of deliverables as inputs to a change the consultant needs to consider root causes of problems, not just symptoms. The consultant also needs to have considered systems issues – that is, how one part of a client's business system affects another. Ideally, the engagement is scoped broadly enough with sufficient time and resource to do all this. One way to do this is to scope an engagement around an outcome, and not simply the production of one or two documents. If the consultant is focused on an outcome, and if a client is willing to pay to achieve this outcome, then the engagement has to contain all the prerequisites for change.

Finally, the change needs to work when the consultant has gone, so sustaining it must not be dependent on the consultant, unless the client specifically chooses to involve you on a longer-term basis.

Next-steps plan

There is one effective and often valid way a consultant can sidestep the production of all the prerequisites to implement a set of recommendations, and that is in the production of a next-steps plan. The consultant must fulfil the conditions of any proposal, contract or other agreement with the client, but rarely does this entail producing every single prerequisite to implement change. Where the consultant is not responsible for producing the prerequisites, they can be listed in a next-steps plan.

There are many advantages to developing a next-steps plan for both the client and the consultant. Having some form of plan means the client knows what to do next, and is not left at the end of the engagement with a sense of 'what do I do now?' A next-steps plan is useful for the consultant as it can help with selling on, but it can also help to close an engagement neatly. Earlier in this chapter I talked about the consultant needing to tie up all the loose ends, but avoiding constantly refining deliverables and making an engagement unprofitable. One tool in achieving this is the next-steps plan, as it is often possible to tidy up some loose ends simply by listing them as actions to complete in a next-steps plan. Of course, a client will only let a consultant go so far in doing this.

> a next-steps plan can help with selling on, but it can also help to close an engagement neatly

There is a balance to be found in terms of the detail in the next-steps plan. At its simplest, the most all-encompassing next-steps plan can be written simply as one action for any set of recommendations. That one action is 'develop a plan for implementing the recommendations'. At the other extreme, a fully detailed plan for a significant change could be months of work for several consultants. Usually, unless the next-steps plan is an explicit deliverable agreed with the client which the client is paying for, it is best to veer towards a simple list of the most important following actions. This avoids the consultant engaging in excessive work, but also ensures the client is not left without an understanding of what to do next.

There is an art to producing a good next-steps plan. The consultant must avoid unethical urges to simply list actions that ensure the client has to buy more consulting services, but it is often reasonable to include some actions that may result in reusing the consultant. The plan has to be comprehensive and understandable, but unless the client has engaged you explicitly to produce it, it cannot be lengthy or overly detailed. In practice this is usually achievable, and it is possible to produce a next-steps plan that is not overly onerous for the consultant, but which adds significant value to the client on any engagement. If done well, the client and the consultant's commercial interests can be aligned.

Identify and help overcome resistance

Any recommendations which provide a challenge to a client, because they come up with novel ideas or concepts, question current strategy or ways or operating, or query basic business principles or assumptions, are almost always going to face some resistance. Resistance comes in many forms. At one level it is a positive sign. Great consulting is challenging, and if there is no resistance then there is probably not enough challenge. But resistance must be managed because it will get in the way of accepting findings and implementing advice. It also must be listened to as sometimes it derives from sensible roots.

To help clients optimally, consultants must think in terms of two types of resistance. There will be resistance at the point at which consultants give their findings, but also there may be resistance later on when the client comes to implementing those same findings with or without the consultant. Even if consultants are not involved in the implementation, they can advise the client about possible resistance. A consultant should try to help the client understand why resistance is important, identify what resistance exists, learn from the resistance (as some may be well founded), and finally help the client to deal with it.

If a consultant's recommendations are to result in real change there will be resistance. Change cannot be undertaken without some shift in the power balance in an organisation. This may be a significant loss of power for some individuals, or may be modest and sometimes only perceived by some people (e.g. if job titles are realigned there may be no power shift, but people can perceive it negatively). The client must accept this and be willing to deal with the resistance or else the change will not occur. A client who wants to upset no one in an organisation when implementing change will never do anything significant.

Change is not done to people, it is participated in and either accepted or rejected. Rarely does it fail because the wrong order was given, but because people have chosen to ignore the orders. Staff will accept change if they are engaged and want to or need to accept it. To make this choice, people have to feel comfortable making the change work, and that includes everyone, not just the senior managers. So, one of the building blocks of avoiding resistance is spending time explaining what a change is to people, why it is being pursued and how it will work. Contrary to popular wisdom, people are usually willing to change. People change all the time, sometimes in imperceptible ways, but over time it adds up. What people mostly resist is being forced to change.

Change means doing something differently. Change is not hard because designing a new way is hard, but because it entails unlearning and giving up existing ways. It is often easy to design a better process, organisation structure, IT system, strategy, or operational metrics. What is far harder is to make them work. Giving up a habit is far harder than making a new one. This is especially true when the change may be perceived to be asso-

❝ giving up a habit is far harder than making a new one ❞

ciated with a loss of face. Implicit in adopting any new ways of work is a criticism that the old ways must have been wrong if they are being replaced. This feeling of criticism can generate a powerful emotional resistance to change. If consultants are involved in change they must manage this process. Partially this must be by creating an incentive for the client staff to change and creating discomfort with the existing status quo. The more urgent and powerful the feeling of discomfort is, the easier it will be to overcome the status quo.

Resistance does not only occur because of actual or perceived power shifts. Acceptance or rejection of a consultant or a consultant's findings is also related to perceived competence, and trust and relationship. This is one of the reasons for stressing the need for a client to have confidence in a consultant's recommendations. The more a consultant is trusted, the easier it is for a client to accept even the most difficult of recommendations. The less a consultant is trusted, the more likely even the best of recommendations will be ignored.

If there is resistance to your work, try to find the underlying reason. Resistance is better dealt with by removing the underlying cause than by treating the symptoms. If you just fight it or ignore it, resistance can get worse. Always try to determine what is causing it, and, based on this, determine what you will do about it. Identify it, listen to it, be willing to change your views if you find the resistance is based on sensible thinking, and then deal with what resistance remains.

It is important to identify what resistance really is, as opposed to what just feels like resistance. Do not confuse resistance with a lack of understanding and vice versa. Either may show as the other. Similarly, do not confuse rejecting your work because it is flawed with real resistance, or vice versa. If you mistake resistance for flaws, you will rework and expend effort unnecessarily because you will not do anything about the resistance. If you mistake flaws for resistance, you will do a poor quality job.

Try to acknowledge alternative views, and give the important stakeholders a forum to discuss their view with you. For the people who resist you, spend time bringing them on board, go round them and let them adopt change at their own pace, reduce their ability to affect the change, or remove them (a valid choice – but not the consultant's). The options depend on the pace of change required and their individual criticality to the organisation. It also depends on the amount of consultant time a client wants to pay for. Dealing properly with resistance can conflict with consulting timelines as it is resource-intensive and can be prolonged. However, if a client really wants to make substantial change, the resistance must be handled.

Try to help with emotional responses, listen and explore logical responses, but don't get lost in them. If your recommendations affect many people, you cannot talk to each and every individual, and sometimes resistance must be conquered with robust and directive client management. Such directive management makes people choose to change simply because the penalties of not changing are too great. However, it does not always work.

One critical place to identify and resolve any resistance is with your real client. It can be surprising, but one of the hardest sources of resistance may be the person who engages you and is paying your consulting fees. The first question to analyse is: 'Does the client really have the desire for this change to be sustained and accept the associated level of pain?' Often clients say they want, for example, better customer service, whereas what they really want is an irritating problem to disappear painlessly. The client may not be able to improve customer service without some pain, and if they will not accept the pain then the change will never happen. Also you must consider your client's own personality and management style. The underlying issues that caused a client to require your help in the first place may get in the way of accepting or implementing your advice. For example, an indecisive client will respond indecisively and a disorganised client will be disorganised in implementing. Although it requires great sensitivity, helping a client to understand their own weaknesses or styles, and how they affect their ability to progress with a change, is huge added value.

Summary

If you have read the book in chapter order you have now completed the second section of the book made up of Chapters 5 to 8. In these chapters I have explained the steps in the consulting engagement process. Consultants' work revolves around the steps of winning, delivering and closing engagements. An ability to perform the tasks in Chapters 5 to 8 is essential to working as a consultant. Perform them well and you are likely to be a successful consultant. However, there is more to consulting than the engagement process, and the remaining chapters in this book describe some of the more advance concepts in consulting.

The main points from this chapter are summarised in Figure 8.2.

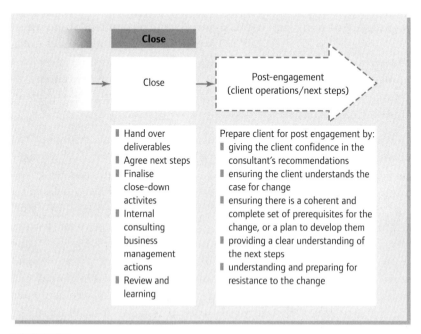

Figure 8.2 Closing engagements and sustaining results

three

High-performance consulting

9

Developing long-term client relationships

I n Chapter 4 I introduced the consultants' engagement process. This process focuses on an individual engagement – that is, a single consulting project with a start and an end. There is another way to look at consulting, and that is from the viewpoint of the relationships between consultants and their clients. Engagements come and go, whereas a relationship can continue for the whole of a consultant's career. Relationships are essential to client-centric consulting, as without a relationship you will not understand the client's issues and needs.

Many people entering the consulting profession are surprised about quite how much consultants talk about and apparently value relationships. Yet consultants rarely discuss why relationships are valuable to them, which relationships should be developed and how relationships should be developed. It is taken for granted that this is understood. This chapter provides an introduction to this critical part of the consultants' world.

Having a wide set of relationships is essential to your success as a consultant. Consulting is reliant on relationships. It is great to develop powerful insights, tools and methods, as these encapsulate your expertise, but without relationships you will never be accepted or engaged with as a consultant. Occasionally, a major consultancy will look to recruit a specialist or a guru in some field or another who can raise the consultancy's capabilities in that specific field, but consultancies only need a small pool of gurus. What consultancies really value, and what they have a much bigger appetite for, are people with broad networks of productive and reliable business relationships.

The value of relationships to consultants

Relationships are the fuel that nourishes a consulting business. Experienced consultants understand the value of relationships, and at times can seem obsessive about them. This fervent attention is not overkill, and in this section I describe the value of strong personal connections in order to encourage all consultants to invest time in developing a broad and productive network of relationships.

In the boom times, relationships assist consultants and consultancies to maximise their revenues. In the difficult periods, relationships are central to keeping consultants busy. Relationships help in identifying opportunities, selling engagements, maximising fees, reducing the cost of sales, as well as the efficient management of and reducing the risk from live engagements. If there is a magic potion that makes consulting work, it is relationships. I advise most new consultants to worry more about their relationships than their service lines. Service lines can be enhanced over time, relationships are essential to getting going as a consultant.

> if there is a magic potion that makes consulting work, it is relationships

The starting point for all consulting engagements is the identification of possible consulting opportunities. As discussed in Chapter 2, the opportunity derives from an unfulfilled customer need. To know that a customer has an unfulfilled need usually requires you to be in dialogue with a customer, and you are much more likely to be in dialogue with a customer you have a relationship with. You avoid all the problems of cold selling when you have a positive relationship with a client, as you can ring them up anytime and simply ask how things are and if there is anything to discuss. There are different ways of phrasing these questions depending on the nature and depth of the relationship, but however you ask, one of the primary advantages of existing relationships is the ability to develop and maintain awareness of client opportunities. Better still, when you have really good relationships, some clients will actively come and find you to discuss potential engagements.

Consulting opportunities do not often arise as an immediate urgent request. It does happen, but in my experience only a small minority of engagements start this way. Few clients wake up in the morning with a sudden desperate need for a consultant. Opportunities develop over time. Relationships enable you to maintain an ongoing dialogue with clients, so you can be involved as opportunities unfold and consolidate from vague ideas into clear concepts.

You can find work without established relationships, but it is much harder. It is possible to predict and recognise some needs by general observation or knowledge of a market. For instance, a financial compliance consultant will know that banks have new compliance needs every time there are changes in the financial regulations. But even so, a general understanding of a need is not the same as knowing if an individual customer has a specific requirement for assistance, and it still leaves the challenge of making a cold call to a client.

Positive relationships significantly ease selling. When you have a strong relationship you are more likely to understand a client better. Even in what are meant to be open competitive situations, such as tenders, the consulting organisation with a better client relationship has a significant advantage over a company with no relationship. The established consultant has access to hints and peripheral pieces of information, which when combined enable a proposal to be better targeted at client needs. When an established consultancy loses a tender to a competitor without an existing relationship, it is usually because the established consultancy has either previously delivered a suboptimal engagement or, more often, has become complacent.

Relationships do not ease sales just because a client is more likely to buy from and support someone they like, but also because the client wants to minimise risk. Consultancy is inherently ambiguous and subject to elaboration as an engagement progresses. Until the end of the engagement, a client is not precisely sure of what they will get and how good it will be. This is a situation in which trust is critically important. It is far more comfortable for a client to agree to purchase imprecisely specified service from someone they know rather than from a stranger.

Relationships can assist in approaching a client with a cold sale, which the client has not directly sought, or may not initially even realise they want. Cold selling in consultancy is problematic, and the usual response to an attempt to cold sell consultancy is complete client rejection, or possibly no response at all! If you have a good relationship, a client will at least listen to alternative consulting services they may not have previously thought about. In other words, a long-term relationship can give you the ability to sell the services you have, rather than what a client initially may be considering. This could include creating demand for innovative service lines. However, care is needed as this risks veering away from client-centric consulting and should only be pursued if it is appropriate for the client.

A client is significantly more likely to be willing to take a risk with a consultant with whom they have a good relationship, based on previous positive consulting interactions. In these situations, the client is more likely to be willing to try out new service lines which have no track record, and is more likely to be open to radical advice. Such openness does not only affect the ability to sell to a client, but will affect the whole engagement process.

Greater familiarity between a client and a consultant can enable the more rapid delivery of value-adding advice, and can ease change and implementation of consulting recommendations. A consultant with an established relationship in a client organisation will find it easier to gain consensus and acceptance of their findings. The consultant is more likely to have open access to information and data – especially less tangible information like feelings and emotions, which may be withheld from someone with a lesser relationship. The consultant will find it easier to engage with the client and gain access to resources, and the client will feel more relaxed in arranging meetings with more senior managers and executives. Generally, the consultant is more likely to be listened to and to be trusted.

Strong relationships are also beneficial for the consultant's risk reduction. The consultant is more likely to have better information with which to avoid problems. Also a client is less likely to become annoyed if an engagement does not meet their expectations and more likely to resolve issues by open dialogue with the consultant.

Having a set of deep relationships is a valuable asset for a consultant. Without any relationships a consultant will struggle to win or deliver any consulting engagements. However, I want to end this section by mentioning a few relationship traps to avoid. The first risk is that if relationships are very strong and long lasting, there is a hazard that consultants can take a client for granted, become complacent and even lazy. We all make assumptions about people with whom we have strong relationships and this can lead us to lose our client-centric viewpoint and simply assume the client will continue to deliver opportunities to us. New consultancies often are brought into a client, when the client becomes fed up with a deteriorating level of service from an existing consultant. A common situation is when a consultant who has regularly worked with a client, rather than seeking to add value, starts to milk the client for as much as possible.

> ❝ there is a hazard that consultants can take a client for granted ❞

Additionally, it can be increasingly hard to take a truly independent and impartial line of advice with a client with whom you have a very strong relationship. Becoming too close to a client can start to bias advice in favour of the individual client manager, rather than for the benefit of the whole client organisation.

A consultant who develops a very strong relationship with a client can find that they are working with the client for an extended period of time. This tendency needs to be avoided. Working only with one client tends to blunt your consulting edge, but also it is a commercial risk for your consulting business. All clients eventually terminate consultants, and if you have only worked with one client for years and years your ability to find other work and the freshness and usefulness of your network of relationships outside this client is limited. As a consultant you do not need to, or probably want to, work with every possible client, but you need more than one. A handful of clients or more, as opposed to a single client, will keep your skills more current and reduce your commercial risk.

Developing networks

The general principle that good relationships, if appropriately used, are of enormous value to a consultant is easy to accept. Look at any of the major consultancy companies and the best paid and most senior staff are often the ones with the most productive relationships. However, the general idea is harder to put in practice than it may initially appear. It is one thing to want a great network, it is quite another to have a set of truly productive relationships. It is not enough to know people, you must convert a personal connection into useful information and opportunities.

A consultant should seek a wide network of relationships. The ideal relationship is strong enough for a client to trust you and share information and problems openly with you, but even relatively shallow associations can be helpful. I have been involved in many pieces of work that have started with a fairly tenuous link with the client: it was sufficient for the client to know about me and to start a conversation with me about whether I could help them. Irrespective of how deep the relationship is, it must be made to work. A productive relationship is not a passive connection between people – it is an active communications channel.

Relationships form networks, and generally the larger the network the better – that is assuming the relationships are positive! The advantage of a large network is that you do not only have access to your own relationships, but many people will allow you to access their relationships as well. There are online tools, social networking sites and so on, which allow you to see how big your network is and to expand it actively. However, whilst such online tools can be useful in creating links, having a link with someone you have never communicated with may be a potential relationship, but it is not yet a relationship.

A network of relationships will develop automatically as you go through your working life. The successful consultant does not just let relationships occur, but actively seeks and manages relationships. The consultant should identify people who could be valuable to have relationships with and targets them. Sometimes this requires the deliberate engineering of situations in which you can introduce yourself and talk to potential clients, which can seem initially awkward, but most professional people accept that everyone needs to build a network. The aim of every conversation with someone in your network should be to ensure the door is open to future conversations.

Having started a relationship the consultant manages and maintains it. Managing a network can be as simple as maintaining a list of people you have relationships with and periodically contacting them. There are some old friends who you may not speak to for 20 years, but when you meet them you will carry on as if there was no break. But your network of professional relationships is not like this. It needs active engagement with people for connections to be kept fresh. Stale relationships with individuals you have had no interaction with for many years are much less powerful. It is easy to forget to keep in touch with some people you should have maintained a relationship with and regret it.

Potential clients are an important aspect of any network of relationships, but you should not just focus on clients and potential clients. Firstly, there are other consultants. Of course, at one level other consultants are competitors, but for every time I have lost a piece of work to another consultant in my personal network I have probably won several. Consultants need other consultants and can help each other out all the time. As well as sharing opportunities, consultants are a great source of information and advice. Secondly, there are people who may never be clients, but have an influence on clients. There are managers and staff who do not control consulting budgets, but are respected by and influential with clients. The classic person who is underestimated, but hugely valuable, is a senior manager's PA or secretary. The PA never buys consultancy, but whether or not you get a meeting with a manager, and whether it is soon or in the distant future, is often at the discretion of a PA. Treat them with the respect they deserve. Thirdly, there may be people who can be sources of useful information. For example, if you consult in a specific sector it is helpful to know people you can discuss trends and issues with in the sector. They may never directly gain you any work, but your up-to-date pertinent knowledge will be an asset.

Although you have to target your efforts on to the most valuable parts of your network, as no one can meaningfully keep in touch with everyone, essentially all contacts are good contacts.

"essentially all contacts are good contacts" However, do not confuse a large contacts list of people with whom you have a tenuous link with a set of powerful relationships. Having someone's business card can be useful, but it is not the same as being able to call someone whenever you want to discuss something or to propose engagements. My belief is that a relatively compact set of strong relationships is more valuable to a consultant than hundreds of vague contacts.

Consulting companies often value the large network of relationships they have. However, relationships are not owned or controlled by the company directly, but by individuals in the company. No amount of contact databases, business management or customer relationship management systems is going to change the fact that relationships are owned by individual consultants. If those consultants leave, at least part of the relationship leaves as well.

Brand specialists will talk about a consumer's relationship with a brand, and it is possible to think in terms of a client's relationship with a consulting brand. However, I do not think clients have deep relationships with professional brands such as consultancies – unless the client is a former employee of the consultancy. Clients have an experience of a consultancy, which if positive will influence them to buy again, but this is different from a relationship between individuals. As there are many consultancy companies with strong brands, relying on the brand to sell is risky. A competing consultant with a strong personal relationship is always going to win over a competitor relying on a relationship purely with a brand.

A strong relationship can give you access to all sorts of useful information and opportunities, but do not take relationships for granted. No one has exclusive ownership of a relationship. Some people have better relationships than others at a particular point in time, but that is only true for that moment. Relationships are not static and they change with experience, all the time.

Clients usually have multiple relationships with different people in a consultancy. This should be encouraged, as different types and styles of relationship suit different situations. A client may enjoy the interaction with the business development or sales manager, but the client usually knows when it comes to added value they need to be talking to the expert and not the salesperson. The salesperson is an important doorkeeper and a route to the right experts at the right time. If a consultancy allows an individual manager to 'own' a relationship completely, then if that manager leaves the firm, the relationship goes with them.

Developing long-term relationships

How do you develop productive relationships? Just being known about is better than being anonymous, but it is not the same as having a relationship. Every time you interact with someone, you modify your relationship. Productive relationships are not given away and nor are they a gift, they are something you develop and earn. Relationships are created by your behaviour and the perceptions of this behaviour of the person you are interacting with. A relationship builds from the way you communicate and your client's experience of interacting with you. Let's consider the way you should interact with a potential client you are meeting for the first time, and then how this should be managed in the longer term.

The starting point for a relationship is the first impression. First impression count and the very initial interaction will colour your relationship with clients. You can overcome a poor first impression, but it is hard work. It is much easier to start with a great first impression. This first impression will develop before you have even opened your mouth, and will be influenced by factors like how you enter the room and how you look. If your first interaction is not face-to-face, you will make an impression by how you sound on the phone or how your email or letter looks. If you are meeting a potential new client for the first time, it is worth considering what first impression you want to give and how you will give it.

Relationships are affected significantly by how you communicate. Communication is a two-way process, and as important as what you say is how you are perceived by the other party. You are much more likely to develop a positive relationship with someone you show attention to and listen to, and someone to whom you give the impression of warmth, friendliness and positivity. Do not be in a rush to impress new clients with what you know, but help them to warm to you by giving them attention and listening to what they say. You need both to care about what they say, but also to appear as if you care. Showing respect and that you value the other person's words are essential for good relationship building.

You want to appear sincere and genuine to a potential client. You are trying to create a level of trust. One approach that can help to do this is what communication specialists call self-disclosure. Self-disclosure is telling the other party something about yourself of a personal nature. It does not have to be deep or secret, but by sharing aspects of our lives we grow relationships. There are many social and cultural norms to be adhered to, but sharing and showing a little vulnerability helps people to warm to each other. Watch a great salesperson and often they exhibit self-disclosure. An example may be saying something like, 'Oh well, I am worried about my children's exam results.' Don't go too far, as revealing too much inappropriate personal information is unsettling and off-putting.

You must adapt to the situation and judge what is appropriate to which occasion. If a client has asked you in for a general conversation for the first time, a little social chit chat is helpful to break down any barriers. If a client has an urgent pressing issue and is under significant pressure, then avoid the chit chat and move straight into listening to their business problems.

Once you have met a client, communication still plays a critical role in developing relationships. As a relationship deepens you should find that your conversations are becoming more varied and covering a wider range of topics, including personal topics. Generally if your conversations are not becoming more varied, you are probably not developing a good relationship. Similarly, the frequency of interaction should increase. This seems obvious when considering a simple example. You probably have a weaker relationship with someone you discuss printer toner cartridges with every six months, than with someone you discuss all your stationery requirements with every month but with whom you also chat about family, sport and the weather. As a relationship develops, so should the content and frequency of your conversations.

There are social rules we all adhere to in having any form of interaction. These are culturally specific and will vary depending on the depth and

> **one valuable skill is observing and adopting the local rules of interaction**

length of your association. Relationships are greatly affected by the way the parties understand and share the same conventions and follow the rules. If, as a consultant, you are going to work in different cultures, one valuable skill is observing and adopting the local rules of interaction.

Another factor that will influence your relationships with clients over time is the consistency of your communications. There must be a degree of stability in the way you communicate and the content of your communications. Communications can change over time, but the change needs to be gradual. There must also be consistency between what you say and what you do. People are expert at noticing differences between our pronouncements and our actions. As well as consistency, a client needs to feel you have some commitment to a relationship and that what you say will be backed up by experience. Inconsistency and a perceived lack of commitment to your words will result in clients feeling you are inauthentic and untrustworthy. Sincerity and trustworthiness are important for consultants.

So far, I have focused on communication aspects of a relationship, and these are crucial to developing and maintaining relationships. To some extent relationships are about communication, but they are also about experience. Your relationships will be influenced significantly by your client's experience of working with you and their expectations of future engagements. If you consistently deliver great work and are enjoyable to work with, your relationship will tend to deepen. You must seek to inspire confidence and build trust in your work. This can be achieved by consistency, appropriate levels of openness and your responsiveness to your client needs.

One challenge with relationships is that it is difficult to maintain the same standards all the time. Everyone sometimes lets their quality level deteriorate a little, or lets their guard down and says something that should not have been said. You must minimise these situations. It is an unfortunate aspect of human beings that we are more intolerant of a few mistakes than ready to give credit for positive interactions. It is extremely easy to make one minor mistake, such as an inappropriate comment in a staff canteen that is overheard by a client or member of client staff. Such mistakes can cause tremendous collateral damage. Relationships are not constant – ideally they get better, but they can get worse!

Do not despair if something goes wrong and damages your relationship, because relationships are malleable. If you do make a mistake and it will be found out, then you must be the first person to admit it. It is a funny thing, but being open about mistakes quickly can actually improve relationships. No one is perfect, and everyone knows this. Admitting to mistakes can be a painful process, but if it is done well it can, in the longer run, improve the situation. Most people respond well to a full apology and open admission of a mistake, as long as it is not repeated.

Your aim should be to develop a relationship which increases your credibility and trust with the client over time. Every time you do something that enhances these, you are strengthening your relationship. Every time you do something that reduces these, you are weakening your relationship.

Selecting the clients to have relationships with

The fundamental reason why long-term relationships are possible is because as a consultant you are providing what the client perceives as a valuable service. But consulting is not a service that can be provided without the involvement of the client – it is a highly interactive service. Therefore to have a long-term relationship not only requires activity from your side, but also that the client behaves in an appropriate fashion and actively engages with you. You should seek out clients who are willing to develop a relationship with you, and avoid those who will not.

There are many characteristics of a good client. Obviously a good client must be willing and able to buy your service. They also have to need your services. There is little point investing effort in developing a deep relationship with someone who will never have any need for your services.

Similarly, there are practical reasons which make some clients better than others. This includes providing the necessary resources, giving access to the right data, and making any decisions quickly and on time. Good clients are responsive to invoices and pay them within agreed payment schedules. Good clients also make appropriate demands upon consultants. Such demands can be high, given the level of consulting fees and the often lofty promises made by consultants, but in the end they need to be realistic and achievable. Good clients limit changes or additions to the engagement. Consulting engagements are often unclear at the start, and it is inherent that as the engagement progresses and understanding increases then areas where misunderstanding existed are found, or new issues arise. The client does need to be reasonable about how much modification can be absorbed in an existing engagement's scope. A good client organisation has a degree of consensus about your work, and you do not find yourself constantly given contradictory instructions by different members of client staff. These factors are looked at again in Chapter 12.

Beyond these practical characteristics, good clients are people you can have productive relationships with. It is useful to remember that a relationship is a two-way association. Although as a consultant you are the person selling the service, and therefore you are the person who needs the relationship more, clients need and want relationships with people who can assist them productively and add value to them. By developing a relationship with a client, and giving a client access to your network, you are not only increasing your opportunity of future revenue streams – you are also adding value to the client.

> **it is useful to remember that a relationship is a two-way association**

In your work as a consultant there will be times when you have to work with clients you do not develop a long-term bond with. But over your career the most useful clients will typically be the ones who you develop a strong relationship with. Such clients do not develop a relationship because you choose to develop one with them, but because they simultaneously choose to develop a relationship with you. Seek out a variety of relationships and do not expect every productive interaction to lead to you gaining a new friend. Some doors are open, some can be opened, and some stay closed. Choose the clients who open their door and allow you to develop a productive relationship with them.

Summary

Productive relationships are central to success as a consultant. They help in finding, winning and delivering work, and without such a network of relationships you will struggle as a consultant.

■ You should seek out the relationships you want, and once achieved actively manage them.

■ The client relationships you develop are a result of how you communicate with a client, and what the client's experiences and expectations of working with you are.

■ Seek out clients who are willing to develop a relationship with you, and avoid those who will not.

10

The ethical dimension

U ntil comparatively recently, few people regularly used the phrase *business ethics* and few worried about managing a business ethically. This is not to deny that individuals in business had ethics or that some commercial enterprises have a long history of shaping their work based on clear moral stances. But this was usually about individual views and not a universally shared acceptance of the need for ethical business practices. This has changed. Study for any MBA, and sooner or later you will find yourself considering business ethics. In any modern company today it is ethics as well as commercialism that influences decisions and actions. The management consulting industry is no exception.

Of course, there has always been a foundation of rules defined in the law. Further rules exist in commercial regulations, which have become generally more specific and onerous over time. Remaining compliant with the law can be considered as an ethical issue, but this is not the concern of this chapter. With the number of consultants there are in the world, no doubt some are charlatans who take a relaxed attitude to adhering to legislation, but I think these are a small minority. Legal and regulatory compliance are not trivial issues, but I am going to assume that if you know the law you want to remain compliant with it. But is that sufficient? The answer is easy and simple: no. Ethics goes beyond legal issues. It is not difficult to imagine many scenarios which are legal, but which most people agree are unethical.

Thinking about ethics opens many complex debates – for instance, absolute moral principles versus relative and culturally specific values.

There are deeply conflicting views on whether an action is ethically sound simply because it adheres to some fundamental principle; or if actions should be judged on their intentions or on their consequences, irrespective of underlying moral principles. No matter how clear you feel you are on ethical principles (e.g. 'stealing is always wrong'), you can very soon find yourself challenged in valid ways (e.g. 'Ah, but what about the pen you are writing with – didn't you take that from the office stationery cupboard? Isn't that stealing?'). These are deep waters and areas where there is definitely no universal consensus. Other than acknowledging the complexity of ethical considerations, it is significantly outside the scope of a book like this to even discuss issues of this complexity. My aims are much more modest. I want to raise the issue of ethics so that it is a conscious part of your consulting perspective.

Ethics can be trivialised or on the contrary made overly complex. In this chapter I will show that ethics should not be a trivial concern for the consultant, but neither should ethics be an intensely complex piece of analysis. Commonsense, pragmatism and reasoned judgement lie at the heart of most good ethical decisions. I have split this chapter into three sections reflecting these introductory thoughts:

- ▓ *Ethical basics*: What are the basic guidelines we should try to adhere to as consultants?
- ▓ *Application of ethics*: Having ethical concepts is one thing, applying them is another. This section considers two specific aspects of consulting – the privileged position of the consultant, and the relationship between the consultant and client.
- ▓ *Ethics and dilemmas in consulting*: If all we needed to do was list some ethical rules and adhere to them, life might be comparatively simple. The real challenge is when different ethical guidelines or other objectives conflict, and deciding how to deal with this.

Irrespective of what you take from this chapter and how much consideration you choose to give to ethical issues, there is a simple practical stance to take. You always have a choice as to what work you do and how you interact with a client. Part of this is an ethical choice. Engagements can usually be shaped in different ways and ethics taken into account during this shaping. In the rare case that the engagement cannot be shaped appropriately, never forget that you can always say no to any engagement you feel ethically compromised on.

Ethical basics

A simple way to think of ethics is to look at the concepts which enable you to decide how to do good and, as important, how to avoid doing harm. Considering the consultancy context, what does this mean in practice? I have chosen seven examples which reflect a simple set of ethical guidelines or can be seen as areas of temptation for consultants:

1 Ensuring fair fees for the engagement.

2 Performing only appropriate engagements relative to skills and experience.

3 Only performing work that the client needs and is in the client's interest.

4 Avoiding building a dependency of the client upon the consultant.

5 Respecting client information.

6 Using fair contracts.

7 Avoiding conflicts of interest arising from simultaneous commercial involvement in a consulting and client business.

Let's explore each one of these in a little more detail.

Fair fees

The fees a consultant charges are part of a commercial relationship between the client and consultant. We should not confuse what is commercially reasonable with ethical fairness. If you have a particularly rare and valuable skill that you have developed over years of consulting, it is perfectly reasonable for you to charge a fee rate in line with what the market will bear. If you are lucky enough for this to be 10 times what your less skilful competitors can charge, this is purely a commercial issue.

> ❝ fairness is concerned with how the fees are presented and handled ❞

Fairness is concerned with how the fees are presented and handled. The client should have an understanding of what the fee rates will be at the start of the engagement, what any extras that will be charged for are, and what the total level of fees for the engagement are likely to be. If the engagement changes, then there is time for debate on the fees again. If the client wants to enter an uncapped time and materials engagement, then again there is nothing unethical in charging the client for every second you have worked, as long as the client appreciates what they are committing to. Similarly, you should not be charging clients for any time on an engagement where you are developing your company's intellectual property and not directly adding value to the client.

One particular issue associated with fees is the charging for time working in a client office or on work related to a client engagement, when the consultant is not actually progressing the engagement but is engaged in business development. Your sales activities should be at your cost, not charged as hours to the client. Of course, you will recoup this one way or another from the client, otherwise you would not stay in business, but that should be recouped from the margin you make on your legitimate chargeable hours.

An area that often causes tension between clients and consultants is the recharge of expenses. Part of this comes down to the apparently lavish lifestyle of some consultants. This is not an ethical issue. What your expenses policy is remains an issue for you and your company. A client has the option when signing up to your services to negotiate what are acceptable levels of expenses to them. You may damage your relationship with your client by having an overly lavish expenses policy, but that is your choice. However, where it becomes an ethical issue is when expenses recharged to a client were not actually accrued related to the engagement. Typical examples are:

- Charging all expenses for travel and accommodation to a certain geographic region to one client who is currently being billed for a live engagement, when one of the reasons for travel was to visit other clients for sales meetings, without the opportunity to recharge travel costs to the latter group.
- Inviting clients out for drinks or dinner, and then recharging them for the privilege.

Performing appropriate work

The second ethical issue involves performing only appropriate work. But what is appropriate work? All consulting engagements require competencies and knowledge. These include any combination of functional, sector, geographic, and service line skills and experience. Loosely defined, appropriate work is engagements that you have the correct skills and experience for. What skills are appropriate depends significantly on the role you are taking on in an engagement. If you are selling yourself as an expert then it is not unreasonable for the client to expect you to have in-depth expertise in a specific area or business. On the other hand, if you are putting yourself forward as a process consultant or facilitator, then whilst you must have process consulting and facilitation skills, specific functional or industry knowledge is less relevant.

It is relatively easy to convince some clients that you have skills which you do not, and unfortunately there are many consultants who seem to just about get away with this. I call this type of consultants *chancers*. They will win the work and take the chance that they will get away with it, irrespective of real competence. These chancers may not sell on very often, but survive on the basis that the pool of clients with problems is very big and they may never need to work with the same people twice. Such chancers are more common in certain parts of the world, where clients have less experience of working with consultants.

What actually is an appropriate level of skill or experience is clearly a judgement. No engagement is a copy of a previous one. Even if it could be, the client situation will vary in some ways, so there are elements of unpredictability, exploration and learning on each engagement. There will be clear-cut cases when you are confident your skills are sufficient and there will be situations which you walk away from because you are not the right person. But there are many ambiguous situations when it is not certain, and in my experience this constitutes a large proportion of engagements. There is a fine difference between a legitimate stretch in your skills and a leap into the unknown. If you are even the slightest bit unsure, the most ethical position is to explain to your client what you do and do not have experience of, and how confident you are of being able to stretch this to meet the situation. Then leave the choice to the client. Clients will usually respond positively to consultants who are open enough to admit their limitations as well as their expertise. Such openness can be the basis of a long-term trusting relationship.

A related but slightly different issue is using the client as an experimental testing ground for a new service line, or using the client engagement as service line development. Consultancies do need to develop service lines, and client experience forms the base of such service line development. This is reasonable. It is even reasonable to develop the service line as part of the work, if this is agreed with the client. It becomes unethical when:

■ As part of the engagement's sale it was claimed that there was a service line when it does not exist, and it is developed 'on the hoof' while on the engagement: in this situation, the client is subject to risk and being charged for the service line development.

- You claim that a service line provides proven value, when in fact if it is a new service line and so effectively an experimental product whose value has no evidential base.

- You claim you have a service line, when in reality you have minimal understanding of a topic but have read an article or two and sound convincing to the client.

An appropriate service is also one in which the consultant has access to sufficient data and information to draw the right conclusions from. If you do not have or cannot find the skills to analyse the situation, then you are not offering an appropriate service. Without the right data, no matter what skills or experience you have, the results of your engagement are unlikely to be correct.

Consulting services are appropriate only if they are based on an understanding of the specific, unique situation of the client. Of course a consultant brings experience from other situations, but simply giving exactly the same advice or the same plan in every situation is not appropriate. Value-adding consulting is always bespoke. Providing a 'cookie cutter' approach is not adding value. There is nothing wrong with a company that sells a standard service to a client which is not tailored to the individual situation. But it is not management consulting – the very word *consulting* implies consultation and hence dialogue and interaction. If you are selling a plain vanilla service then good luck, but do not call it management consulting.

> " value-adding consulting is always bespoke "

Only doing necessary work

The third issue for ethical consideration relates to only doing work that a client needs and is in the client's interest. One situation in which this matters is with follow-on work, when you have been fortunate enough to complete an engagement successfully and part of the recommendations are for subsequent work using your skills. There is an obvious moral hazard when the person with an interest in future work is also the person advising a client as to what the future work should be. I do not see any problem with advising follow-on work that requires your skills, or winning it. The problem comes only if the advice you gave has been deliberately skewed to favour the sell-on. The easiest answer is to point out your inherent conflict to the client. Most clients see the conflict of interest, and pointing it out does not change anything other than making it clear that you are being open and honest.

There are some situations in which the bias is more covert. A classic example is that some consultants design engagements to overcome client issues by starting with the generation of hypotheses. The hypotheses are used as a starting point to explore what the client issues and solutions might be. The engagement then seeks data to prove or disapprove the hypotheses. This is common practice, especially amongst the more strategic consultancies. There is nothing intrinsically wrong with it, as long as the selection of hypotheses and the search for data is not biased to come out with a result that is in the consultant's commercial interest. Unfortunately, sometimes the selection of hypotheses is biased. This problem can run very deep. Some consultants so strongly believe their own skills, service lines and views on management that the bias is unconscious. Unproven assumptions are made about how a business should and should not be run, and these are reflected into the hypotheses and data collection approach selected. There is then an inherent bias which results in recommendations that unsurprisingly(!) match other services the consultancy can offer. This problem can be compounded by some consultants' lack of understanding of the difference between a hypothesis, a conviction, an evidence-based conjecture and a fact.

Another problem can arise when the strength of a consulting company's brand is used to pressurise a client to undertake work. When a partner or other senior member of a major consultancy looks a manager in the eye and says 'we are advising you to do this', this can be the quality advice of a good consultancy sticking to its guns, but it can easily veer into an implicit threat. The unspoken statement is really: 'Follow our advice and the risk is not yours, go against it and everyone will know it was your choice – if it goes wrong you will pay the penalty.' Great care is needed here, because in some situations this is a legitimate position to take. To me, the difference between an unethical threat and a reasonable statement comes down to intentions. If it is given as a valid warning to the client, then it is ethical. If the threat is given purely to bully the client into purchasing your services, it is not.

Often consultants remain working with a client well after an engagement has really finished. Sometimes they stay beyond the time they are required, without adding value that is commensurate with their fees, simply because the client has not got round to terminating the engagement. If you keep on working beyond the natural end point, you should question whether you are still really offering sufficient value to the client. If you aren't, then move on.

Avoiding client dependency

My fourth ethical concern is client dependency on the consultant. It is quite easy, with some clients, to develop a dependency on your skills. It may be accidental, but it can also be engineered. There is a point on any engagement, whether it is an engagement delivering recommendations, a plan or implemented change, when the question to answer is 'so what should the client do next?' Answering this question is the source of many ethical challenges. A dependency on the consultant can be developed by not providing all the information to enable a client to progress work, so they have to keep coming back to you for more. It can also be through inappropriate advice, for example selling proposals or ideas that are unnecessarily complex relative the client's level of skill and which you know they will need your help to implement.

As so often with ethical issues, there is balance required. A client may legitimately want to retain your skills for a period of time because they continue to add value in various ways. This is the basis of long-term consultant–client relationships. But, this is quite different from the deliberate manipulation of recommendations or plans relative to the client's skills so that they need to retain you – either to interpret the recommendations to plans, or simply because they are written in such a way that you are the only person who can fulfil them.

Handling confidential information

The fifth point on my ethical list relates to the correct use, and avoiding the misuse, of client confidential information. This must be based on a general respect for the confidentiality of data you collect as part of the engagement. This is another complex issue, as clients have to have sensible expectations with respect to information as well. Of course, you cannot take specific data and sell it to your client's competitors. Also consultants should not be secretly collecting data on client sites which then will form part of their consultancy's benchmarking database. But your client hired you because of some specific expertise – expertise you developed at other clients. It is inherent in hiring a consultant that they will learn whilst working for a client, and what they learn will be used on future clients. Consultants should not be embarrassed about this. It is effectively part of the definition of the profession of consultancy. If a client does not like this aspect of consultants, then

> ❝ clients have to have sensible expectations with respect to information ❞

they have a simple commercial decision – there is no compulsion to engage consultants. But there is a significant difference between learning on a client's site and actually walking off with specific client ideas and business information which you use to support selling to or delivering engagements for other clients.

Using fair contracts

The sixth ethical issue boils down to the consulting contract. Clients should know better, but it is easy to fill contracts with all sorts of inappropriate small print. Of course, a client should really have the contract checked (see next page). But the fact that important clauses are hidden in the small print and not explicit in the proposal reflects the suspicion that some consultancies are trying to pull the wool over their client's eyes. I have noticed two areas where I think some consultancies push the boundaries of ethics:

1 *Ownership of intellectual property (IP)*: Many consultancies, including some of the blue chip names, have contractual clauses stating that they own the IP from any consulting engagement. What grates with many clients is that the IP (if there is any) was developed when working with client staff. Ask anyone if they think it is ethical that person A owns the IP for a piece of work they developed in conjunction with person B, when person B paid for all the work. Most people will say no! Yet this is precisely what giving ownership of IP to the consultant means. Of course, consultants may bring IP on to the client site which they should retain ownership of, so it can be difficult to disentangle really original IP arising from an engagement with what the consultant owned before. However, whenever I am employed to choose and manage consultants, I insist that any clause giving the consultant full ownership of IP is taken out or at least renegotiated for shared IP.

2 *Recharging for expenses and supporting activities*: The actual amount charged to a client may significantly exceed the pure consultant time costs. There are expenses on top, sometimes administration fees and all sorts of other fees. Often these fees are reasonable, but sometimes they are completely unreasonable. I have heard of partners in some firms recharging proportions of their club fees to clients. Also some simple administrative support can be very profitable for consultants – for example, photocopying at massively inflated rates, well above the usual commercial rate. I have seen six-figure charges for photocopying.

Conflicts of interest

The final ethical concern relates to conflicts of commercial interest. This is almost turning the ethical problem around, as its root lies with the client. I have come across situations where company directors are simultaneously directors of consultancy companies and lobbying for the use of the consultancy in the business they are a director of. I have come across a senior IT manager pushing the services of an IT consultancy that he had a direct shareholding in. These are clear ethical breaches, and probably fall foul of most organisations' corporate governance regulations. Requiring staff to register such commercial conflicts of interest and penalising rapidly and heavily for breaches is usually sufficient to remove most of these temptations. One possible solution that clients and consultants can adopt is to simply rule that any company the individual works for cannot be provided services by the consultancy they also have a commercial interest in.

I want to end this section on ethical guidelines by looking at it from the opposite perspective. Whilst you have an ethical responsibility as a consultant, the client also has a responsibility to behave in a sensible and competent manner. Clients have lawyers who should read the small print and accept the contract, modify it or suggest a completely different contract. Managers should only ask for appropriate services for their business, and in the end it's their job to buy what their business needs – not only yours to ensure it is right. Managers should review findings, recommendations and plans and ensure they are fit for purpose for their organisation. You are not selling door-to-door products to vulnerable groups. You are selling a professional service to a commercial enterprise, and the working principle of *caveat emptor* (buyer beware) must to some extent hold. (This point is revisited, from the client perspective, in Chapter 14.) However, ethics cannot be shrugged off with the view that the clients are 'big boys' who should know better than to accept unethical practice. As a consultant, you have a clear ethical responsibility to your client.

Application of ethics

Ethics is interesting as a theoretical subject and one for debate with friends over dinner. But what makes ethics real is its impact on the decisions we make and the actions we take. There are two factors which can make the applications of ethics in consulting quite complex:

1   the privileged position of the consultant
2   the lack of clarity over who the client is.

As a consultant you operate in a privileged position of trust. Imagine the scenario of a client you have worked with on and off for many years. A client who values your skills and the way you execute engagements. You are regularly advising the client. You are a *trusted advisor*. As a trusted advisor to the client you face one of the classic moral hazards in business. It is your advice that often leads to you gaining more work. You will know when you are selling on if it is right for your client, and if it is right for you. That is the opportunity to make the right ethical choice. If you do not know, you are not thinking clearly enough, as it is usually obvious. When you legitimately sell on, your interests and those of your client align, and this is a good outcome for both of you. When your interests are not aligned, don't try to sell on.

> when your interests are not aligned, don't try to sell on

The privileged position can run deeper than this. We now enter distinctly muddy waters – and that is whether as a trusted consultant you have a *duty of care* to your client. Technically, duty of care is a legal term referring to the need for professionals to conform to a reasonable standard of care when executing their profession. I do not literally mean a legal duty of care, but the ethical duty of care a consultant has to their client. What is the difference between a commercial duty and a duty of care? To me, your commercial duty is to fulfil the terms of your contract and proposal. A duty of care goes beyond this and means upholding the standards expected of a profession. By duty of care I mean a responsibility actively to ensure your client gets the best advice, irrespective of the precise boundaries of your engagement, and to execute all your work to a high-quality standard. If you have a duty of care you cannot turn a blind eye to anything you think is substandard or inappropriate, irrespective of the scope of your consulting engagement.

There are several dangers once a consultant reasons they have a duty of care. The first is simply that you can get lost flagging a myriad of problems to a client. No business is perfect and there are always hundreds of substandard ways of working. If not, there would never be the possibility of any business improvement. Additionally, the label 'duty of care' is often used spuriously by consultants to barge into all sorts of areas of the business that really have nothing to do with their work. Therefore consider seriously whether you have a duty of care to your client or not. If you do, it is not a stick to beat the client into doing work they would not otherwise accept, but it is a responsibility to work professionally and advise on related matters that you are competent to advise them on.

What about the lack of clarity over who the client is? Throughout this chapter I have considered *the client* as the focus of our ethical considerations. But as I described in earlier chapters, the identification of the client is not a trivial matter. Consultants tend to think of the client as an organisation, but an organisation is an abstract entity. On the other hand, consultants may think of the client as an individual, but the interests of no one individual in an organisation may actually align perfectly with all the interests of the organisation. So, there is the odd situation that an organisation is made up of people, you can only interact with people and judge the organisation's interest from those people, but the organisation's interest may not completely align with any of those people's interest.

Of course, for many engagements we can, in practice, say that there is no ethical dilemma. The scope of the engagement is such that the interest we should consider as described by individuals in the organisation is to all practical purposes the interest of the organisation. But this will not always be true. Consider the following questions:

- If your work leads to someone being made redundant, have you harmed the client? Usually consultants answer no. Often this is right – but thinking about the grounds on which this judgement is made is often not as clear cut as it should be and can be suspiciously abstract.

- Should you go above the individual who engaged you to their boss without their knowledge, to comment on the individual's skills and ability? This sometimes is legitimate and sometimes unethical. Which it is must be determined by assessing the reasons you have for going to the boss and what alternatives are available to you. Generally, it is best to avoid such action except as a last resort.

- Does the engagement you are working on help a senior but incompetent manager to keep their job? At one level, if managers had all the skills required, consultants would not be needed. But if the primary reason for the engagement is to support a person who should not have a job, then this must be regarded as unethical.

- Are you providing advice for the benefit of an individual client manager over the organisation as a whole? This is veering not only into ethical issues, but potentially into straightforward corruption.

■ If the engagement results in recommendations on redundancy or job changes, are you giving unbiased advice, ignoring your commercial interest? You can envisage consultant's advice being biased against staff who oppose or inhibit the consultant's work or ability to win further work. Sometimes, as part of a change activity, people do need to be moved into different roles or removed from an organisation, but this must only be because it is in the organisation's interest. Doing it for the commercial interest of the consultancy is never ethical. I am sure this practice is rare: it is completely unacceptable.

Some consultants avoid the issue of conflicting client interests by saying that they are working for a higher authority; no, not God, but the shareholders' interests. This is just dodging the issue, and is one of the great intellectual evasions of consulting. Generally, a consultant is not engaged by the shareholders. The consultant has probably never spoken to the shareholders and does not understand their interests other than some vague and generic need to increase value in some way or another. Thinking that you are working for the interests of a group of people you have never spoken to, never specifically analysed, and whom you have no relationship with, has to be considered as highly dubious.

So what classifies an engagement as in the interests of the organisation? The answer can only be for you to make a judgement of the situation based on the information that is available to you. Moreover, if you assume that you have a duty of care to the client, you should not only consider the information that is available to you, but also actively seek out the information you require to make the ethical choice.

Ethics can seem a burden, yet can also be an advantage or selling point for consultants. As always with consulting, for every problem there is also a commercial opportunity. Understand the ethical issues and how to make balanced ethical decisions well, and there is an opportunity for ethical consulting as a service in its own right. Many clients face a range of ethical issues which they are not equipped to handle and benefit from consultants to help them along.

> ❝ for every problem there is also a commercial opportunity ❞

Ethics and dilemmas in consulting

So far in this chapter I have described basic ethical guidelines for consultants and considered aspects of being a consultant that must be taken into account when making ethical judgements. This final section goes beyond and looks at situations in which different ethical guidelines are conflicting, or when the consultant faces a conflict between ethics and other considerations.

There are many ambiguous situations when it comes to ethical decisions, where clear thinking and sharp judgement is required. With some dilemmas there may never be a truly satisfactory answer, only the least wrong one. But the ability to make a balanced decision in such situations, whilst not unique to consulting, is a regular part of the challenge of being a successful consultant.

There are three common situations where dilemmas involving ethics arise:

1 balancing the interests of different stakeholders
2 constraints the client puts on the engagement
3 the conflict between commercial interest and ethical guidelines.

Let's look at each of these in turn.

Balancing the interests of different stakeholders

Balancing the interests of different stakeholders, both within the client and also within the consulting organisation, is a very common challenge. We have already discussed the concept of a client as being complex, and that there may be more than one client. When the role of the client is made up of different people, they will often have different interests and hence there is a risk of conflict. Examples where this can cause dilemmas for the consultant are:

- When two (or more) client representatives want different and incompatible things covered in an engagement. Often, different client needs can be catered for in a single engagement, but it is possible that they can conflict irreconcilably.
- If an individual member of a client organisation, who is paying for your work, wants you to do something that is not in their business's interest.

There is no single solution to these sorts of issues, but the answer is to be found by a combination of the following:

- Having a clear primary client who arbitrates and makes decisions when there is a conflict of interest.

■ Not hiding or ignoring the issue of conflict. Be explicit with your client: it is the client's problem and although you can help they must in the end fix it. If you try and ignore or hide a conflict, this may often lead to greater problems, which you are then party to.

■ Negotiating a solution that is acceptable to all parties, involving the different clients in the negotiation. A single meeting bringing the interested parties together is usually the best way to do this.

Finally, if nothing else works and you are left with either an impossible engagement, one in which you will not be perceived to deliver value, or one in which you feel unacceptably ethically compromised, walk away. This may not be easy to do, and I do not underestimate how difficult some clients can be if you say you do not want the work. But you should uphold your own standards.

Constraints the client puts on the engagement

The second type of dilemma which faces consultants is connected to the constraints clients put on engagements. As part of scoping an engagement, or during carrying it out, the client may specify a range of factors which constrain the consultant's freedom to decide how to pursue the engagement. Many of these requirements will be perfectly reasonable. For example, the client may need the work completed within a certain timeframe. Clients will usually have a limited budget and the engagement must be performed for whatever the client can afford. The client may be a busy manager and so may want to limit how much time the consultant can have to work with them. Similarly, clients have limits as to how many people they can allocate to work with consultants. These types of constraints are all part of a normal consulting engagement.

Most clients are reasonable and will negotiate on such constraints and listen to reasoned argument from the consultant. But in the haste to earn money or for an easy life, consultants can sometimes agree to all sorts of conditions which, in reality, are unworkable. Generally, this is a mistake. From a commercial perspective the consultant needs to think through any constraints and decide if it is still possible to complete an engagement and be paid for it profitably. The ethical perspective is different. Even if you can complete the engagement and are paid for it, you must decide at what point is the engagement so constrained that it will add no value to the client? A sensible consultant is only interested in commercially viable engagements. An ethical consultant is only interested in engagements that are of value to the client. It is possible, if sometimes difficult, to be both sensible and ethical.

Experienced consultants can think of many examples of client behaviours which reduce the value the consultant may give. Some clients regularly engage consultants, never listen to the consultant's advice, but still pay the bill. I have no problem with clients who engage, debate and disagree with the consultant's findings – but if the client simply ignores the advice all the time, you are taking money from an organisation for nothing. Another example is that it is not unusual for clients to want findings without giving you enough time to do proper research or analysis. Of course, it is always possible to give some advice on even minimal information. But its validity and value are questionable. Consultants can be tempted to take the risk and provide advice without sufficient information, when in reality the answer should be to decline the work unless sufficient time is allowed for data collection and analysis.

Conflict between commercial interest and ethical guidelines

Throughout this chapter I have looked at examples of the possible conflict between commercial and ethical interests. I would like to complete the chapter by looking at two further conflicts of this kind in a little more detail. The first concerns the sustainability of consulting advice, and the second the application of knowledge from one client to another.

To add value to a client, a consultant must not only create whatever the agreed deliverables are – reports, plans, recommendations and implemented change – but also needs to ensure that the result is helpful to the client. For something to be helpful, it must be usable and appropriate to the client. Additionally, recommendations must be practical and workable in the client's environment. There is no point giving advice which you know will not be possible for the client to achieve. Your aim should not merely be to fulfil the letter of the proposal and deliver whatever you agreed to deliver, but the contents of the deliverables must have a lasting impact on the client.

> " for something to be helpful, it must be usable and appropriate to the client "

Effective consultants base their knowledge on the experience they have gained working in many businesses and many different situations. That is often the reason for engaging a consultant. The client starts by thinking, 'I have a problem of type X, which I do not know how to handle.'

The client then goes on to think, 'I will get help from a consultant who has dealt with problems of type X in many situations.' The ethical problem arises from the issue of understanding when it is appropriate to take knowledge and experience from one client and apply it to another. If you are a public sector consultant, there is probably no ethical issue, but as a consultant advising clients in the commercial field, there is. Is it ethical to help multiple clients by taking the knowledge from one business and selling it to their competitors? Even if we exclude directly sharing current business data, the consultant still has an ethical dilemma. Management approaches, business processes and other intangibles are the source of most competitive edge in business, but these things are the very currency of consulting.

One possible ethical line to take is to avoid working with direct competitors, at least in areas of the business that provide competitive differentiation. If you work for company A, you will not work for their main competitor, company B. This may be fine if you are a sole trader who has a much larger list of possible clients than capacity to do work, but this is impractical for a major consulting firm with tens of thousands of staff. The big firms, simply because of their scale, must at times work for direct competitors. In some industries there are fewer and fewer major players. To survive as a specialist consultant, you are bound at times to provide services to competing organisations.

An answer may be to challenge the validity of massive consultancies providing services to competing businesses. If you are so big that you must provide services to competitors, perhaps you really are too big to maintain a clean bill of ethical health. I think this is a valid challenge, but I know it is impractical. The huge services firms are here to stay. A more realistic answer is the concept of a *Chinese wall*. A Chinese wall is the term used for an internal division within a business in which certain information may not pass. Individuals working on one side of the Chinese wall may not work on the other. Companies such as financial services and auditors, where information from competitors or information about possible market sensitive changes are handled, use Chinese walls all the time. I applaud the concept. In practice, I am cynical about how strong such walls really are.

I think the solution must lie in an open dialogue with the client. If the client challenges you, you should commit to keeping their real secrets secret, but you must also be open to the fact that sometime you are likely to work for a competitor. That is just the way the world is and the nature of consulting. If the client expects you to bring direct experience of competitors, then they have no ethical grounds for complaining if you share your ever-growing experience with their competitors as well. If a client wants you to guarantee your experience is never used elsewhere, you need some guarantee from them as to an ongoing income stream!

Summary

Ethics provides you with an understanding of what you should and should not do, and how you can achieve good and avoid harm.

■ There are a range of situations in which consultants have the opportunity to do good, and conversely there are situations in which consultants can be strongly tempted to undertake activities which are in their interests but which do harm to their clients.

■ Each situation is unique and a range of factors must be considered before deciding what the most ethical approach to take is. However, making ethical decisions is a central part of being a good and client-centric consultant.

■ Ethics is a complex matter for consultants because of the privileged position they occupy with a client, but also because the needs of different stakeholders may be very varied and yet must be addressed.

The language of consulting

anguage is the main tool of the consultant. Quite simply, the way you talk, present and write will determine how successful you are as a consultant. The language you choose tells a listener a lot about you and indicates how client-centric you are. Great consulting communication is all about clarity of thought and an ability to express things in ways that are meaningful to your clients.

Everyone wants to and must communicate, as it is an integral part of everyday life. We use language all the time, often without thinking about it. Language is the mechanism for interaction between people, and consultancy is concerned primarily with interaction. Some professions can get away without needing to worry too much about the finer points of communication. If you are making a physical product, it is the product that matters, not how you talk when you are doing your work on a production line. Consultancy is different. The product is often just words, in the form of reports and presentations. Even when a consultant is employed to manage change, a significant part of the management of change is how you influence and direct people using language.

Great communication skills will enhance any consultancy. Although it should not be encouraged, even relatively weak sets of recommendations or engagement proposals can convince clients if they are well presented. Conversely, poor use of language can destroy the best consulting opportunities. It is of no use at all being the world's greatest subject matter expert, if you cannot share and explain what you know. The most successful consultants are not necessarily the best experts, but they are the most capable of effectively imparting what expertise they have and influencing others.

Communication is central to everything the consultant does. Whether it is understanding a client's issues, collecting information, developing reports or feeding back to a client, these are all activities which are based on communicating. Consultancy is a business that is dependent on relationships, and what and how you communicate will determine the relationships you build. Communication is vital to sharing ideas, developing consensus, challenging assumptions and influencing people – all tasks essential to consulting.

Obviously, a consultant must be able to write and to present. The fundamental capability to put pen to paper or use a word processor is rarely a problem for consultants. But consultants suffer from the same issues that dog many aspects of business communications. Unfortunately, whilst there are some exceptions, business speakers and business writers on the whole are not models of brilliant communication. Business language can be dull, it often utilises clichés and relies on jargon. It suffers from too much output and not enough listening, and it regularly results in miscommunication and ambiguity.

Not everyone is a natural orator or a gifted writer, but whilst those talents will undoubtedly help, they are not necessary. Speaking, writing, presenting and listening skills can be learnt and improved, and a few simple concepts can help to enhance the capabilities of most consultants. This chapter provides some pointers to improving your communication skills. It describes what communication is, and suggests a simple way for you to plan and execute your communication. It also discusses one of the central but underestimated language tools of the consultant – asking questions. Finally, the chapter looks at some of the traps in using language that consultants should avoid.

> **❝ not everyone is a natural orator or a gifted writer ❞**

Communication

What is communication? This is a surprisingly hard question to answer in a way that everyone will agree to. Communication is one of those concepts that we all intuitively grasp, but struggle to give succinct and meaningful definitions of. The problem this poses is that if we cannot easily define the concept, we cannot be sure we all share the same meaning.

Essentially, communication is the transmission of information from one person to another. This definition is typical, reasonable and technically correct, but it is not enlightening and I think it misses two of the most important points. The first is that communication is a goal-directed activity. We communicate for a reason. When you think about this, it is obvious. But it is a point often forgotten. One of the reasons communications fail is because the speaker or writer is not clearly conscious of or focused enough on the desired goal. Secondly, communications should be something you take pleasure in. What makes the great speakers and authors great is that they enjoy using language. Yes, they are adept with all the tools of communication, and, yes, they are aware of the goal they are trying to achieve, but at the same time they delight in the act of communication. This seems all too often to be forgotten in business.

There are a host of different ways to communicate. Most obviously there are the written and spoken word, but within these categories there are a range of communication skills to be applied. Ways of using language include: asserting, explaining, recommending, questioning, answering, reinforcing, summarising and reflecting. Communication has specialised techniques, such as negotiating, persuading, asserting, confronting and developing relationships. Some activities, like training, facilitating and interviewing, are essentially applications of communication. Critically, communication is a two-way process, and a key part of all interaction is listening, which is especially important to consultants. Although this chapter focuses on language, communication is not just about words – body language, gestures, tone, pace and so on are all essential components of how well you communicate. Individuals tend to have biases to some forms of communication rather than others. As a consultant, it is helpful to develop the ability to use the full range of communication skills.

Each of these aspects of communication is the subject of many books. Consultants tend to be practical people and focus on improved communication via presentation or writing skills courses. It is worth making the effort to understand even a modicum of the academic theory of communication (e.g. Hargie, see page 279), as this can be enlightening and give many ideas on how to improve your communication skills.

A consultant working in a professional domain is primarily interested in being effective. Hence, if you understand what communication is, the next helpful question is: what is effective professional communication? When asked to describe what makes good communication, it is common to use criteria, usually expressed as adjectives, such as clear, lucid, intelligible, absorbing, accurate, coherent, informative or enjoyable. It is certainly worth thinking about such criteria, but I believe that effective professional communication can be defined in terms of two statements. Effective communication:

▦ is carried out to meet understood objective(s)
▦ achieves its objective(s).

As consultants our most important goal is to communicate effectively and this is the emphasis of this chapter. However, it is worth bearing in mind what the difference between effective and excellent communication is. Being effective is good enough, but understanding what excellent communications are gives you something to aspire to. What I think separates excellent from merely effective communication, is that excellent communication:

▦ is pleasurable or engaging for both the speaker (writer) and listener (reader).

Not everyone is or will become excellent at communication, but irrespective of how well you use language, you can improve your speaking and writing skills. Improving communication skills requires that you actively seek feedback, which at times can be painful, and that you learn from the feedback. My first consulting report was thrown back to me across a desk by a partner in Coopers & Lybrand, covered in a mess of red ink and exasperated comments. Excruciating as that experience and others were, the feedback was valuable and worked. I now have several books published, each of which has sold thousands of copies, and have been translated into multiple languages. Yet I am still aware of how much I have to learn and I seek feedback on written materials and presentations all the time. Partially this is to improve the individual document or presentation, but more importantly it is to continue to improve the effectiveness of all my communications.

Planning and executing communications

To explain how to improve your communication skills I am going to use a simple model of communication. There are many more complex models, which are useful for discussing specific aspects of communication or understanding detailed mechanics. But I want to use a model which is easy to understand, practical and useful to consultants. The model I am going to use is the *communication wheel*. This is a model I

❝ the model needs to be interpreted flexibly ❞ developed some years ago when working with groups of experts to help them think about and achieve better communications, and to help them avoid some communications blunders typical of their professions. As with all simplifications, the model has some flaws, and needs to be interpreted flexibly and with the application of a little common sense. But I have found it a very effective way to help people improve their communications.

This model is shown in Figure 11.1. In this section, I will briefly explain each part of the model, to enable you to identify any areas of weakness and to focus on enhancing them.

The model has several features. Firstly it is shown as a circle (or wheel), which represents the fact that any single act of communication may result in further communications. Communication is an ongoing process, each interaction can encourage further interactions, and this is the basis of dialogue. The model has an outer wheel and a central hub. The outer wheel is concerned with transmitting information, but communication is a two-way process: as well as transmitting you receive or listen. The importance of listening is indicated by its position as the hub of the communication wheel. The outer wheel has six steps, each of which I will briefly discuss

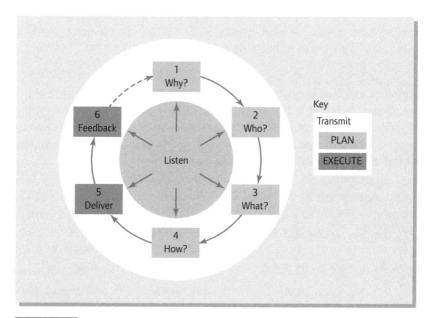

Figure 11.1 The communication wheel

below. The first four steps are about planning communication, and the last two are about executing communication. The model can be applied to all sorts of communications that consultants are involved in, whether presenting, speaking in a meeting or writing a report. This model can be used to help improve formal communications, but it can also help with the most informal of conversations.

Let's briefly explore each of the steps.

1 Why?

The first step in communicating is to be clear about why you are doing it. Communication is a goal-directed activity, and unless you are clear about the goal you will not successfully communicate. Yet all too often we start conversations, write documents or develop presentations without being absolutely clear about why we are doing this. In the process of consulting there are often many goals that each communication must achieve and this can result in messy and confusing interactions with clients.

Occasionally, the goal of communication is to share some information, but more often as a consultant it is more complex than this. You communicate to persuade a client to take action, to have decisions made, to gain support or consensus, or perhaps to impress a client. Providing information when, for example, your goal is to influence a client to take an action, may not be enough. Unless your design your communication around your goal, it is unlikely to succeed.

With the spoken word, goals are dynamic and can change as a dialogue unfolds. A skilled speaker is adept at modifying goals as a conversation continues. However, it is best to be consciously monitoring where a conversation is going compared to the initial goals. Sometimes a change in goals is a correct response to additional information that becomes apparent during a conversation. Often, especially in intense or heated conversations, we accidentally lose sight of our initial goal and start just responding to each individual part of a dialogue. Everyone finds that sometimes they start a discussion and part way through think 'where is this going?', having lost track of what it is all about and what outcome they want. Journalists and politicians are adept at deliberately making their interlocutors lose track of the objective of the dialogue.

The starting point for all communications should be to understand what the goal is. You can understand this by asking yourself questions, such as:

- What are you trying to achieve?
- What do you want to be different when you have communicated?
- How will you know this has been achieved?
- What next steps do you want to get from this interaction?
- If there are several goals, are they compatible and are any more important than others?

If you cannot answer these sorts of questions, do not be surprised if your communication is ineffective.

2 Who?

Communications must be appropriate to the person or group being communicated to and in the style they prefer. This person or group is your audience. Effective communication is meaningful and appealing, from the audience's viewpoint. Client-centric consultants always seek to communicate in the most appropriate way for a specific audience. This means that you must be prepared to tailor whatever you want to say to the audience, and the same point may need to be said in different ways to different audiences. It is important to remember always that you are not communicating to yourself. Fine words that you like are worthless unless your audience likes them too. You must use terminology that is meaningful and appealing to your audience, as it is only what makes sense to your audience that matters.

> ❝ it is only what makes sense to your audience that matters ❞

There are many factors that need to be considered when thinking about audiences. What are their media preferences:

- Do they prefer the spoken or written word?
- Is there any specific terminology that should be used or avoided?
- What style of communication do they like?
- Do they prefer the big picture or details?
- Do they respond best to facts or emotions?
- Do they like ideas that are action-orientated, or do they favour more conceptual information that makes them think?

The better you understand your client's communication preferences, the more likely you will be able to influence them.

However, as you tailor your approach to your audience don't lose sight of *why* you are communicating. There is a risk that you can forget what you want to achieve, in delving too deeply into how people like to be communicated with.

Many people wanting to improve their communication skills will focus on their language and use of words. For a consultant, a far better and often simpler way to improve communication skills is to think more clearly about these first two steps of the communication wheel. Simply by having clarity over why you are communicating, and by understanding who your audience is and what their communication preferences are, you will significantly improve the effectiveness of your communications. If you focus on these two points alone you may never become a great or memorable speaker, but you will be effective and sufficiently influential for consultancy needs. Everything else is finesse, these are the fundamentals.

3 What?

The next stage of the communication wheel is about developing the specific messages you want to communicate. What are the points you need to get across that will help you to achieve your communication goal? This is a step worth being patient about starting. We are all tempted to jump into the action of writing documents or creating presentations. My advice is to hesitate a little. Do not work out your messages before you know why you are communicating and to whom. A message is only relevant when you know who you are communicating with. If you do not know what you want to achieve and who you will be influencing to achieve this, then there is little point in working out messages.

Effective professional communication is simple and concise. What you communicate should be made up of a central message, any supporting messages that reinforce the central message, and key information that verifies these messages or helps them to be understood. This information should be at an appropriate level of detail for the intended audience. There can be a temptation to write lots to try and impress. In reality, the most powerful information is concise. Everything that does not contribute to the central message of a report or presentation should be discarded. A well-written and concise document is of far greater value to your clients than an elongated and rambling tome.

However, whilst brevity is to be preferred, a coherent communication is more than a set of messages strung together. Any communication must include appropriate levels of context and scene setting. This depends on the audience and their familiarity with the subject. Critically, any communication, whether it is spoken or written, needs to have a logical and understandable structure to aid comprehension. This means some of the words in any communication are not about transmitting the messages you want transmitted, but will be information related to the process of communication and understanding. This includes explanations of what is being communicated, such as 'I am now going to talk about ...', or signposts to the structure of communication, such as 'once I have completed the introduction I will ...'.

The ordering of messages is important to enhance impact and influence your client's reactions. To improve the structuring of your messages you can use the classic consulting approach of Minto's pyramid principle. It is an excellent way of structuring your thinking, and if you are unfamiliar with it I recommend investing some time in reading up on it. I am also a great fan of mind maps, which can help in structuring very diverse information. (For both topics, see the references on page 280.) It is interesting to note that both the pyramid principle and mind maps are primarily about structuring thinking, which can then be applied to how you write or present. They are not purely writing techniques. This point underlies the principle that it is clarity of thought that makes great professional communication, not a huge vocabulary, understanding of grammar and syntax, or ability to drone on and on.

Finally, words are not the only form of communication. When speaking you must consider your body language, as well as your dress and appearance. There are also factors like pitch, tone, speed, volume, pauses and so on to get right. For the written word, characteristics like document format, layout, font, colour, tone, style, as well as the use of visual aids, all have a direct influence on the effectiveness of your communication.

4 How?

The final part of planning your communication is to determine how you will communicate. What media will you use? Will you communicate formally or informally? There are many factors to consider, including audience preferences, but also what is most appropriate for the situation. For instance, very sensitive information must be transmitted in a different way than general information relevant to all members of an organisation.

An important consideration is the timing and level of repetition of communications. Timing is crucial to effective communication. Simply, there are good and bad times to communicate. You should also bear in mind that messages, especially if they are complex or radical, can take several attempts to be heard and understood. What this means is that important messages should be repeated consistently and often in different media. Anyone who has worked with clients on change programmes knows the importance of frequent, repetitive and consistent communication.

❝ important messages should be repeated consistently and often in different media ❞

Communicating once is never enough for any important messages in an organisation. If you ever feel tempted to say 'but I told you that', then probably you have not communicated a message enough times.

Some messages take time to sink in and people need the opportunity to discuss and challenge. Without the ability to explore and challenge information, people are less likely to understand or accept it. Hence, when planning how you will communicate, make sure there is an opportunity for your clients to question and discuss anything you propose or recommend.

Having thought about why, what and how, a good test of any communication materials you have developed or conversations you have planned is to ask yourself 'so what?' If you communicate what you plan to communicate in the way you plan to do it, what will it achieve? If you cannot answer the question 'so what?', then it is likely that the communication will be ineffective.

5 Deliver!

If you are clear about why you are communicating, and who you are communicating with, have designed a concise and effective set of messages, and have developed appropriate materials to be delivered at the appropriate times – you will effectively communicate. You never know how your audience will respond until you have communicated, but the better prepared you are, the more likely you are to succeed.

In reality, you do not always have time to think through every aspect of every communication. Some client conversations just happen without time to think through how you should respond. There is no easy answer to this, other than the points that I have described will work for all types of professional communication. If you practise them, they will become automatic, subconscious and fast enough to use in the most unexpected of situations.

6 Feedback

You never know if you have successfully communicated until you have feedback from your audience. The more prepared, the greater the likelihood of success, but you must not assume you have achieved your communication objectives until you have a definite response from your audience.

Ideally, this response is formal feedback or directly checking your audience's understanding of what you have said. Often this is not possible or appropriate and you have to look for more subtle clues, such as body language and behaviour following your communication. What you are seeking is to determine whether your messages were understood and whether they were accepted. Most of all you should be seeking to determine if you will achieve the goal that your communication originally set out to achieve. Client behaviour is the most important element of feedback. Normally, you communicate to generate some form of response in your client – if you do not get this response then the communication has failed.

Feedback is also essential for improving your own communication skills. If you never get any feedback, all you have is your own opinion on how well you communicate, which is liable to be wrong. It is amazing how many people assume they are good speakers or writers, but do not seek feedback. Without feedback, an assessment of how well you communicate is just that – an assumption.

7 Listening

As a consultant you will have a significant amount of information to disseminate. You will want to share ideas, explore concepts, influence and guide clients. To achieve these you will be writing and speaking, but to be able to transmit relevant information you must start by gathering information. This is done by listening. Listening is one of the most underestimated skills, and one we generally spend least effort to improve, and yet people who listen well are at a significant advantage to those who do not, especially in a profession like consulting. As an example of this, often in client sales meetings we are so engrossed in making our sale that we miss comments from the client which indicate what they really want, and hence lose the sale. Always listen.

In terms of the communication wheel I use listening as a generic word for all ways of receiving information, including hearing, reading and observation. Irrespective of how you listen, having information enables you to moderate your ideas and behaviour.

Listening is not only essential to gathering information. Listening is an important part of developing relationships and of encouraging people to listen to you. People rarely form relationships with other individuals who do not listen to them. People are less inclined to listen to anyone who will not listen to them.

It is common to assume that listening is automatic. It is not. Hearing sounds and seeing writing on the page is automatic. Listening is not merely the use of your senses, it is a mental activity. Your brain is not a passive recipient of stimuli – it interprets and filters, often subconsciously. Hence, listening is not foolproof – you will filter out information, your concentration will lapse and at times you will be distracted. Even if you physically receive information, it does not mean you have actually taken it in. This is one reason why you should seek feedback and test understanding after communicating – to make sure the information was taken in, and was interpreted in the way intended. If you are the listener, and it is important that you understand, you can check your understanding by summarising or reflecting back to speakers. A response in the form 'let me just summarise what I heard ... is that correct' is a powerful way to check your listening.

> **" you brain is not a passive recipient of stimuli "**

The guidelines for listening are:

- concentrate on listening
- don't listen by accident
- seek to improve your listening skills.

Whenever you need to take in information, be conscious of your physical and mental state and try to overcome feelings or office environmental factors which are stopping you listen. Never be afraid, for example, to halt a meeting to resolve an irritating noise that is stopping people listening. Also, try to learn about your own listening biases. This can be hard, but is very revealing. What sorts of information do you find easier to take in and what do you struggle with? What are your limits? If you can only read in 15-minute bursts, there is no point scanning your eyes across text for hours at a time. What sort of information do you find easy to absorb, and what takes more effort?

If you only listen to the words, you will only gain a partial understanding of other people's viewpoints. There are many important areas for observation in any conversation. What are the speaker's eyes, body language and gestures saying? Is there any fidgeting and activities not related to conversation – do they indicate anything? When you are listening in a group, observe the positioning or seating arrangements, and the level of interaction between people in conversation. But don't listen just to the content or just interpret the body language! You need both. Also, whilst we all have an innate capability to interpret body language to some extent, care is needed with the interpretation: it is subjective and culturally specific. Try to look for clues that information is or is not being accepted, and if it is not obvious, seek feedback by asking questions like 'does everyone accept this ...?' or even better actually test understanding by asking more specific questions. Unfortunately, this is not always possible.

All aspects of communication are interrelated. Every time you communicate, you need a listener. Help them to listen by communicating in a way that will make it easy for them to follow what you say. This is partially about being clear and engaging, but it is also about removing any obstacles that stop them listen. Conversely, every time you listen, your response has an effect on the person you are listening to. If you really want to understand what someone has to say, listen in a way that encourages them to be open with you.

Questioning

There are many aspects of communications I could have written about in this chapter, but there is one I am going to focus on a little more and that is questioning. A consultant must be competent at writing reports, developing and giving presentations, and in general conversation with clients. If you are not, you need to develop those skills quickly, and there are a myriad of books and courses on these topics. The precise communication needs will depend on the type of consulting you undertake and the preferences of your client base – but you will always ask questions whilst engaging with a client. However, questioning skills vary greatly between consultants, and rarely is a competency in asking questions set as a criterion for being a consultant. It should be.

Simplistically, you can think of a question as a request for information. But questions perform a much wider role in our conversations than this. Posing questions shows interest and is therefore important as part of relationship building. The questions you ask reflect the way you think, and hence will influence how clients judge you. There are usually multiple ways of requesting information, and the precise way you do it, and the clarity and style of question, mirrors your thinking. Questions can also lead or influence another person's thinking, although this also depends on how the question is asked as well as the words used. Depending on the tone and where the emphasis is placed, a simple question like 'why did you do that?' can be interpreted as showing real interest and request for information, as an indication of disagreement or as a reprimand.

The precise wording of questions is important. Compare two similar questions, such as 'do you like working in this department?' versus 'what do you like about working in this department?' It is easy to mean to ask one of these, but actually to ask the other. The type of response and the information it contains may be very different.

There are many types of questions, and as a consultant you should consider the best way to find out whatever it is you are seeking out to find out. Common types of questions are:

- *Closed questions*: These are used when you want simple yes/no answers or factual information. Examples include: 'have you finished?' or 'how long have you been on the project team?' Such questions do not encourage the speaker to open up, merely to answer the question. If you are struggling to get a dialogue going with a client, it may be that you are asking too many closed questions.

- *Fact finding*: These are more detailed closed questions. You may get a longer answer, but you still are trying to find out facts. For example: 'what is your exact role in the department?'

- *Open or exploratory questions*: These are used to encourage dialogue and to find out opinions. For instance: 'how do you see the strategy progressing?' Open questions are powerful and helpful for relationship building. However, they are less useful if what you really want are specific facts or you want to end a conversation.

- *Follow-up questions*: These are used to probe further once an initial question has been asked. Consider: 'how does that link to the other team members?'

- *Prompts*: These are simple statement to encourage the speaker to provide more information. A typical example is to ask something like 'and then?' They almost sound too simple, but can be very helpful in keeping a conversation going and continuing to show interest in the speaker's words. If a speaker clams up, a few friendly prompts can encourage them to keep going.

◼ *Leading or loaded questions*: These are questions asked when the questioner already has an opinion and is seeking to lead the person being questioned to share the same opinion. They are not really about gathering information at all. Examples might include: 'don't you agree that the project is badly run?' or 'what do you think of John, isn't he a brilliant manager?' Consultants should use such questions sparingly, if at all. They will bias the information you gather, and clients often see through them and may perceive you as prejudiced if you use them too often. Inexperienced interviewers often ask leading questions, and effectively tell the person they are interviewing what they want to hear.

◼ *Confrontational questions* (as loved by journalists and sometimes politicians): These are directed to gain an emotional response. For instance: 'why don't you just fire him?' or 'why on earth did you do that?' As much as the wording, confrontational questions depend on the tone they are asked in. Consultants should usually avoid confrontational questions where possible, but it is easy to ask one when you are surprised by a client's response to a previous question.

Consultants should take care in phrasing questions, and in using the most appropriate type of question. The tone, pace and speed of questioning are also critical. In the haste to get information, it is easy to start firing off lots of questions without giving someone a chance to answer them. If you want information, ask one question at a time and leave time to listen to responses. On the other hand, firing lots of questions at once can be used as a deliberate technique to confuse people. Stakeholders who oppose your work or want to be difficult may sometimes use this technique. As a consultant you should avoid it.

Consultants should base advice and decisions on facts and concrete observations, and a key source of this is questioning. In Chapter 6 I described how you need both qualitative and quantitative data. Even with qualitative data you should seek to be precise. Precision comes from the type of questions you ask, and assessing whether the answers given are precise enough. Probe with questions like 'when?', 'who?', 'precisely in what situation?' General statements, like 'the culture is the problem' or 'department X does not help', need to be turned into concrete specifics.

Questioning is such a standard part of everyday conversation that it is taken for granted. Take the time to think about your questions, and if you do not get the type of response or level of interaction you expected then think about what in your question prompted the response you did get. Improving questioning skills will pay dividends to all consultants.

The consultant's traps: jargon, misuse of words and the ambiguity of language

If you want to excel with communications as a consultant, there are three traps to avoid. These hazards are not unique to consulting, but are prevalent within the profession. They are all related, yet slightly different aspects of using language. Each of them can be an accidental hazard, but may sometimes be deliberately used by consultants. The three traps are:

- using jargon
- misusing common terminology
- miscommunicating as a result of the ambiguity and subjectivity of language.

Jargon

Jargon pervades the business world, and consulting is a profession that wallows in it. Consultants seem to love inventing and using jargon. It is a habit that should be discouraged. There are a number of reasons consultants use jargon. Four of the most common seem to be:

1   it is an efficient shorthand

2   a consultant is trying to impress a client with their cleverness

3   a consultancy is trying to give an impression of novelty or uniqueness to a service line or intellectual capital by branding it with unusual words

4   a consultant does not understand and is trying to cover up.

Jargon can be excused when it is used as an efficient shorthand that an audience all understands and is comfortable with. Jargon often encapsulates complex concepts within a single phrase, and hence provides an efficient way to communicate. The problem is that not everyone understands the phrase in its context as jargon, and so when it is used the listener may be left in the dark or completely misunderstand. When a consultant is talking with other consulting colleagues then arguably they can use whatever jargon they like. Generally, jargon is acceptable when it is used between two people of equal technical expertise, or similar cultural or organisational background. However, using jargon is a habit, and the more it is used the more difficult it is to talk without using it or even recognising the fact that your vocabulary is littered with jargon.

Consulting and business jargon are interwoven, and fads in business generally result in new jargon with consultants. Examples of some of the more hideous pieces of consulting jargon I have come across include: *paradigm shift, archaeology of data, control architecture* and *integrated talent management.* To the user, such phrases may be an important part of their language and their way of thinking. But there are usually simpler alternatives, and in using jargon a consultant fails to remember or consider the client's perspective. Some readers may not regard these phrases as bad jargon, which stresses the point that what is and is not acceptable jargon is in the mind of the listener. As a consultant, you want to speak in the language that most appeals to your listener.

Even relatively common words from certain specialisations may appear as jargon to clients. For example, consulting project managers regularly get excited about the difference between *project* and *programme managers* and may be upset if they are referred to by the wrong title. Clients rarely care about the difference. Whilst clients are perfectly capable of understanding these words, an obsession with precise terminology can be a barrier and shows a lack of empathy with clients. IT consultants often talk about architectures, as in *process architecture, systems architecture* and *data architecture.* These are helpful concepts in the context of a discussion between knowledgeable participants, but can baffle the uninitiated, and even between experts can mean different things. Likewise, common business terms such as *stakeholder* may not be the everyday language of some clients.

Complex or obscure words are often used by some consultants as a way to impress clients, or to give an impression of some new thinking. Often this thinking is just the repackaging of old ideas. A classic example of this is the word *transformation* instead of *change.* Initially, the word transformation was meant to indicate a particularly radical change, but increasingly it is used by consultants to refer to almost any change.

> ❝a real skill is to explain complex ideas in everyday language❞

In truth, few clients are impressed with 'consulting speak'. Clients may be frightened by jargon into buying your services, but this will not be the basis of a long-term relationship. Obscure jargon may occasionally impress, but more often it puts people off and shows your inability to understand the client. A real skill is to explain complex ideas in everyday language. It is always better to explain complex issues in everyday language than to show off and use words which other people do not understand. Jargon increases the risk of misunderstanding and ambiguity, which may come back to bite you. Jargon is especially unwelcome when it is used to hold clients deliberately at a distance from a real understanding of advice being given, or to exert power over the clients.

Sometimes clients become accomplices in this problem by accepting jargon. It is the responsibility of everyone to question unknown terminology – either to improve understanding or to expose nonsense. But everyone has sometimes silently listened to unfamiliar jargon, perhaps too embarrassed to raise the 'what does that mean?' question when someone uses a term that is not understood by all. Jargon can enable an authoritarian yet, in reality, vacuous speaker to get away with a lack of content. Rather than seeing the speaker's vacuousness, clients occasionally end up impressed. The fact that this can work, does not mean it is an approach you should follow. Client-centric consultants never want to position themselves in this way.

A good test for someone who claims to be an expert is to ask them to define a piece of terminology they use regularly. Even common business phrases like *change management* will stump some people, and this is a sign of a lack of real understanding.

Consulting jargon should be avoided with clients. Use clear and straightforward language in a client-friendly manner. A client-centric consultant always avoids pointless jargon. All terminology should be meaningful to the audience you are talking to. The only jargon a client-centric consultant uses is the client's own jargon. One sign of a strong affinity with a client is when you adopt the client's language. As a consultant you will jump from business to business and each one has its own jargon. When you first work in a new organisation, that organisation's jargon may inhibit your own understanding, but competent consultants are never afraid to ask 'what does that mean?' and actively seek to pick up local jargon and linguistically blend into the organisation.

As a consultant your role is to educate, improve, help, facilitate and make change. Hence, obscure consulting jargon is particularly inexcusable for the management consultant, as communication is your core tool in achieving this role.

Misuse of common terminology

Somewhat similar to jargon is the misuse of what are actually useful words and phrases. I am not talking about the language pedants who will decry someone who writes 'practice' or 'stationary' when they should have written 'practise' or 'stationery'. These may be mistakes, but they do not seem to diminish communication. What I want to focus on is the misuse of words and phrases that block communication and, worse still, inhibit clear thinking.

This is best shown with a few examples.

Examples

The words *opinion* and a *finding* are often confused. As a consultant, when you say 'in my opinion', you are giving a personal opinion, which may or may not have some basis in fact but will be supported generally by your expertise. On the other hand, a finding is a conclusion drawn from a sufficiently relevant sample of data. If you present opinions as findings you are misleading your client. A client has every right to conclude that something which you present as a finding has an evidence base and to ask to see the evidence.

Another classic example of misuse of language in my experience is the phrase *best practice*. Consultants regularly claim to be presenting something as best practice. Clients and other consultants often accept things as best practice. This should always be questioned. Who has decided or determined it is best practice? Occasionally it is best practice, but more often it is simply standard or accepted practice that has become prevalent over time for lack of an obvious alternative. Confusing best practice with standard practice is just lazy thinking. This is an example where the misuse of the phrase not only miscommunicates to the listener, but also often reflects weakness in the speaker's thought. There is a risk that calling something best practice is not based on an attempt to make an approach sound good to a client, but is actually believed by the consultant to be best practice.

Similarly, when a consultant talks about helping a client with *change* this can mean many different things. It could be about the identification of change, the planning and preparation for change, the implementation of change, or making the change sustained. If you use the term without specifying which you mean, you and the client may form very different impressions, which will lead to longer-term difficulties.

I enjoy the flexibility of language, and understand that language is dynamic and ever modifying. I accept that old familiar words will gain new uses, which I may not like, and that new words, which I don't understand, will come into common usage. But as a consultant you need to ensure that you are communicating what you seek to communicate. Be precise in your terminology. When you use phrases which in themselves make claims, such as best practice, make sure you are using the phrase when it is appropriate to do so.

Ambiguity of language

I want to end this section with a very short point about the inherent ambiguity and indeterminacy of language. A language like English is extremely powerful and flexible. However, language is inherently indeterminate, and its flexibility makes the indeterminacy greater. By indeterminate I mean that there can never be absolute certainty that a group of people sharing a conversation are talking about the same things.

To minimise problems with language, always strive for clarity. Unless you are working with people of a very similar background, avoid jargon and use words correctly. Challenge the word or phrase where you think its application is inappropriate. But even when you have used the best phrased wording, you must accept that your listener or reader may not have understood you in the way you intended. You must always avoid assuming that someone has understood you, or that you have understood someone else.

Ideally, you should always check understanding. There are situations in which you can only say something once, but as a consultant you generally have an opportunity to enter into dialogue with your clients. When you have presented important findings or made key recommendations, test that your client has understood. This should be part of your ongoing discussions with them.

Summary

Language is the central tool of the consultant, and the way you talk, present and write will determine how successful you are as a consultant. The key points to remember are:

- Communication is a goal-directed activity; therefore always start by being clear about why you are communicating and what you want to achieve. Effective communication:
  - is carried out to meet understood objective(s)
  - achieves its objective(s).

- Once you understand why you are communicating, think about who you are communicating to. Messages must be said in the most appropriate way for an individual audience, avoiding jargon and misuse of terminology. This means the same message must be said in different ways to different audiences.

- Having communicated, you should always seek feedback, even if it is only observing the body language or behaviour of your audience. Without feedback, you will not know if your communication has achieved its goals.

- Listening and questioning are core skills for all consultants, and consultants should seek to improve both the effectiveness of their listening and their questioning skills.

12

Knowing when to say no

In the preceding chapters I explored various ways to make consultancy an effective and commercially viable business. With the exception of Chapter 10, this has been a largely positive outlook on how to be a successful consultant. But success does not only come down to executing your work in the best way, it is also about choosing the right work, and part of choosing the right work is understanding which engagements to reject. This chapter explores when you should say no to an opportunity.

Delivering consultancy is a partnership with a client. A partnership is a relationship both parties voluntarily select to enter. Clients do not just choose us, we choose our clients. Of course, there is always a commercial reality. Sometimes you can pick and choose, but everyone needs to earn an income, and you cannot always be overly selective in your work. However, you do not *have* to accept any work, and some engagements you should not accept. Generally, you should be seeking to have a sufficient pipeline of work that you can focus on the engagements you want, rather than having to accept anything that comes your way. You should target the most attractive engagements, and filter out the ones you do not want. My experience is that consultants deliver the best quality results when they feel they have a choice over what work they do.

This chapter firstly explores what opportunities you should reject as a consultant, and why. Then it describes at which stage in an engagement process you should say no to an opportunity, and looks at the tell-tale signs that should ring alarm bells about an engagement. Finally, there are a few pointers on how to say no to clients.

What can you say no to?

It may seem that in rejecting a possible engagement all you are doing is declining an individual piece of work and hence losing the opportunity to earn the fees associated with the engagement. The truth is somewhat more complex. For instance, it is usually not sensible to pursue engagements which are not commercially viable for you, but, on the other hand, consulting is a business based on relationships, and every time you say no there is a risk you damage the relationships you have.

The best place to start is by considering what you are actually saying no to when you say no. There are multiple reasons for saying no and multiple things a consultant can say no to. There are many scenarios that can be imagined, but the most common possibilities include:

■ rejecting an individual engagement because you are unavailable, do not have the right skills or the terms are unattractive

■ rejecting an individual engagement because of the approach a client insists on

■ declining an opportunity for a subsequent engagement

■ avoiding a client organisation totally

■ choosing not to work with an individual manager within a client organisation.

Let's look briefly at each one of these, and the potential benefits and risks associated with them. Later in the chapter I will look at how to diminish the risks. In general terms, the risks are all avoidable if you position your reason for rejecting the work well enough. However, clients' responses and interpretations of your actions are not always predictable and care is needed to tailor your justifications to the situation.

Rejection owing to availability, etc.

In saying no to an individual engagement the consultant is effectively saying: 'I am happy to work for you, but I am not willing to do this specific piece of work.' The benefits of this depend on why you chose to reject the opportunity. However, in rejecting a piece of work you are inadvertently exposing yourself to certain risks. A client may well respect your decision, but there is a real chance it will irritate them. Think of your own likely response:

> ❝ declining work may be interpreted as rejecting a client altogether ❞

what is your reaction when any business declines to provide you with a product or service? Generally, it is negative. Even if we logically accept it, emotionally we do not like it. Declining an individual piece of work may be interpreted as rejecting a client altogether. Also, assuming the client will progress with the engagement, they will use another consultancy. If this consultancy performs well, you may be displaced in the client's view as a favoured partner for future engagements.

Rejection owing to approach

If you are rejecting an individual engagement because of the approach a client insists on, the consultant is saying something along the lines of: 'I am happy to perform the engagement if I have the opportunity to shape the approach. I do not think I can add value in the way you would like me to work.' Again, the benefits you achieve depend on your reasons for being unhappy with the approach. The risk is that the client interprets you as saying: 'I don't think your approach will work', which of course, may be true! The client approach may be unworkable or inappropriate, but more often it is just unviable for the consultant. A more important risk is that the client interprets your statement as meaning something along the lines of, 'I am much smarter than you and can see a way of doing this which you are not clever enough to understand.' This is unlikely ever to be popular, and if a client gets it into their head that this is what you are implying, you will significantly damage your relationship with them.

Declining a subsequent engagement

Declining an opportunity for a subsequent engagement is also fraught with risk. There are many perfectly valid reasons for rejecting a subsequent engagement – most obviously, you may not have the skills to do it. If you are a strategy consultant you could have a brilliant strategic insight which is of huge value to the client. You may not, however, have the right skills to execute this strategy and so the follow-on is not the type of work you should be doing. However, there is a major risk in rejecting follow-on work. The client is quite likely to interpret your decision to decline the work as you saying: 'I don't have confidence that what I am recommending will actually succeed and I do not want to be around to see the mess.' Declining follow-on work risks undermining the client's faith in your current engagement.

Totally avoiding a client organisation

Totally avoiding a client organisation is relatively straightforward. Whilst the consultant may find a tactful way of saying it, the message is: 'I do not want to or cannot work for you.' If you do not ever want to work with this organisation, this is a fairly low-risk strategy to take. After all, you do not really mind what the managers in that business think as you do not plan to work with them. With the movement of people from one organisation to another there is a risk that managers later turn up at one of your key clients and may not respond too favourably to you. This is a modest risk, and as long as you avoid the organisation rather than explicitly reject them, then the likelihood of detrimental effects elsewhere in your business is minimal.

Choosing not to work with an individual

In contrast, choosing not to work with an individual manager within a client organisation has some significant pitfalls. There may be many reasons for not accepting a specific manager as a client. Some people are simply nightmares to work with and take particular pleasure in making consultants' lives difficult! It may be due to some personal grudge against consultants, a style taken with all suppliers, or a belief that this is in the best interests of their organisation. Irrespectively, there are some managers you do not want as clients. Tread carefully. If it becomes explicit that you are avoiding an individual manager you can damage your wider relationship with a client organisation. You definitely do not want to convert the manager's generic dislike of consultants into a targeted aversion to you or your firm.

These are five examples of typical grounds for saying no to an opportunity. There are many variants on these themes, such as 'I am not willing to work with this team on the engagement', but the most significant risks are similar.

Why should you say no?

There are many reasons why you may wish to say no to an opportunity to earn fees. In Chapter 10 on consulting ethics, one solution to an ethical dilemma was rejection of the work. But ethical reasons are neither the only nor the most common reasons for rejecting work. At the forefront will be commercial issues – there is little point performing commercially unviable work unless it has some longer-term benefit or fulfils a personal ambition or desire. Even if it does, such commercially unviable work can only make up a small part of your overall work or you will soon go out of business.

There are a few absolute justifications for rejecting client work which do not need to be analysed or assessed in any great detail. If you are in one of these situations, the first thought is to reject the work; the second is to worry about any mitigating actions. I have never experienced it, but I can imagine scenarios in which a client is asking for help to cover up deliberate legal or regulatory breaches. There may be engagements or clients whose business clashes clearly and significantly with your ethical guidelines or creates other conflicts of interest. If you are not willing to reject an engagement in this situation then there really is little point in pretending you have ethical guidelines. For instance, most of my colleagues will happily provide consulting to defence companies, but I have some who will not, because the nature of what the defence industries do clashes with their ethics and beliefs.

You may also reject an engagement or a client because of agreements you have made with other clients. These agreements are usually of the form: 'Having done this work I will not work with any of your competitors for a period of x months/years afterwards.' I try to avoid such agreements and generally they run counter to the ethos of being a consultant. However, there are some situations in which the client may be fully justified in requesting an exclusivity agreement – for example, if you help them launch a completely innovative new product. You would be sensible to agree to it, if such an engagement is commercially appealing.

The clear-cut cases may be easy to make a decision on, but in real life decision making is often more ambiguous. Even when the nature of a situation should point towards rejecting an opportunity if you know all the facts, the facts are not always apparent. For example, a client is unlikely to say, 'Oh, by the way I'm breaking the law – can you help me cover it up?' Usually, things are less black and white. Let's therefore start to explore some of the greyer reasons, beginning with those of the most benign nature.

Non-contentious grounds for saying no

There are some quite non-contentious grounds for saying no to an engagement. The most obvious is that you are not available or do not have enough time to do the work. This may seem unproblematic, but even this needs careful positioning as some clients may interpret it as: 'I have another client who is more important than you.' Be honest, say you are busy, but put it positively: 'I have made a commitment to another client. I would like to help you, but I cannot break a commitment once I have made it. If you could delay my involvement, I'd be very happy to help you.' Another reason for avoiding an engagement is that it is not the sort of work you do, either because you do not have the skills to do it, or perhaps it is in an industry or geographical area you do not work in. For instance, I like foreign work, but I turn down a fair amount because the travel commitment restricts my ability to do other things I want to do.

> ❝ be honest, say you are busy, but put it positively ❞

Commercial terms

A very common basis for declining an engagement is the commercial terms. These may make the engagement commercially unviable or unacceptable to you. Perhaps the client will not pay a competitive day rate, or maybe will not cover expenses, which are high because of some feature of the engagement. Another related reason for rejecting an engagement is commercial risk. You may be unsure if the client will pay the fees. Working for foreign companies is inherently no more risky than working for ones in your own country, but if a foreign client does not pay, then your ability to seek redress may be limited. Hence you may wish to avoid unknown companies in far-off locations.

The risk–reward balance of the engagement may be wrong. This is often true with fixed price engagements. On the surface such engagements can look lucrative, but if you are unsure about how many requirements the client may place on the engagement, and the client is completely unwilling to flex the fees at all, there is a risk that you can end up working very hard for no profit. There is a more straightforward commercial decision as well. If you have a strong pipeline of work and have been earning good fees recently, you may reject work simply because it does not interest you and you have no need of it.

Avoiding certain clients or sectors, or nature of the work

I have never explicitly rejected a client totally, but like many of my colleagues I avoid certain clients or categories of clients. Some consultants lack interest in certain sectors. For example, I have many colleagues who avoid public sector work. Public sector work is important to consultants and to society as a whole. However, some consultants just don't enjoy working for public sector clients because of the culture and working style, and consequently avoid it. Consultants also keep away from some clients because of the client's reputation. It can surprise clients, but consultants talk to each other and some clients are known to be hard work or slow payers, and so on. I have a few clients I tend to avoid for these reasons. It is not that I will not work for them, but I prioritise other clients above them.

You may also choose to decline work because of the nature of the specific engagement. Although consultants have a reputation amongst some clients of positioning themselves to do anything and everything, most consultants are well aware that they have a limited area of specialisation. There are many types of engagements I could not do, or could not add sufficient value to, because I do not have the right skill set to do it. If I am asked to do such work, I say no.

It's not in the client's interest

A more subtle reason, and one which client's will find harder to accept, is when you have the skills to do an engagement, but do not wish to do it because it is not in the client organisation's business interest. You can do the work, but you do not think it will have any effect on the organisation and hence the investment will be wasted, or worse you actually think it will be detrimental for the organisation. The individual client may have a grand vision of the future to which the engagement contributes. You understand the engagement, but think the grand vision is unachievable or not worth achieving. Various consultants will respond in different ways to such a situation, but many will not accept the engagement.

How the engagement will be run

So far I have talked about reasons related to the client or the type of engagement. There are also reasons for declining engagements because of *how* the engagement will be run. As I have stressed many times in this book, consulting is a partnership and, although you may be a brilliant and resourceful consultant, in almost all engagements you need some input from the client. You will need information, resources and some of the client's own time. As well as resources you may need decisions made, and in the pressure of an engagement probably need them made promptly. If you are not going to get the information, resources, client time and decisions, you should reject the work. Unfortunately, this is difficult to ascertain up-front, and in most instances you won't know that the situation is like this until engagement has started.

The client's responsibility

Sometimes you should say no, even to the best work, because it is in the client's interest for you to say no. There are some types of work that clients need to do themselves. If they don't do it they will not learn and will not accept the results. There are many situations in which a client wants us to tell them what to do, whereas they really must work it out for themselves. A process consulting style of engagement may be appropriate, but an expert telling them what to do is not. There are also activities which it is only appropriate for the client to do, and no matter how much they may wish to abrogate responsibility to you, they cannot. For example, consultants should never perform staff appraisals (unless they are working in an interim management role).

When to say no

You know what to say no to, and why you should say no, but when should you say no? There can be a temptation to wait to decline work for as long as possible. You may delay because of the natural human tendency to avoid a difficult conversation. There are some advantages in delaying a decision to say no. The longer you wait, the more you will understand about the client and the engagement, and therefore the better information and grounds you have for rejecting an engagement. This is partially about you not rejecting work prematurely that turns out to be viable and acceptable, but also the better your understanding, the better explanation you can give to your client as to why you are rejecting an opportunity. However, generally I counsel that the earlier you decline work the better.

> there are some advantages in delaying a decision to say no

From your commercial perspective you want to spend the minimum amount of time in finding, focusing and framing an engagement you will not pursue. Developing a proposal can take a significant amount of time and if you are not going forward with the engagement, the earlier you decide the better. It is also in the client's interest that you decline work early. The earlier a client knows, the better chance they have of finding an alternative consultant, and the less time they have wasted briefing you on the work. Usually, it is far easier to minimise the damage and risk by an early exit rather than a late one. Best of all is not to get involved, and not to chase the opportunity in the first place.

Of course, there are situations in which everything about the engagement looks wonderful and it is only part-way through that you realise it is a disaster. Typically, the further you are in the delivery phase the more difficult it is to extricate yourself and the less point there is to doing so. Even if an engagement is commercially unviable, if you have done 90 per cent of the work you might as well finish it. Just grin and bear it, and learn for next time! When cases hit the press as examples of poor work from a professional services firm, it is usually when the client and consultant start arguing late in the delivery stage. This is best avoided.

Tell-tale signs of a poor opportunity

If you are going to say no, you want to do it as early as possible. But early on in the initial interactions with a client it may not be apparent that the engagement is not one you should be accepting. In the propose stage of an engagement the information is never perfect. The work is characterised by uncertainty and there are no foolproof ways of checking if a client engagement will succeed or not. So, what indicates that you should be saying no? There are some tell-tale signs to look out for.

Firstly, you should eliminate any work which, irrespective of other engagement characteristics, you will reject. If you have absolute no-go areas when it comes to working with clients, ask straightaway if these are going to be a feature of the engagement. There is little point expending any effort on work that you are not willing to do. Examples of this could be an engagement which requires you to travel to places where you are absolutely unwilling to go, or to work times when you are certain you are unavailable. If you have any suspicion of this, just ask the client.

Clients with astronomical and ever-growing expectations are indicative of problems ahead. There is nothing wrong with ambition, and if you are charging premium rates a client has a right to expect good value in return. But you are human, and if they want you to deliver a lot, the client must also put in a lot. In the haste to sell, there can be a temptation to promise too much to clients. If client expectations are too high you either need to bring them back down to earth or you should try and sidestep the opportunity.

Another bad sign is if clients repeatedly avoid providing information. This may refer to money. For commercial reasons a client may not want to tell you the precise budget they have, but they should be able to confirm that there is a budget, and you should at least be able to have a broad conversation about the order of magnitude of their expectations. Similarly, you may need information and resources from a client to develop an effective proposal. If the client will not provide adequate resources at this stage, it points to a risk that they will not do so during the delivery phase either.

You can meet clients who have fixed ideas about how long an engagement will take or how much it will cost. This is fine if the client accepts you have to shape and scope the engagement to fit their budget, but if they expect significant flexibility combined with a limited and fixed budget then you should avoid the opportunity.

Some clients keep the conversation about potential engagements going on and on, but never let you get to a sale. You may not be able to complete a proposal as the grounds keep shifting and you are spending too much time framing and focusing the work. Alternatively, you deliver a proposal but never get a decision or approval to start, or the client questions anything and everything. If a client is spending a lot of money on consulting support, it is fair for them to question the proposal and ask for refinements and modifications. But there is a difference between improving an engagement and unending alterations, which can become nit-picking.

At some point, cut your losses and run. There is a balance to be found, as proposals do sometimes take a long time to come right, and if you stop progressing the work too prematurely you may lose out. But don't fall into the trap of assuming it will come good at some point. You can burn significant effort and some clients really are just:

- Fishing for information. The client is picking your brain for ideas. You can give a client a lot of information and advice for free in shaping proposals.
- Looking for a competitive quote to get a better deal from another, preferred consultant.
- Incapable of making a decision in a fast enough time.
- Thinking that as you are a supplier, the cost of sales is your problem not theirs. There is some truth in this, but like any business the cost of sales has to be recouped and if you have a client from whom you cannot recoup the cost of sales, then it is a client you do not want.

■ Appearing busy to appease some of their internal stakeholders without any intention of ever committing.

You can turn some such clients to your advantage. For instance if a client really cannot make up their mind as to what they want, offer to facilitate the process of determining what is needed, as a paid-for engagement.

Another time to avoid an engagement is when the client wants, or is hinting that they want, something unethical or illegal. This has never happened to me, but I have heard of consultants being asked to help with some dubious assignments.

The final sign of a poor opportunity is if you just don't seem to be hitting it off with your client. I do not mean that you and all your clients have to be close friends. A consultant–client relationship is a professional relationship and you should be capable of working with people you would not instinctively socialise with. But successful consultancy does rely on a positive relationship, and if you do not warm at all to each other then it is a bad sign. If your client does not like you they are less likely to accept your findings and may not trust you. If you do not trust your client it can make your working life unpleasant.

> **" if you do not warm at all to each other then it is a bad sign "**

The way to approach all opportunities is to be structured in your thinking, and to observe and listen to what is going on. In the propose stage, your role is to seek as much information as you can to decide whether you will proceed with an engagement. As you engage with the client, manage their expectations about what you are and are not willing to do. If there are any signs that cause you concern, probe and get more information. How much risk you are willing to take is up to you personally. I tend to be cautious, as a consulting reputation takes a while to build and is easily damaged. If I cannot answer to my own satisfaction whether the engagement is viable relative to my standards and my needs, I tend to decline the opportunity.

How to say no

Saying no is surprisingly hard sometimes. Most consultants don't like hurting people, don't like letting clients down and don't want to damage relationships. Each of these can result from saying no. (If you do like doing these things, your career as a consultant may be short.) You definitely should say no if it is right for you to say no, but you must do so in the right way.

How you say no depends on a number of factors. Important considerations are your relationship and your past positioning with the client. Generally, the better your relationship the more open you can be, and the easier it is to discuss your reasons. A client you have a strong relationship with will accept most reasons for declining work. How you have historically positioned yourself is important both in terms of what you have said generally about your services, but also what you have said specifically about the current opportunity. Clients have a tendency to remember what you have told them.

If you told a client from the start that you will not be available after June, then even if there is a sell-on it is clear you cannot do it. Just remind them: 'As I said back last October, I am not available from June onwards, so you need to find someone else to complete the follow-on work.' If you have regularly told a client you only ever do consulting of type X, and the engagement is of type Y, it is easy to point out why you can't do it. But your historic positioning cuts both ways. If you have stressed you will do anything for the client or you always have a pool of resource available to perform engagements for them, don't be surprised if they are annoyed when you reject work for a reason that conflicts with your original positioning. If you have chased a client very hard for work, and then do not want it, you are likely to irritate them greatly!

The reason for saying no is important to the way that you decide to tell the client. Some reasons are absolute, and irrespective of client impact and response you will not do the work. Most are less clear cut. An engagement may be commercially unviable, but if you do lots of engagements with the client, and they are otherwise highly profitable, you may choose to accept the work to maintain the relationship. In this case, you should help the client to understand that what you are doing is an exception.

Once you have made a decision to decline some work, start immediately to determine how you will tell the client. You are not only trying to avoid the work, but trying to do so in a way that does not damage your relationship with the client. Start by thinking from the client's perspective. What is the impact on them of you rejecting the work? Will they understand and accept your reasons?

The possible client effects from a consultant rejecting the opportunity of work are varied. It may be embarrassing for the client if a consultant says they do not want their business. It can cause difficulty for the client if they need the work done and there is no viable alternative. It may simply be annoying, as they have to go and find someone else. Try to:

- Avoid surprising a client. The more surprised they are, the more likely they are to be annoyed. Occasionally, they may be pleasantly surprised, but if so you should probably be worried about your services!

- Manage the client's expectations. The more a client is prepared for you saying no, the less likely there will be any damage to your relationship.

- Help the client, if appropriate. For instance, try to find an alternative consultant to work on the engagement. This is good for your client and helps in your relationships with other consultants.

- Give the client a reason they can believe and can explain to anyone else who asks why you will not do the work. The client may have to talk to more senior managers, and you want them telling the senior manager something positive. If you do this well, you can actually enhance your reputation with the client.

Clients find some reasons valid and easy to understand: for example, 'I do not have the skills to do this work for you.' You may not like admitting skills gaps, but it is easy for a client to understand and accept. If you present your reason badly, the client may perceive it as consulting nonsense. For instance, in saying 'the engagement does not fit with my portfolio of services', you may actually be admitting you don't have the skills, or honestly pointing out that you want to focus on particular types of work. Unfortunately, this does sound like a made-up and feeble excuse. Stick to simple and direct language, as this is less likely to leave a bad taste in a client's mouth.

> " stick to simple and direct language "

You may be tempted to lie about why you will not do an engagement. Saying 'I am too busy' is more palatable than 'I won't work for you because you are an irritating client'. Perhaps this is unethical, but it does little harm and avoids a mutually embarrassing situation. But keep lies, even white lies, to a minimum. It has the risk, as always with lying, that you may be found out. If there is one thing that is likely to destroy your relationship with a client permanently, it is being caught out lying to them.

What if it is too late to back out from the work? Imagine you are well into an engagement and it is an unrecoverable disaster. In this situation, you need to start a damage limitation exercise. You may not be able to save your relationship with the client. Therefore, your main concern should be to extricate yourself from the engagement in the best way possible for both yourself and the client, even if this is a situation of finding the least-worst solution. In parallel with stopping work with this client, you want to try to avoid knock-on impacts elsewhere. Ask yourself: what is the likely response of other managers in the client organisation or in other organisations? Be prepared for other clients asking questions about why the engagement has stopped. Try to develop a clear and honest description of what went wrong that does not affect your reputation or your clients. It may be satisfying, but it is unprofessional and usually counter-productive to bad-mouth clients in public. Therefore have a positive description ready if anyone asks. You will do yourself more good if you can immediately give this clear description than if you are left fumbling for words.

Overall, as a consultant you may find that over the course of your career you say no to a lot of possible work. If you are really successful you will not be able to do all the work for all the clients who will want to work with you. Always be prepared to say no. If you do it clearly and honestly, avoiding jargon, and help the client to understand why you cannot do it in the most positive way, then you are unlikely to have too many problems.

Summary

- You do not have to accept any work, and some engagements you should not accept. You should always be willing to say no to client engagements.

- If you decide to reject a client opportunity, it is important to work out how you will reject it, as the rejection may damage your relationship with the client. Sometimes, saying no can actually enhance your relationship.

- Choose the timing of saying no. Generally, if you are going to say no, say it as early as possible.

13

Key consulting tips

With a complex topic like management consulting one of the challenges for an author is deciding what to leave out. There are various topics I have rejected from this book because I think they are of marginal relevance, critical only to a subset of consultants, or not the sort of ideas that are best conveyed via the medium of a book. That left me with a long list of thoughts or tips that will be useful to consultants but which do not fit neatly into any of the preceding chapters. They are very varied points but the features these tips have in common is that they are either helpful, but not obvious, when you start consulting, or they present useful but unusual ways to think about the world of consulting. The tips are a direct result of my experience as a consultant and I hope you find them useful.

Tip 1

Don't make yourself indispensable to a client.

It can seem a good idea, from a commercial perspective, to make yourself indispensable to your client. If you do a great job, a client may welcome your ongoing and continuous involvement with their business. This can result in strong revenues from the client and it removes the need for unprofitable and time-consuming business development. Unfortunately, a permanent relationship has a number of drawbacks.

Before explaining the disadvantages, it is important to understand that in giving this advice I want to differentiate here between the individual consultant and a consulting company. A consulting company will benefit from a permanent relationship with a client, but the interests of the individual consultant are not the same as those of the whole company. I also want to make a distinction between repeat business, where you periodically sell to and work for the same client, and continuously working with a single client. The former is a sign of success, but the latter is problematic.

The first drawback is that if you personally work for only one client, you are not only indispensable to them, you will become dependent on them. All consulting engagements are eventually terminated, and if you have a relationship with only one client you will find it more difficult to find other work. When you want to leave, the client may not willingly let you. If you work for a big consultancy and your client insists on your continued presence, you may be left in a client organisation for a long time to maximise revenues and to maintain a client relationship. This is not good for your career prospects or your skills development as a consultant. An engagement can start to feel like a prison sentence rather than an opportunity for value-added consulting. If you do pull out, you leave the client with a problem. How will they cope without you? The client may end up feeling betrayed by you because of the challenges they face operating without you. Even internal consultants need to try and work across a business and not for a single client manager on a continuous basis.

What is a reasonable length for an unbroken involvement with one client? That is a 'how long is a piece of string?' type of question. My guidance is that value-adding engagements often take several months, but if a single engagement is stretching into years then you should question whether you are still adding value and improving as a consultant.

Always think about your exit plan from an engagement: what will you hand over to whom and who needs to have what skills transferred to take over from you? A consulting company wanting to maintain the revenue stream should try to rotate a different consultant into a client every few months. Soon after you begin an engagement, start sending those subtle messages that you will not be around forever, as it can take several weeks or months to extricate yourself smoothly from a client.

> ❝ always think about your exit plan from an engagement ❞

Tip 2

Give your clients the credit they deserve.

Your client runs a great business, otherwise they could not afford your fees. As a consultant, it is easy to see all the things your client is doing wrong, but if they did everything right they would probably never need your help. Give them some credit, as without it you risk becoming arrogant. Arrogance in a consultant is unpleasant, and usually unwarranted.

Your client has probably achieved things you have not. When you are speaking to the chief executive of a big firm, do not just think about the mess they are making in some aspect of the business you are an expert in. Think about how they manage tens of thousands of staff and budgets of billions of dollars – something most consultants have never done. There is a lot of things consultants don't do and don't have to worry about that clients must do every day. Give great advice, be critical where you need to be, but remember that a little humility never goes amiss.

Tip 3

Understand the client's personal interest.

Why does the client, personally, want the work done? As discussed in Chapter 2, there are many different reasons why clients engage consultants. Try to get below the superficial level and understand why the particular client you are working for now wants the engagement done. What is in it for them as an individual?

This tip is not concerned with determining whether the engagement is for personal interest, as arguably in the end everything we do is for personal interest (even if that is limited to wanting to avoid a punishment). Try to establish whether the personal interest of the client is aligned with the rest of the organisation's needs. If it is not, it is best to try and avoid the engagement.

A related issue is to learn to differentiate between the issue a client wants resolved and why they have chosen you. You may have been chosen for a range of reasons beyond the current issue. You must primarily focus on the issue the client wants resolved, but if you understand what it is about you that made them choose you as the right person to work with, you have an advantage. Leverage this understanding to enhance your relationship.

Tip 4

Client trust is more important than charisma.

There is an image of the great consultant as vibrant and charismatic. Forget charisma – think about trust. A client trusting you is always more important than great charisma or personal confidence. Charisma and confidence can help, but too much charisma can make some people wary. A client is looking for someone they can happily work with day in, day out, which does not necessarily mean the person with the most alluring or magnetic personality.

Trust is the keystone that will enable you to develop productive client relationships and overcome any lack of confidence or charisma.

Tip 5

Add extra value.

Value is delivered to clients from all sorts of help provided by a consultant. Much of the value of consultants does not come from the primary work in delivering an engagement, but comes in peripheral activities. These can be small tips, advice, pointing at useful articles or books, problem solving, simple tools or even just helpful chats now and again.

If you want to sell-on to a client, then delivering a great engagement to the letter of the proposal is a good start, but clients like working with people they know will willingly add that little bit extra. Of course, you must avoid the scope of your work expanding too much, but willingness to do that little bit more is a virtue. The trick is to find things that are easy for you to give, which add value to your client and which you have the opportunity to provide simply by being around. An old article from

Harvard Business Review that is relevant to the client right now may add significant value, but takes little effort on your part. Just because something is easy for you, does not mean it is not valuable to your client, and, conversely, just because something is hard, does not mean it is.

Tip 6

Be flexible, but stick to the brief!

Tip 5 is important, but needs to be balanced with the fact that you have limited time on an engagement and already have lots to do. To consult profitably requires that there is a limit to how much you deliver outside the engagement brief.

Clients expect a degree of flexibility in consultants, and often this is essential. At the point an engagement starts, you may have won a fee-earning assignment, but its precise shape and content may not become apparent until a few more days or even weeks of work. Whatever you do, stay close to the original brief, unless you agree a defined and properly priced modification to it. For example, don't drift into promising a business change, when what you are being paid to deliver is a report. It's very easy, in the pressure of trying to keep a client happy, to end up promising all sorts of additional extras, which you will never manage to deliver within the time or budget of your existing work.

Tip 7

Manage your engagement timescale from day one.

Consultants regularly run out of time towards the end of engagements, and end up working from early morning to late at night just to get the final report completed. There are various reasons for this, and some consultants seem to thrive on adrenaline and caffeine at the end of an engagement. Generally, this is just bad planning and poor time management. Most of the activities that delay you at the end of an engagement –

being asked to interview one more member of client staff, having to rework a report following a review by a senior manager in your own firm, or clients rejecting your findings – were predictable or at least clear risks from the first day of the engagement.

As all good project managers know, slippage on engagements starts on day one. It's far easier to catch up on lost time at the beginning than the end. Catching up on one lost day when you have 10 weeks to go is easy. Catching up on one lost day when you have only one day to go is a nightmare!

Keep the pressure up from day one. Predict the problems you may have when finalising an engagement and leave time in your plan to resolve them. It will make your life much less stressful and enjoyable, and usually it enables you to deliver a better quality result to your client.

| Tip 8 |

Take care with risk-reward engagements.

Risk-reward engagements are a type of commercial arrangement in which the consultant agrees to link their fees directly to the value delivered or benefits received by the client. The consultant is therefore taking a risk on the outcome of an engagement, and as a result is looking for the balancing opportunity for increased reward. A classic example is a procurement project, where a consultant is engaged to reduce a client's procurement spend and, rather than being paid normal day rates, negotiates to take a percentage of the procurement savings as a success fee. On paper a risk-reward deal sounds fantastic. The client only pays for what you deliver, and there is an opportunity for extra margin to be made if you manage the engagement well. Risk-reward arrangements have been shown to work in many situations, and as a result of them there are a number of satisfied clients and profitable consultancies. It is a great value proposition, but take care before you get involved in one.

The often unforeseen problems with risk-reward deals come down to difficulties with measuring the success of the engagement and how you handle the situation in which you significantly over-deliver. There is also the rather obvious risk that you may under-deliver and not get paid, which is inherent in the structure of a risk-reward contract, but I assume you would not enter into one if you did not understand and assess this specific risk!

Risk-reward deals can easily end in acrimony and argument. If you are very successful you may earn a lot, but if you earn too much it can damage your relationship with the client – even if it was the client who suggested the deal and who benefits overall. For example, if your work results in you being paid several times what you would have earned if you were paid your normal day rate, then clients can end up resenting this. I have been involved in projects where the consultant performed what was according to normal fee rates hundreds of thousands of pounds of work, to be paid in millions of pounds based on the risk-reward metrics. Clients should not resent this, as they also benefit. You can argue it is in both parties' interest and you would be correct. However, there is little point being correct if you irritate a client so much that they will not work with you again.

> *risk-reward deals can easily end in acrimony and argument*

Additionally, you will obviously focus on delivering the maximum amount to achieve the maximum reward. The problem is that businesses are multi-dimensional and too much change in one area, such as reduced procurement costs, often has a detrimental effect elsewhere in a client's business. Clients often feel all you care about is the reward, which of course is true, as that was the point of the deal!

Successful risk-reward engagements require a mature relationship with clients, who will perceive the benefits to themselves if they end up paying you more. If you do want to enter a risk-reward deal, make sure the client understands the implications, there is a reliable measurement process in place and the timing of measurement is agreed up-front.

Measurement must be in place at the start of the engagement, or else there is no baseline for comparison. The timing of measurement is crucial. Any change takes time to bed in and problems may not be initially apparent. Collecting data on success at the wrong time may present an overly optimistic or pessimistic picture of engagement success. Avoid this problem by agreeing at the start when and what you will measure as the basis of payment.

Tip 9

Be clear about the different types of risk.

When you talk about engagement risk there are two separate aspects of risk: client risk that you will not deliver or will give suboptimal advice, and consultant risk that you will not deliver in the client's eyes or will lose money on the engagement. You must clearly differentiate between the two. The implications of the two types of risk are different, and the way each type of risk is communicated, managed and mitigated will be different. Client risk is largely the client's issue to deal with, but you should be conscious of the client's need to avoid risk, and be engaging in such a way as to give them confidence that the risk is minimised. Consultant risk is yours alone to manage.

Tip 10

Manage your relationship with client staff sensitively.

Client staff will often think of themselves as representing the client and perceive you as just another supplier, whereas you may see the same client staff just as a resource to be used by you to deliver the engagement. There is an inherent conflict in these views and managing it requires a fine balance.

On some occasions you may end up 'managing' client staff within the scope of the engagement. Remember, staff are not your personal employees. How they feel and what they say about you can influence your client's judgement of you. However, don't treat them with kid gloves or you will not get the work you require done. It's great to be popular with the troops, but it may not get the work completed.

If there are problems between yourself and client staff, discuss it with the client as soon as possible. Don't simply ask the client to remove any staff you are having trouble with as this makes it look as if you are a weak manager, but let the client know there is a potential problem brewing.

Tip 11

You cannot have zero impact on a client organisation.

Sometimes clients want consultants to have zero impact on the organisation. The client may be concerned that the consultant may cause some negative impact, especially if the engagement is dealing with some sensitive issue such as cost reduction or due diligence associated with potential mergers.

It is essential to act with sensitivity and respect a client's need for you to minimise impact. You can reduce your impact, but you cannot have zero impact. Even an activity like data collection by consultants is visible to the organisation. It is very difficult to do it and carry out an engagement in secret. It is quite possible that staff will not know why an engagement is being pursued, but the fact that something is happening will become apparent to staff sooner or later. Therefore never promise to a client that you can work in such a way that no one in the organisation will have any knowledge of your work.

Tip 12

When in a team, work as a team.

Engagements often require a consulting team to work on them. When you are working on this type of engagement, engage the whole consulting team, accepting the strengths and weaknesses of different consultants. Delivering such a consulting engagement is like taking part in a team sport. You always want the best team you can get, but, like pulling a sports team together, the nature and timing of an engagement means that there is often not a perfect match between the skills required and the consultants available to deliver the engagement.

Continuing the analogy of the team sports, some consultants will be playing out of the position they are best suited to. If you are the lead consultant on an engagement, you must learn to get the best from the team you have, helping those who are in roles they are not familiar with to contribute to the overall engagement goal.

Tip 13

Be authentic.

If you are advising a client to act in a certain way, you should act in that way too, otherwise your advice seems insincere. Human beings, including clients, seem to have almost perfect radar to pick up inconsistency of behaviour and hypocrisy. Yet consultants and consultancies are often loath to take their own medicine, and act as if it is not relevant to them. The worst financial systems I ever worked with were in an audit-based consultancy and one of the most inefficient management processes I saw was in a six sigma consultancy. The line management of staff by senior managers and partners in some consultancies I have come across would not be tolerated in many other organisations. The strange thing is that these consultants not only gave advice contrary to their behaviour, they believed it. If you believe your advice – take it yourself.

> **if you believe your advice – take it yourself**

If you point out the difference between consultant behaviour within their own companies and client recommendations, the consultants usually mumble something about 'cobbler's children' (from the old story that a cobbler's children have the worst shoes). This is just labelling the problem – it is not a valid justification!

Tip 14

Learn on engagements, but don't treat them as a time to learn.

What makes you valuable as a consultant is your ability to advise and get things done. These capabilities improve with time and engagement experience. All engagements provide an opportunity to learn. But remember, the client is not paying you to learn or develop intellectual capital – the client is paying you because you already know.

On every engagement think about who is getting value and who is learning. It should be the client more than the consultant. Any value and learning for the consultant should be collateral and not primary. If learning is your primary goal, you have lost the point!

> **Tip 15**
>
> Keep the expenses reasonable.

Many consulting contracts are specified on a fees-plus-expenses basis. Consultants are often away from home for long periods of time. Consulting organisations often set expectations that consultants will be well looked after when working. These factors can result in consultants generating huge expenses bills.

Don't go crazy on expenses, or stray outside the expectations of the client, or differ widely from how client staff operate. Yes, you have a right to be recompensed for reasonable expenses when away from home. But if the chief executive flies economy class, then it is not helpful for consultants to fly first class and bill for that. Do not hide behind the wording of your contract, as the details of what are and are not reasonable expenses are often not thought about when developing an engagement contract.

When you arrive at the client's workplace, work out what is acceptable and what is not. If you are unsure, spend conservatively. If you make a mistake – apologise – and if you underestimate what is acceptable to spend, it is never a problem to start spending more! You can do a lot of damage and cause significant resentment if you charge for what the client perceives as excessive personal expenses. Clients do not see their role as providing for well-paid consultants to live in luxury.

> **Tip 16**
>
> Avoid ostentatious signs of wealth.

If you do become a hugely successful consultant, have a fleet of Ferraris and Rolls-Royces, then that is absolutely fantastic for you. But don't turn up to client sites in one of them. Clients like to know a consultant is successful as it gives them confidence they are working with someone who knows what they are talking about. But there is a difference between turning up in a well-appointed executive car and showing off. Clients do not like thinking that the consultant working with them is significantly wealthier than they are, and got that way by charging their organisation. There are lots of ways of reinforcing your experience and competency – ostentatious wealth is not the best. Save it for your family and friends at the weekend.

Tip 17

Be clever, don't just look it.

Consultants can become obsessed with how clever their work looks rather than how clever it really is. There is some truth that clients can be impressed with reports or presentations simply because they look good. A well-prepared document with excellent graphic design can gain artificial credibility because of how well it looks rather than what it contains. There is nothing wrong with trying to make your presentations look exceptionally attractive, and in modern business it is expected, but do not use it as to hide a lack of thinking. Sooner or later, and often sooner, you will get caught out.

An example of this is in the application of tools – such as spreadsheet-based analyses of client data. Many problems can be solved with simple intuitive tools. When you present a tool it should be because it is good, not because of the 'now that's clever' response. Such responses are short-term. The tools must actually add value!

Tip 18

Knowing 'what' is useful; knowing 'how' is valuable.

It is helpful to understand the difference between *know-what* and *know-how*. An example of know-what is telling a client 'the relevant regulation is subsection 4.2 of the 2006 regulations', whereas an example of know-how is telling the client something in the form of 'the best way to conform with the regulation is to train all your customer-facing staff in a half-day course as we have specified'. Know-what is facts, figures, information and data; know-how is approaches and experience of what works and an ability to make things happen.

❝❝ the real value comes from know-how 🟐🟐

Years ago an encyclopaedic knowledge of a business topic was valuable. The person with the most comprehensive set of know-what in an area was sought after and treated as a guru. But increasingly most business information can be easily referenced. A 15-minute trawl on the internet can provide huge amounts of useful information that would have taken weeks of research not that long ago. Hence, simply knowing things is more and more just a basic requirement to consult, it is not a differentiator. Clients need consultants to have access to know-what, but the real value comes from know-how.

Know-how must be real. If you claim to have know-how to make things happen for a client, then you must be able to make things happen and not, for example, simply have the ability to list the sort of things a client should be considering. Clients will soon find out whether your know-how is real or bluffing.

Tip 19

Focus and simplification are of most value to clients.

Value to clients often comes from expressing the problem they really have in simple terms, or explaining how to implement a solution in an easy to comprehend and unambiguous fashion. Being able to express a knotty set of problems that a client has struggled to understand on a one-page diagram is of huge value. Similarly, showing a logical plan for overcoming a problem that can be grasped in a few minutes is worth a lot to a client. In business, the aim is to get results in the most effective way, not to worry about understanding every aspect of every issue. Accurate simplification is powerful.

Simplification is also required so that you can complete your engagement within a reasonable amount of time. To do this, you need to prioritise where you will focus your energies. A consultant must focus on an engagement and remove or ignore peripheral issues. For example, a business problem may have 20 contributory causes and you have time to focus only on the most critical three. When you do prioritise, keep a log of how you made your prioritisation decisions, and ideally keep your client involved in such decision making. Whether you focus on the three causes with the biggest impact on the problem, or the three which are easiest to resolve, will significantly alter the content and outcome of the engagement. A client may challenge, at a later date, your decision to focus on those three aspects of a problem and not the other 17. Unless you can give clear and appropriate reasoning, which the client agrees with, you can end up with an ever-extending and loss-making engagement.

Tip 20

Understand the limitations of simplification.

There is a balance to tip 19. Consultants love developing simple theories and models, and generally clients like them and find them useful. But there is an inherent risk in making the true complexity of real life appear simple. There is always a risk of underdetermination by the data, i.e. there can be competing theories, models or other simplifications that equally well fit your understanding of the situation. The problem can be compounded by a consultant who, after using a model which is intellectually appealing and gives some useful results in one situation, fails to see that what they have is just a model and not the *truth* that applies equally well to all situations.

Making complexity simple can add huge value and give powerful insights, but you must always remain modest enough to know that at best the theory or model will approximate to reality and is not reality. Business theories are not scientific laws. You must be alert enough to identify when simplifications and models do not work. By all means see the value in models and other simplifications – but also see the limits.

Related to simplification is the modern tendency to reductionism. A reductionist breaks a problem into parts, treating the problem as the sum of its parts. Some problems can be resolved by breaking them into small simple components and resolving the individual parts. However, some business problems are related to the complexity of a business and the dynamic interaction between its components. In these situations, trying to resolve real issues by solving small parts may never work.

Tip 21

Be wary of following on from someone else's findings, recommendations or plans.

In Chapter 4, I introduced the concept of the client's change process. This can be summarised by saying that most activities have followed on as a result of some previous activity, and the activity that is currently being done will flow on to another. Hence, you may be involved in some strategic thinking which follows on to an operational review, which then follows on to some change planning, and then carries on as a change implementation project.

As a consultant you will be involved only in a part of this process, and often will have to carry on using data, findings, recommendations or plans someone else has developed. For instance, a client may have developed a change plan, but realise they do not have the skills to implement it and ask you to help them run the implementation project.

There is always a risk in taking over from someone else. You may not agree with the prior findings, or what was suggested by the previous person may not be right. Taking the previous example, a client invites you in to complete a project they have planned but do not have the skills to implement. On the surface this may sound fine, but think about it for one minute. If the client does not have the skills to implement the project, do they really have the skills to develop a plan for it? Almost certainly not!

You cannot always start from the very beginning of every change cycle. You will not always be involved in the first stages of strategic thinking through to the end of change implementation, and may just pick up one part of this work. Therefore you must be able to take over from someone else, but at the same time you should be wary.

The solution is not to reject engagements that require you to take over from someone else's work, but always to build in the opportunity to review previous findings, recommendations or plans. Clients do not always like this, as they can see it as simply an attempt by you to increase your fees. But reviews do not need to take long, and if you have an open

❝ reviews do not need to take long ❞

conversation with a client about your need to manage risk then they will normally accept this. It is usually in the client's interest too, since anyone who is involved for part of a change process, but hands over to someone else, may have little incentive to make sure what they propose will actually work. If the client will not allow you the opportunity to review the previous work, it is often better to decline the engagement than take the risk.

> **Tip 22**
>
> Successful engagement findings and recommendations should match the client's time horizon.

Different people work to different time horizons. We all know people who cannot plan or think beyond tomorrow, and others who are not interested in anything that is not measured in months or years. Typically, more senior managers think in longer timescales, but this is not universally true.

If a client only thinks in terms of weeks or months there is little point providing advice that will take years to implement or vice versa. The client will be incapable of utilising your advice, no matter how theoretically perfect it is.

Summary

In this chapter, I have described a number of tips gained from my experiences as a consultant. No doubt in 10 years' time I will be able to add to this list as my experience and knowledge continues to grow. Many of these tips will apply to all consultants, but of course the lessons I have learnt are a function of the type of engagements I have undertaken. The best tip I can give to all consultants is to be observant and learn from the experiences of working on multiple engagements across a variety of clients. It is this diversity that gives consultants their value, in being able to consider a client situation from a broader perspective than the client.

If you have read each of the preceding chapters you have read all the contents of the book directed primarily at consultants. As your career progresses, you will learn, develop and build your own set of tips and techniques. They will be the basis of your growing success. And if you have any different tips, I for one am more than happy to hear them.

The client's perspective – buying consultancy

This book is primarily for consultants, but I know the readership includes buyers and users of consultancy. Therefore, in this last chapter, I have taken a client-centric viewpoint, and describe tips and techniques concerning selecting and controlling consultants. These tips should not only be useful to clients. By thinking through these points consultants who want to adopt a client-centric approach will be better prepared to deal with any client objections to proposals and, most importantly, more able to fulfil client needs.

When writing this chapter I thought of the Latin phrase *caveat emptor* (let the buyer beware), because the buyer does need to beware when purchasing consultancy. There are knowledgeable clients who can handle every consultant and get the most from them. But like going to the dentist or the garage, the consultant is the expert in a field (or should be), and you are in their hands. Naturally, you have your own knowledge and experience to check a consultant's advice: you can robustly probe and challenge it, perhaps even test what they tell you, but in the end, for pragmatic reasons, you may have to accept much of it in good faith. This means the consultant is in a privileged position. Any time we buy services from someone in such a position we are sensible to be wary. To paint a slightly bleaker picture, whilst many professional management consultants are paragons of virtue and ethical behaviour, a few are not – and you can pay a price for naivety.

There is a more positive mindset to adopt. Consultancy is most effective when there is a productive relationship and working partnership between the consultant and the client. These tips can be thought of as review points that help in ensuring there is a productive partnership. All these tips relate to areas which it is reasonable to have an open and constructive dialogue between consultant and client as prospective business partners.

There are complex issues to consider when buying and getting the best from your consultants that are unique to your context, but there are some key tips common to every situation. To keep the detail to a reasonable level, I have assumed a relatively simple situation in which you wish to engage a consultant: you have a problem or issue and you want a consultant to give advice on how to solve it. My list of 20 key tips for anyone engaging a consultant or consultancy is shown in Table 14.1.

Table 14.1 Client tips for buying consultancy

	Tip
1	Start with an understanding of why you are buying consultancy.
2	Take time clarifying the scope and deliverables of the engagement.
3	Don't forget you always have a choice – not to buy or to use someone else.
4	Check the proposal matches your needs and expectations.
5	Agree the billing arrangements up-front.
6	Clarify who is the client.
7	Decide how much freedom you will give the consultants.
8	Expect a lot – but don't expect miracles!
9	Confirm precisely who is in the consulting team.
10	Read the small print in the contract.
11	If you don't trust the consultant, don't buy.
12	Before saying yes, be clear about what happens when they finish.
13	Plan check points in the engagement.
14	Prepare for the consultants' arrival.
15	Keep an eye on who the consultants are talking to within your organisation.
16	Pay for work, not for sales activity.
17	Delivery is a partnership.
18	Check back against the proposal.
19	Check the deliverables – don't just accept them.
20	Only pay the bill if you are happy with the work and the invoice is reasonable.

Let's go through each of these in a little more detail

Tip 1

Start with an understanding of why you are buying consultancy.

Consultants are often engaged on the vaguest of pretences. I have had many discussions with clients who have a confused understanding of what it is they want the consultant to do. Perhaps there is a tangled knot of issues, or the problem is felt rather than verbalised. Clients can be tempted to hire consultants because they are under pressure and have a general feeling of discomfort which they would like to go away, rather than for a clear reason. The difficulty with this situation is easy to understand. If you do not know clearly what your problem is, how can the consultant clearly provide an answer? In general terms, the vaguer your thinking is, the more risk there is that the consultant will not provide a solution of value to you.

In the ideal situation you can concisely and unambiguously define the issue you want the consultant to resolve in a sentence or two. The more specific and precise you can be, the more specific and precise the consultant will be in helping you. The shorter the definition of your issue, the less chance there is for misinterpretation.

There is a related point. You should not only understand what your issue is, but also have a rational justification for why using a consultant is an effective and efficient way to resolve it. I am a strong advocate of consultancy, but it should not be the answer to every problem. You have some capable people already within your organisation. Whatever your issue, why not see if they can resolve it? In addition, if your problem is clear-cut and of a common nature – why not try buying a book? It will be much cheaper. I am not trivialising the situation: often the most sensible way to get a rapid solution will be to hire consultants. But you should give your in-house staff a chance first, at least on some occasions.

> you should give your in-house staff a chance first

If you cannot clarify what your objective in hiring a consultant is, you can ask for a consultant to help facilitate developing the definition. It is often effective to engage consultants to help you structure your thinking, or to identify and scope a problem. If you do this, be clear that the reason you are using consultants is precisely that: to identify and scope a problem, not to solve it. Good consultants are adept at helping clients understand problems. The same consultants may then be used to go on and solve the problem. But it should be a separate piece of work, and remember that the skills needed to facilitate the definition of a problem are not always the same as those required to solve it.

| **Tip 2** |

Take time clarifying the scope and deliverables of the engagement.

In tip 1 I described how it is important to understand your objectives. The way a consultant will meet your objectives is by carrying out an engagement to a certain scope and producing a set of deliverables.

The scope should be determined as a process of discussion and exploration between yourself and the consultant. A broader scope may mean a better quality of outcome, but it is also likely to mean a longer and more expensive engagement. What factors you need to consider when setting the scope will depend on the nature of your issue, but also how constrained you are in terms of time and budget. Such factors can be described in terms of questions, such as: which areas of the business must the consultants interact with to understand your issue fully? How many people should they interview? Is there anyone you do not want them to interview? Do you have an absolute time or cost limits? What corners can be cut, and which must not be? Are there any previous reports or documented analysis available? Are there any reasonable assumptions the consultants can make to speed up the work?

The deliverables can take many formats. In traditional consulting engagements the deliverables are a report, but they may also be a presentation of findings, a workshop or some staff training. The point in checking deliverables is to ascertain to your own satisfaction that the set of deliverables the consultants is proposing will enable you to resolve your issue. You may be tempted to expand the deliverables, and it is always worth pushing consultants to maximise the value they provide to you, but if you push too hard you may simply get an increased price.

> **Tip 3**
>
> Don't forget you always have a choice – not to buy or to use someone else.

I have observed that clients often find themselves engaging consultants reluctantly, because they feel they have a unique problem and only this consultant can solve it – or they are in a hurry and this consultant is available now. The client may be under pressure from a more senior manager to get on and solve the problem. However, the client is not comfortable with the consultant or their fees.

The truth is that rarely does a consultant have an absolutely unique skill set. Even when they do, ask yourself – do you really need it for this piece of work? For all really important work, get a competitive quote. This is not just an issue of fees, but more importantly to check whether you are offered the optimal service.

> **Tip 4**
>
> Check the proposal matches your needs and expectations.

Assuming that you have given a clear scope and objectives for an engagement, the consultant should be in a position to write a proposal that meets your needs. Life is rarely this simple. It is only when writing a proposal that a consultant realises there are gaps in their understanding. It is only when reading a consultant's proposal that you determine that what you thought was a clear and unambiguous definition of needs was not really understood by the consultant.

A proposal should do several things. First of all, it should play back to you what the issue is that you want the consultant to solve and, without being a history of your organisation, identify any relevant background information, constraints or assumptions. Secondly, the proposal should define how the consultant intends to resolve your issue. Finally, it should include the commercial terms. There may be other items in a proposal, but these three items are core. You need to be happy with all three. Even though you are not the expert, you do need to check how the consultant intends to resolve your issue and ensure you have some confidence that the consultant's method will work within the culture and context of your organisation.

Consultants find it irritating when a client constantly quibbles over every single detail in a proposal. This is largely a commercial issue – consultants cannot afford to spend a huge amount of time writing proposals as no fees are being earned whilst doing this. Do be reasonable and only quibble if there is a real need to, as it is helpful to start an engagement with a good relationship with a consultant. But in the end you are the client – the consultant is just someone trying to sell you a service. If you are unhappy with the proposal, ask for it to be changed. If they will not or cannot, there are plenty of other consultants out there.

Tip 5

Agree the billing arrangements up-front.

Clients can be surprised by the timing and scale of fees when the invoices arrive. As a client you should check up-front what you will be paying for and when. The sorts of items that can cause surprises are administration and expenses costs, which often can add 20 per cent to the overall fees. You may find fees for people you have never heard of, such as the consultant's quality assurance team or a junior consultant who had to do some background research for the engagement back in the office. Remember a consultant will charge VAT and this will usually be on top of the quoted fees for the engagement.

Part of the billing problem is the concern amongst clients that consultants will try their luck and add additional charges to the engagement. This is a risk to avoid. But there is also a risk the other way. It is almost impossible to specify absolutely a consulting engagement with total clarity up-front. Like most service contracts there is a degree of ambiguity. Consultants often experience scope creep, where the client constantly adds extra work into the engagement. This is difficult to manage as the client's requests are often individually reasonable, but once several have been made the consultant is

> 66 consultants often experience scope creep, where the client constantly adds extra work 99

in danger of an unprofitable engagement unless fees are increased. You may not be concerned whether the consultant makes a profit or not, but you should be. A consultant working on an unprofitable engagement is more likely to cut corners to get the work finished quickly.

The best way to avoid any conflict is to agree what will be paid for, when invoices will be raised and to agree a process to discuss any exceptions or changes to this. If you are on a restricted budget, you can always negotiate a cap on things like expenses, or even ask for a fixed rate for the whole engagement.

Do not expect fixed fees to be a solution to all problems. If you do negotiate a fixed rate, do not then track how much time a consultant is spending on a piece of work as this is no longer your concern. Your concern should be: 'Have I got a quality result for the fixed fee I am paying?' Also, if you ask for a fixed rate, do not be surprised if, when you ask for additional areas to be covered in an engagement, the consultant asks for additional fees.

Tip 6

Clarify who is the client.

When you involve consultants in your organisation you may consider yourself to be clearly their client. This may seem obvious to you and not in need of any clarification. This may be true, but it is worth directly confirming with the consultant that you are the client and they are taking instructions from you and you alone. For all sorts of reasons (see Chapters 2 and 5) consultants have a very fluid concept of who the client is on many engagements. Their idea of the client can vary between the person who engages them, other managers in the organisation, the organisation itself (whatever that means) and sometimes other stakeholders such as shareholders.

If you have engaged the consultant, and it is your department's budget that is paying their fees, and if what you are asking them to do is reasonable and in the organisation's interest, then you are correct to consider yourself as the client for this engagement. No one else is. Of course, sometimes it is not directly your budget, and sometimes what you are asking the consultant to do is in your personal interest as well as the organisation's. It is fair to say that then the concept of client is less clear cut.

Why worry about this? One reason is that you do not want the consultant seeking changes to the scope or incurring extra fees because someone else in the organisation has asked them to do additional work. You also do not want the consultant to be drawing conclusions based on information or assumptions you regard as invalid. Further, you do not want consultants going behind your back and talking about you to more senior managers (although, in reality, this is very rare).

'Who is the client?' can be a difficult question for a consultant to answer, as there may be many people who validly consider themselves as the client of a consultant. This is especially true if a consultant has a long-term relationship with an organisation and knows many different managers there or is running several engagements in parallel within your organisation. As a client you should understand that difficulty and make it clear that you personally are the client on this engagement.

Tip 7

Decide how much freedom you will give the consultants.

There are different ways of getting a consultant to resolve a problem for you. At one extreme you can tell them the problem and leave them with complete freedom as to how they resolve it. At the other extreme, you not only tell them the problem but give them detailed step-by-step instructions as to how to do it. In most cases a client works somewhere in the middle. Usually you can give some freedom or discretion as to how people working for you complete their tasks, but there are some constraints in any organisation which mean they have to do certain things in certain predefined ways.

Try to see it from the perspective of a consultant. Generally, if you define the problem the consultant will come up with a solution in any way they see fit. As the consultant is the expert this is reasonable, because they should know the best way to do something. You may have to put some limitations on how the consultant works for legal, regulatory or your own organisation's rules. For example, you may tell a consultant that their work must be done in compliance with the relevant health and safety regulations. You may want to put additional constraints on the consultant for political or organisational reasons. For instance, you may say, 'Please, do not involve the sales department in this piece of work.' Additionally, you may be tempted to tell the consultant how to do the work. You could say something like, 'I want you to do this by running a workshop for three days in March.' There is nothing wrong with any of this, but the less freedom you give the consultant, the less of their expertise you are letting them use. On the contrary, the more discretion you give to a consultant, the more able they are to add value and use their specific skills and creativity, and come up with an innovative and powerful solution to your issues.

To give someone discretion, we normally have to trust consultants. If you do not trust your consultant you have probably hired the wrong one (see tip 11). If what you really want is someone who will not only try to help, but will help by working in the precise way you define, with little or no discretion, don't pay for a management consultant. Save the money. There are many very competent contractors as capable as any consultant to follow your instructions at a much more economic rate.

Tip 8

Expect a lot – but don't expect miracles!

Successful consultants can charge what are perceived to be high daily rates. They can justify charging such rates because they should add significant value. From a client perspective, if a consultant wants to charge you a high rate it is reasonable to have high expectations of what they can deliver.

Consultants are only human, even if they are highly skilled in a specific area. Be demanding and do not accept any second-rate advice or deliverables. Expect interesting and innovative solutions. But do not expect them to suddenly resolve the fundamental issues that have been at the root of all of your business problems for years and years. If they do, then great, and sometimes they will, but do not risk your personal reputation on it happening.

> ❝ expect interesting and innovative solutions ❞

Tip 9

Confirm precisely who is in the consulting team.

Whenever a major consultancy tells you about the wonders of buying a service from them and all about their fantastic intellectual capital, methods and tools and years of experience, remember that you are paying for people, not a company. Consulting is done by the productive interaction of consultants and clients – human being to human being. Whenever a major firm tells you that it does not matter who they provide as all their staff are brilliant, smile but ignore them. Even in the firms with the highest recruitment standards there are significant variations in skills and performance, and there are massive differences in the relevance of individual consultant's skills to your circumstances. The situation faced by many clients is that a brilliant team arrives to make a sales pitch, but the team who turns up to actually deliver the engagement is not the same.

Before a consulting engagement starts, confirm who exactly is on the team, and make sure that you are happy that the individuals being proposed have skills and abilities that are commensurate with their individual fee rates. If you delay the start of an engagement, do not be surprised if the consultancy firm cannot offer you the staff they originally proposed. Even so, any replacement must be acceptable to you. Secondly, get some comfort that the people being proposed not only have the necessary skills, but are people who you and your team can work with. There is no point paying for a brilliant consultant who cannot effectively work in your culture.

Tip 10

Read the small print in the contract.

You may sometimes feel a little inexperienced about detailed legal and contractual issues and want to believe that a consulting firm would not pull the wool over your eyes. I think most consulting firms do not want to play games with contracts, but for various reasons clients often find themselves surprised when they are subject to legal clauses they signed up to unintentionally. It probably happens because when a contract is drawn up it is not drawn up as a friendly little agreement between a nice consultant and an agreeable manager – the contract is drawn up by lawyers representing two different legal entities. There is an inherent assumption that when two organisations interact they are competent to do so. *Caveat emptor.*

Do not enter into a contract of any scale without getting your lawyers to check it. But you need to read it too. Your lawyers should ensure you do not sign up to a contract that is detrimental to your organisation in ways that lawyers consider are important, but your lawyer may be less worried about some aspects that should concern you.

There can be all sorts of potentially troublesome clauses in a perfectly valid legal contract from a consulting company. Examples include:

- What you pay for (expenses, fees and other costs).
- What you own at the end of the engagement and what the consultants retain ownership over (intellectual property).
- Client confidentiality: what can the consultant do with any information they find whilst performing the engagement?
- Changing consulting staff and whether this needs your approval.

Tip 11

If you don't trust the consultant, don't buy.

Everyone has instinct and gut feelings about certain people. Sometimes, for reasons you cannot quite verbalise, you do not trust someone. Of course you must avoid simplistic thinking and rejecting consultants because of your personal biases, but generally if you do not trust the consultants you are about to hire, then don't sign the contract. There are plenty of consultants in this world, and you can find someone else.

Why do I say this? Because if you do not trust the consultant, you will waste too much time checking their work and fretting and feeling nervous because you are uncomfortable. You are a busy manager and cannot afford this. You do not owe a consultancy work, and should feel no qualms about rejecting a consultant you do not trust.

You can go too far the other way. You should not buy consulting just because you trust someone, and just because you trust someone you should not accept their advice without critical review. You should always be sceptical about any consultancy offering. As a professional manager, you should be a little wary of anything any supplier offers you. Your responsibility is to look after your organisation's interests, and you cannot do that without being constructively critical of what any supplier offers. But there is a big difference between a workable level of ongoing critique of a consultant's work and true distrust.

Tip 12

Before saying yes, be clear about what happens when they finish.

A consultant will work with you for a limited period of time to produce a set of deliverables. One common point of contention between consultants and clients is the situation in which a consultant believes they have finished their work and wants their invoice paid, and the client is not satisfied because they cannot use the deliverables from the consultant.

It is easy for a client to develop a dependency on a consultant or consultancy company. Consultants are often highly skilled and productive, and can produce deliverables, recommendations or implementation plans which are meaningful to them and usable by them given their skill level, but may not be appropriate or easily usable by the client.

Ask yourself: will you be able to use the consultant's advice or are you opening the door to an endless stream of future sales? There is nothing intrinsically wrong with the latter, but you should get into this situation with your eyes open and sufficient budget to deal with it. Will your staff need training to be able to apply the recommendations of the consultant? Again, this is a normal situation, but if it is the case you should ensure there is some degree of skills transfer built into the proposal. Overall, the best approach is to define as one of your requirements for the consultant that any deliverables they produce are appropriate to your organisation and usable by you and your staff given your current level of skills.

I discuss this issue in more detail in Chapter 8.

Tip 13

Plan check points in the engagement.

Many consulting projects are difficult to define in a way that you are absolutely sure that your and the consultant's understanding of the problem are the same. More importantly, in productive consulting engagements understanding evolves as the engagement does. Part of the reason for many engagements is as much to improve understanding as it is to fix the problem. This means the structure and scope of the engagement often changes as progress is made. Having regular check points in a consulting engagement enables you to make changes to the structure or scope in a controlled way. If you are employing consultants, I recommend having some form of review at least once a week.

Additionally, if your finances are tight and the consultants are working on a time and materials basis, regular updates enable you to track expenditure and ensure you are both getting value for money and that the work remains within your budget. You can easily make sure the spend-to-date is reasonable and you are not going to get an unexpected surprise.

Good consultants will ask for this – even insist on regular meetings with their client. Both for cost and scope control, regular updates with any consultants you are employing are essential. Most managers have busy schedules, so plan these check points and fix them in your diary at the start of the engagement.

Tip 14

Prepare for the consultants' arrival.

Consultants are typically expensive beasts to have walking around your organisation. They can add tremendous value, but they can also rack up significant fees doing mundane administrative tasks. Some parts of the engagement can be just as well done by your staff. Of course, you may be working for a cash-rich company that really does not mind a few thousand pounds of extra fees, but this is not true for most clients.

If you can do up-front work it can save you a lot of money and make the consultants more efficient. There are obvious administrative tasks – for example, arranging building passes, car parking spaces, office space and so on. Additionally, usually at the start of an engagement consultants need to collect information about your organisation. Much of this data collection needs the consultants' specialist skill, but some data will be quite straightforward. For example, consultants often need basic company information such as turnover, last year's annual reports, organisation charts and so on.

Of course consultants can perfectly well manage the process of getting building passes and a desk – but do you really want to be paying someone at top rate to do this? Ask what administrative and facility needs are required, and, if they are reasonable, fulfil them. Feel no qualms about saying no if the consultant has unreasonable requests, or refusing ones that do not fit the style of culture of your business. Also, ask them what information they will need to do their work, and, if any of it is straightforward then source it for them. Finally, ask if there are any tasks on their project that can be done easily by a member of your staff.

Sometimes you cannot help the consultants simply because your staff are already too busy. However, you may be able to reduce consulting bills by hiring cheaper contractors or temporary members of staff and getting them to do some of the less value-adding parts of the consultants' work. Consultancy companies do not like this as it decreases their fees, but you are the client.

Tip 15

Keep an eye on who the consultants are talking to within your organisation.

If you are the client for a consultancy team working in your organisation, it is worth keeping some track of who the consultant is talking to in your organisation. You do not want to constrain unnecessarily the consultants, as this may limit the quality of their resulting recommendations, but you need to be aware of a few risks.

Common things to be wary of are:

- Paying for consultants' business development activities (see tip 16) as they spend time talking to other potential clients in your organisation.

- Consultants interacting with managers who, for political reasons or business sensitivities, you do not want included within the scope of the consultants' work.

- The impact and impression the consultants can give in the organisation. It is easy to start false rumours running, for example about impending redundancies, simply because of a consultant's loose talk.

- The impact the consultants have on your reputation. If you are the client, what consultants say and do will, to some extent, reflect on you.

Tip 16

Pay for work, not for sales activity.

Selling consulting engagements is one of the costs of running a consultancy business. Experienced consultants know how to manage the balance between chargeable client work and business development activities such as selling. When a consultant is working in your organisation, they usually have the freedom to move around and talk to all sorts of people. This freedom is often essential to the consultant being able to make quality recommendations. This freedom is also a huge temptation for the consultant, as it is a wonderful opportunity to make new relationships and sell other work.

Don't be paranoid about consultants selling other work: it is perfectly legitimate for a consultant to try and gain other business within your organisation. A consultancy is a commercial enterprise and needs to sell profitably to continue to exist. But you should not be paying for their sales time. Make it clear that you will not tolerate paying for any time that you perceive to be business development activities.

❝ don't be paranoid about consultants selling other work ❞

Tip 17

Delivery is a partnership.

Unless you want completely generic information, consultants cannot deliver meaningful advice on their own. (If you do need generic information, it's much cheaper to buy a book or a report.) The value from consulting comes from bespoke recommendations which are tailored to your specific context: your organisation's sector, its nationality, the way you are structured, your way of working – all those things that make your business unique. For a consultant to understand your uniqueness they need to work with you. Therefore be prepared to give a proportion of your own time to helping the consultants. Consultants will help you, but you cannot simply delegate or outsource the resolution of a problem to them. Additionally, you should be prepared to provide staff time to work with consultants.

Factors to consider in allocating staff to work with consultants are:

- *Data and information collection*: Consultants cannot provide bespoke advice without information about your organisation. The main source of this information is you and your staff.
- *Skills transfer*: You may want to have some skills transfer from the consultants to your staff as an outcome of the engagement. To achieve this, staff must have time to work with and be trained by the consultants.
- *Cost minimisation*: As described in tip 14, the more of your staff you allocate to an engagement, the less consultant time you will require. Usually your own staff are significantly cheaper on an hourly rate than consultants.
- *The limitations of consultants' own skills and knowledge*: There are many things consultants cannot do and do not know about. For instance, many consultants are not ex-line managers and some of their advice will need to be made practical and workable for you to make use of. Only you can do this.

If you are hiring consultants both to advise and implement, then be clear to yourself that all a consultant can do when it comes to implementation is help. The help may be valuable or even essential to implementation, but it is your organisation that must own the implementation project, and your organisation that will live with the results once the implementation is over.

Tip 18

Check back against the proposal.

At the end of a consulting engagement, and at periodic intervals throughout the engagement, check that the work being done is aligned with the proposal. Even if you have set up regular reviews, it is worth explicitly checking back against the proposal. In the intensity of a good consulting engagement it is easy to slowly veer off track compared to what was originally agreed.

There are often valid reasons why the engagement is not following the original proposal. The understanding of the work needed will evolve, and new ideas, different from those originally proposed, are generated. Often a consulting engagement starts trying to resolve one issue and then a different root cause is identified. Hence the shape and scope of the work will change. You should ask for an updated proposal or statement of work. This does not need to be a complex document, and can be something very brief. Without it, you risk ending the engagement in conflict.

Tip 19

Check the deliverables – don't just accept them.

All consulting engagements should result in some form of deliverable. The deliverable may be something tangible like a report; it may be something intangible but measurable, such as an improvement in performance in a department; finally it may be intangible and unmeasurable, such as some skills transfer to staff. Before letting a consultant complete their engagement you should have confidence that the deliverables produced are complete and of a sufficient level of quality. Of course, this is easier for some deliverables than others, but even for those that are completely unmeasurable you should judge completeness and quality. You cannot reject deliverables simply because you do not like them. Ask questions such as: are they comprehensive? Do they cover all the areas expected? Are they of sufficient quality? Are the findings valid? Are any assumptions the consultant has made reasonable?

Tip 20

Only pay the bill if you are happy with the work and the invoice is reasonable.

Once the engagement is over and the deliverables have been handed over, you will receive an invoice for the consultant's work. For large engagements you may also receive interim invoices. Your main responsibility is towards your organisation, and you therefore must only pay the invoice if you are happy with the work and the invoice is reasonable. By

> **if you are unhappy with the bill, tell the consultant**

reasonable I mean that it is in line with expectations and the parameters of the proposal or statement of work. Even if you are happy with the work, you may not be happy with the invoice when you see thousands of pounds for unexpected expenses. If you are unhappy with the bill, tell the consultant, and arrange to discuss it and ask them to explain and justify it. If they cannot, ask for a reduction.

Many consultants will not thank me for pointing this out, but if you are arguing over invoices, ask to see copies of all expenses receipts. It is a fair request, but often extremely painful for the consultants, especially if there was a big team on the engagement.

If you do decide to dispute an invoice with a consultant, make sure that the reason for any discrepancy is not down to you or your organisation. Clients often, unwittingly, ask consultants for all sorts of extras and add-ons as an engagement progresses, and may increase the scope significantly. Also, often consultants' productivity is constrained by being unable to get sufficient time with you or your staff, or slow decision making on your behalf. These sort of factors extend the engagement, and it is usually perfectly reasonable for consultants to expect additional fees in these situations, although this does depend on the proposal and what was agreed at the start of the engagement.

Invoice surprises can be reduced by following the advice in tips 13 and 17.

Conclusion

Management consultancy is a vibrant and dynamic business. Like all businesses it has its ups and its downs, but clients always need help and the range and number of issues they have are increasing. Many clients find consultants useful and continue to buy a variety of consultancy services even in the deepest recession. There are general trends in business which are helpful to consultants. The ongoing tendency to downsize and outsource functions results in increasingly efficient and lean organisations. Efficiency is great for the bottom line, but it also means there is little capacity for dealing with anything out of the usual. Who do clients call when something out of the usual comes up? Often it is a management consultant.

Not all clients are fans of management consultants, and some professional consultants prefer other titles such as business advisor. This can lead to the incorrect conclusion that consulting is a business in decline. It has its challenges but, in truth, there remains a huge and growing demand for *good* consultants – a good consultant being one who adds value in a way appreciated by clients. The most successful consultants are those who offer a genuinely client-centric consulting service.

Management consultancy is, therefore, a great career choice. However, there is a growing body of people who want to work as consultants. Consultancy is a career chosen by many graduates, and it is also a result of mid-career changes. There are increasing numbers of experienced managers looking for alternative careers or the lifestyle flexibility that it is possible to have as a consultant. Additionally, more countries are developing their service industries. Geographies that were once seen as territorial opportunities for consultants are now developing their own competitive and high-quality consulting businesses who are selling back into the consultants' home countries. This is a good trend from the viewpoint of the client, as the greater supply of consultants means that to succeed as a consultant you must increasingly differentiate yourself with better skills and innovative service lines.

As I described in Chapters 1 to 3, to start as a consultant you need a skill that is of use to your clients, but you also need to have or be willing to learn the skills of being a consultant. Even the best and most successful manager may struggle with understanding the processes, tools and art of being a consultant.

Successful consultants build a profitable consulting business by thinking from the client's viewpoint, and developing service lines that are meaningful to the client. But it is no good having skills alone. You must be able to convince a client to utilise them, which requires that you not only be capable but credible. Credibility comes from knowing about clients, understanding their issues and coherently presenting your services as ways to resolve their issues. Of course, you must be able to find clients and potential clients must be able to find you.

There are three main processes you should understand to deliver value-adding consultancy, which I defined in Chapter 4.

1 *The consulting engagement process*: These are the steps you should take to go from selling an engagement, through delivering it to closing it down in the optimal way.

2 *The client's change process*: You should be able to position your services relative to the wider changes the client is undertaking.

3 *The client's operational process*: You should never forget that the most important part of a client's business is usually its day-to-day operations, and any help you give must fit within the client's operational process.

Chapter 5 looked at ways to go about identifying opportunities, understanding client issues, developing opportunities and winning work. The fundamental point, and one that potential consultants often overlook, is that to be a successful consultant you not only need to be able to consult, you must also be able to sell your services. This is not necessarily hard, but it is essential.

Most of your time as a consultant will be spent delivering client engagements, as outlined in Chapter 6. You start engagements by looking ahead and planning what you will do, but at the same time expecting and being flexible enough to requirements to modify the plan. As you progress through delivery, always think from the client's perspective. Is what you are discovering innovative, implementable and acceptable to the client? An engagement needs to be sufficiently wide ranging, but clarity, coherence and usefulness are of far greater value than absolute comprehensiveness. The best consulting ideas meet three criteria: they are innovative, implementable and acceptable to the client.

When thinking about consultancy, novice consultants tend to think in terms of experts providing detailed advice, but there is an alternative way of adding value to clients called process consultancy. This is described in Chapter 7. Instead of advising a client of what the solution to a problem is, the process consultant helps clients to develop solutions themselves. The effectiveness and wide applicability of process consultancy should not be underestimated.

Having delivered an engagement, you must finish it off and close it down. Often it is the way an engagement is closed that a client most remembers, and how you leave a client organisa-

" often it is the way an engagement is closed that a client most remembers "

tion is as important as how you make your first sale. When you leave, the client should have or be capable of delivering a sustained change. If there is no change, you have added no value.

In Chapters 9 to 14 I described some of the higher-level competencies of experienced and successful consultants. You should develop the ability to locate and develop productive long-term relationships. You must some-times be willing to say no to client opportunities, but when you do, think carefully about how you will say no, as doing this in an inappropri-ate way can damage your ongoing client relationship. Consultants face a variety of business temptations, but sustainable consultancies are built on a strong ethical foundation. Working ethically is essential in modern business. Finally, as a consultant one of your main tools is language: learn to use it appropriately and clearly, trying to avoid jargon and other communication traps.

You will never know everything about consultancy. Observe, listen and learn as your experience grows. Share your ideas with other consultants, who are often happy to help you improve on them. Client needs are ever changing, and success is built upon an ability to track these changes and a willingness to adapt your service lines accordingly. I, and most success-ful consultants I know, are always happy to receive comments and suggestions on our approaches.

Good luck with your consulting career.

part

four

Additional resources for consultants

A: The tools, processes and materials of a consultancy business

I often talk with prospective consultants about how to go about setting themselves up as a consultant. The somewhat unbounded question I try to answer for them is 'what are all the things I should think about to set up and run a consultancy?' Although I have titled this section 'tools, processes and materials' the list is broader than that. I catalogue a variety of things to consider, without defining them in detail. This should not been seen as an exhaustive list, but it does contain most of the essentials.

The level of formality with which a business is run will vary from a one-person, self-owned business through to a major consultancy with thousands of staff and many partners. In principle the mechanics of running a consultancy and consulting engagements are the same, irrespective of scale. However, anyone joining or working for a large or well-established consultancy will have all the processes and tools they may want, and so the list is aimed at someone setting up their own new consulting business. I have assumed you will work based in the UK, although most items will be relevant to someone working in any location.

The items in **bold** are essential or at least highly desirable in my mind, from day one. The others are suggestions for you to consider or to develop over time.

Tools, processes and materials required to run a consultancy

Legal structure/company registration
When I started as an independent consultant there was an ongoing debate as to whether it was better to work self-employed/sole trader or via your own company. Increasingly there is no choice, and generally you must have a recognised legal structure such as a limited liability company (Ltd) or limited liability partnership (LLP). This is one area where it is worth seeking specialist advice.

Company name

Tools, processes and materials required to run a consultancy (continued)

Company bank account

Cash float

You will not get paid immediately and will need some money to keep the business running. When you first start it may be some months before the first client payment is made. It is easy to keep the costs of a consultancy business low, but they will not be zero and therefore a modest cash float is required.

I separate this from a personal cash float you may also need, depending on how you will pay yourself during the initial stages of your consultancy. Most consultants, who run their own business, receive a combination of a relatively small salary and dividends from profit. The focus on dividends is due to the inability to forecast the company revenues accurately and hence the need to keep the cost base and salaries comparatively low.

Company credit card

Accountant

Legal support

Whereas you must have an accountant to run a limited liability company, you are not obliged to have any formal legal support and it may be expensive. Obviously larger firms may employ full-time lawyers. This is easy to justify as the risk in some types of consulting is high and it is essential, for example, to ensure that contractual terms are right. For a small firm or a one-person consultancy company your need for legal advice will probably be very limited. Try and develop a relationship with a local business solicitor you can call on if required.

Tax setup

For example: **corporation tax, VAT, National Insurance (employer and employee), employee tax.**

Benefits to staff

For example: salary, pensions, dividends (for shareholders).

Business management processes

For example: engagement process, engagement/client risk assessment template, risk management process, pipeline management.

Accounting system

There are many excellent and inexpensive accounting software packages. However, you do not have to buy a proprietary software package, but to run a company you need some form of accounting system, even if it is simply a spreadsheet for a one-person consultancy.

Expenses tracking

At a minimum you need somewhere to store receipts and a spreadsheet for logging which expenses are allocated to which client or to business development.

Tools, processes and materials required to run a consultancy (continued)

Engagement costs tracking/invoicing

If you are going to charge a day rate you need a reliable mechanism to track the days spent on a specific engagement and any other costs to be recharged to the client. Larger firms use time sheets, but this is usually unnecessary for a very small consultancy.

Standard letter/email templates

For example: invoice templates, letters, envelopes, etc.

Availability tracking

You should have some idea of when you are free and when you are already committed so you know how you can respond to new opportunities. For an individual consultant this can be as simple as keeping a diary. Once a consultancy has several consultants or more, some form of forward utilisation estimates is essential. These should be regularly updated and available to all staff involved in selling.

Business cards

In this era of electronic communications business cards seem a very dated phenomenon. Yet clients still expect them. If you are going to have them, get them decently made and ideally professionally designed. It makes a significant difference to client perception. You can however wait to invest in them until you have generated some fees.

Marketing materials

For example: company logo, website, leaflets.

Sales and other business development materials

For example: **CV**, case studies, service line descriptions, terms sheets.

Professional society membership

This is generally useful, but not mandatory. However, providing some types of professional advice requires you to be a member of the relevant professional society. Some societies have many fringe benefits, for example meeting or working spaces you can use for short periods at zero or low cost. There are specific societies which support consultants, such as the UK's excellent Institute of Business Consultants.

Professional indemnity insurance

Arguably this is not mandatory, but many clients insist on it as part of their contract with consultants and it is strongly recommended.

Facilities and office space

For example: **company address, PC, printer, scanner, desk, stationery, storage space/filing for papers**, projector, etc.

If you plan to work from home ensure you are compliant with property, and health and safety regulations. This is generally not an issue for solo consultants.

Tools, processes and materials required to run a consultancy (continued)

Reference materials

This depends on the specific type of consulting you perform.

Service line definitions, processes and tools

This tends to be the domain of the larger firms. One-person consultancies tend not to bother, as details are all in the head of the consultant. Once there are more than a few people in the organisation then it can be worth documenting formal methods. Also, irrespective of the value to the consultant directly, clients like to see methods and tools and they can increase credibility.

Standard contractual terms

This tends to be restricted to larger consultancies. If you are a one-person consultancy usually you end up taking the contract offered by clients rather than offering your clients a contract.

Relationship management system

As a consultant you will develop a lot of relationships and need to manage them to keep your pipeline of work flowing. At the very least you need a well-maintained contacts list. It is better still to have some form of tracking system logging contacts with key clients/potential clients, and what you should do next. Remember, many of your relationships will be with other consultants.

Agencies/other routes to market

Many consultants gain all their work through their personal network. However, there are a range of agencies who deal with placing interim managers and consultants and these can be a valuable route to market.

Driving licence/car/insured for business use

You can work without a car but it does constrain you, as not all clients are conveniently close to public transport. Note that some domestic car insurance will not cover you for business use, and as a consultant much of your travel is not to your usual place of work, and therefore counts as business use.

Additional items for foreign work

For example: **passport, work visa (if appropriate), travel arrangements**, proof of company's tax status in own country (otherwise you may find yourself liable for local corporation or withholding taxes), letter of invitation (required in some countries).

B: References

I have had an eclectic range of influences and cannot remember, let alone list, all the sources that have stimulated my thinking on consulting. Many ideas have come from working with other consultants, and where the source is a document it has often been an article.

The references I list in this appendix are all useful. They are of one of two types: those that have had a major influence on my approach to consulting or way I think about consulting; and those which include interesting views on and tools for consulting, some of which I personally use. I have also included one of my other books, which may help some readers who want to explore further the critical topics in Chapter 8.

Alexander, Christopher (1964) *Notes on the Synthesis of Form*, Harvard University Press.

Block, Peter (1999) *Flawless Consulting: A Guide to Getting Your Expertise Used*, 2nd edn, Jossey Bass.

Buzan, Tony (2002) *How to Mind Map: The Ultimate Thinking Tool That Will Change Your Life*, Thorsons.

Chappell, Timothy (2008) 'Moral Perception', *Philosophy*, 83 (326), pp. 421–437.

Cope, Mick (2003) *The Seven Cs of Consulting: The Definitive Guide to the Consulting Process*, 2nd edn, Financial Times/Prentice Hall.

Fisher, Roger, Ury, William and Patton, Bruce (2003) *Getting to Yes: Negotiating Agreement Without Giving In*, 2nd edn, Random House.

Freed, Richard and Romano, Joe (2003) *Writing Winning Business Proposals: Your Guide to Landing the Client, Making the Sale and Persuading the Boss*, 2nd edn, McGraw-Hill Professional.

Hargie, Owen (2006) *The Handbook of Communication Skills*, 3rd edn, Routledge.

Hume, David (1999) *An Enquiry Concerning Human Understanding*, Oxford University Press.

Kotler, Philip and Keller, Kevin (2008) *Marketing Management*, 13th edn, Pearson Education.

Minto, Barbara (2008) *The Pyramid Principle: Logic in Writing and Thinking*, 3rd edn, Financial Times/Prentice Hall.

Newton, Richard (2007) *Managing Change Step by Step*, Prentice Hall.

Rankin, Elizabeth (2001) *The Work of Writing*, Jossey Bass.

Senge, Peter (1993) *The Fifth Discipline: Art and Practice of the Learning Organization*, Random House Business Books.

Schein, Edgar H (1987) *Process Consultation: Lessons for Managers and Consultants: Volume 2*, Addison-Wesley.

Schein, Edgar H (1988) *Process Consultation: Its Role in Organization Development: Volume 1*, 2nd edn, Prentice Hall.

C: Sample proposal letter

Address line 1
Address line 1
Address line 1
Address line 1

Phone number
Email address

Date

Dear *enter name*

Re: Ongoing support for the RENEW programme

Thank you for inviting me to work with you and your team over the last few weeks in Ulan Bator. I enjoyed the experience very much, and look forward to the opportunity to work with you again. As agreed when we last met, I am sending you a short letter to outline XYZ Consulting's proposal for ongoing assistance to the RENEW programme.

This proposal follows on from the work XYZ Consulting has undertaken so far for ABC Company. Phase 1 is complete, and I will invoice your London office this week.

I am now proposing an additional four-week phase of support (referred to in this letter as *phase 2*), and outline a possible longer-term engagement to run until roughly the end of March (referred to in this letter as *phase 3*).

Phase 2

The RENEW team is responsible for delivering the major change programme to improve the operational performance of the company. To deliver this programme you need access to project and change management skills, as well as specialist techniques such as process and organisational design. Your team is highly motivated but relatively inexperienced. RENEW is a complex and ambitious programme. Team members have had initial training in project and change management, but will need ongoing support to develop their skills further and successfully deliver the programme.

In addition, you are considering the longer-term needs of the ABC Company. Currently, you have very limited project and change skills in the business. You believe that having an in-house capability to deliver projects and change is essential to the effective ongoing management and development of the business. Therefore, at the end of the RENEW programme, in approximately 18 months' time, you want to have created a team with the capability to deliver any future projects and programmes for the ABC Company.

The aim of phase 2 is to continue to enhance the capability of the RENEW team, and to provide overall direction and support to the programme. Over the next few weeks the programme structure will be revised in line with the findings of phase 1.

The objectives of phase 2 are to:

- Perform a detailed review of each of the six component projects of the RENEW programme. I have a structured quality assurance (QA) process which I use to review projects. (I will undertake the review, and am happy to provide you with my QA checklists and forms as part of the ongoing skills transfer and for future use in the RENEW programme.) The output will be a series of detailed recommendations for each project manager to increase the likelihood of project success. A review of this nature will take two days per project stream, working with the project managers and their project teams.
- Feed back to you any significant issues or risks from my project reviews, and provide an assessment of the team's capabilities to meet the challenges of the RENEW programme.
- Hold a one-day workshop with you and your team, to review progress to date and identify common areas for improvement.
- Finalise the proposal for phase 3. As part of phase 2 we will explore phase 3 in detail.

Taking these objectives in mind, and assuming that each of the project managers will be available to work with me in phase 2, this will take four weeks. Although I will work flexibly, any delay in the availability of project managers to work with me is likely to lengthen phase 2.

Phase 3

Since it is not yet possible to finalise my role in phase 3, this section outlines an indicative proposition that is subject to modification.

In your current RENEW team structure you envisage the role of a programme consultant working with you to help deliver the programme. In phase 3, I will perform the role of programme consultant. My main objectives will be to:

- Support each of the project managers in delivering the component projects that make up the RENEW programme. This will take the place of *ad hoc* support, periodic QA reviews of the projects, and where appropriate more detailed training or one-to-one support in specific aspects of project, change management, process and organisational design, as well as providing an understanding how to manage IT projects.
- Identify and manage programme-wide issues and risks (i.e. issues and risks which are common to many projects or which do not sit within a specific project). The project managers will still remain accountable for the resolution of issues and risks within their projects.
- Report to you on programme-wide issues and risks as they are identified and support the identification of mitigations and resolutions.
- Define the role and develop the plans for your permanent project and change management team to continue after the completion of the RENEW programme.

The nature of this role may need to be modified as the programme progresses. Therefore I intend to work in a flexible manner, expecting these objectives to evolve in parallel with programme developments.

Fees and timing

For phase 2, the fees will be £..,.... We will discuss the commercial terms and start date for phase 3 when I am in Ulan Bator.

Fees exclude expenses, which will be recharged at cost, and VAT. My assumption at this stage is that my billing for phase 2 will be via the UK office of ABC Company, but if we reach an agreement on phase 3 it will be billed directly to your department. As with phase 1, I am assuming you will provide support with visa arrangements.

You are aware I have a number of commitments in the UK, which I need to finalise before I am fully available to work with ABC Company. In terms of indicative dates I will be available to perform the work of phase 2 in the week starting 27 October, and, assuming that is successful and we come to a mutual agreement, I am able to start phase 3 on the week starting 24 November. Although it has not been planned in detail, you should estimate that phase 3 will take approximately four months.

For your planning purposes, I would like to let you know that I will be unavailable for the weeks commencing 22 December and 19 January due to existing commitments.

I hope my proposal meets your requirements. If you have any questions or issues please let me know, and if any of my assumptions are also incorrect please advise me. Once you confirm that you are happy with this proposal we can confirm starting dates.

I look forward to continuing to work with ABC Company.

Yours sincerely

Enter name
Director
XYZ Consulting

Index

Think big
for less